T0339467

Insider Threat

Insider Threat
Prevention, Detection, Mitigation, and Deterrence

Michael G. Gelles, Psy.D.

AMSTERDAM • BOSTON • HEIDELBERG • LONDON
NEW YORK • OXFORD • PARIS • SAN DIEGO
SAN FRANCISCO • SINGAPORE • SYDNEY • TOKYO
Butterworth-Heinemann is an imprint of Elsevier

Butterworth-Heinemann is an imprint of Elsevier
The Boulevard, Langford Lane, Kidlington, Oxford OX5 1GB, UK
50 Hampshire Street, 5th Floor, Cambridge, MA 02139, USA

Notices
Knowledge and best practice in this field are constantly changing. As new research and experience broaden our understanding, changes in research methods, professional practices, or medical treatment may become necessary.

Practitioners and researchers must always rely on their own experience and knowledge in evaluating and using any information, methods, compounds, or experiments described herein. In using such information or methods they should be mindful of their own safety and the safety of others, including parties for whom they have a professional responsibility.

To the fullest extent of the law, neither the Publisher nor the authors, contributors, or editors, assume any liability for any injury and/or damage to persons or property as a matter of products liability, negligence or otherwise, or from any use or operation of any methods, products, instructions, or ideas contained in the material herein.

British Library Cataloguing-in-Publication Data
A catalogue record for this book is available from the British Library

Library of Congress Cataloging-in-Publication Data
A catalog record for this book is available from the Library of Congress

ISBN: 978-0-12-802410-2

For Information on all Butterworth-Heinemann publications
visit our website at https://www.elsevier.com/

  Working together
to grow libraries in
developing countries

ELSEVIER Book Aid International

www.elsevier.com • www.bookaid.org

Publisher: Candice Janco
Acquisition Editor: Sara Scott
Editorial Project Manager: Hilary Carr
Production Project Manager: Punithavathy Govindaradjane
Designer: Mark Rogers

Typeset by MPS Limited, Chennai, India

Contents

About Deloitte

About the Author

Dr. Michael G. Gelles is currently a Managing Director with Deloitte Consulting, LLP Federal practice in Washington, D.C., consulting in the areas of law enforcement, intelligence and security. Dr. Gelles is a thought leader in insider threat associated with possible security risks, asset loss, exploitation, terrorism, workplace violence and sabotage. Dr. Gelles leads consults to government and private sector organizations in the area of insider threat, business assurance, organizational transformation, workforce planning, leadership development and strategic planning with a specific emphasis around people, mission and risk. Dr. Gelles has led the development of a number of Deloitte innovative solutions in addition to insider threat to include multigenerational workforce solutions and developing a secure cyber workforce. Previously, he was an executive in federal law enforcement and the chief psychologist for the Naval Criminal Investigative Service (NCIS) for more than 16 years. In that capacity, he assisted the NCIS and a multitude of other federal, state and local law enforcement agencies with criminal, counterintelligence and counterterrorism investigations and operations. Dr. Gelles has been involved in the investigation and debrief of numerous convicted insiders ranging from espionage to sabotage. He is an author of numerous articles and book chapters, as well as a book on threat management and risk assessment. Dr. Gelles received his Bachelor of Arts from the University of Delaware and his master's and doctorate degrees in psychology from Yeshiva University in New York. He completed his clinical and forensic training at the National Naval Medical Center and his advanced training at the Washington School of Psychiatry. He held past academic appointments in at the Uniformed Services University of the Health Sciences and at the Washington School of Psychiatry.

Foreword

The risks to an organization's critical assets are greater today than they have ever been. With business being conducted globally online, with a global workforce, the advent of technologies that make access to information available from anywhere on any device, the risks to data have increased significantly. Information can be accessed, downloaded, and ex-filtrated in seconds and in those short seconds an organization's proprietary information, client confidential data, can be stolen or exploited before anyone notices. Most important, the exploitation of an organizations' assets can cause irreparable damage to brand, reputation, and public confidence, and in cases of the government, national security and public safety. Therefore, it is paramount to develop an insider threat program that allows the organization to prevent, detect, respond, and deter insider threats.

For the past decade, both private and public sector organizations have invested heavily in protecting their perimeter from external cyber attacks, while remaining vulnerable to the insider threat who can circumvent cyber defenses with malicious intent or unwitting complacency. This book addresses the insider threat: how to develop a program that protects an organization's critical assets through a proactive and holistic view of the organization's policies, business processes, technology, security awareness, and training.

Developing an insider threat program should be viewed as more than just the tactical implementation of a technology that monitors employee activity. When developing an insider threat program, an organization should consider three key elements. First, it is important to understand the normal activities and behaviors of personnel as they conduct business. Next, it is important to define what is outside the norm that raises a level of concern and what could be a risk to assets. Although technology is a foundational element of a comprehensive program, we have learned that taking a critical look at the organization's policies, business processes, communications to the workforce, and training of personnel in handling sensitive or confidential information is critically important in defining an insider threat program. Lastly, the effectiveness of an organization's cyber security protections and understanding of normal job behaviors and activities of personnel when properly correlated through the use of behavioral analytics are the foundation of a mature insider threat program that monitors and detects events.

From our experience, we have learned that there are three key elements of a data protection strategy – a confidential information program, a cyber security program to protect the perimeter, and an insider threat program. These elements are tightly linked to an organization's data protection strategy because key interdependencies exist to protect an organization's assets. Using the "Secure, Vigilant, and Resilient" framework is one way to achieve a closely connected, comprehensive strategy designed to protect an organization's information, client information, facilities, and, most important, people.

A holistic insider threat program mandates a collaborative effort across the C-suite and key executive stakeholders. These stakeholders often include executives from risk, information technology, human resources, legal, ethics, and physical security who can impact change in policy, processes, employee life-cycle events, and physical and information security controls. It is especially critical to have support from the CIO and CISO to provide needed technology controls and data from source systems that capture behavior, that when correlated, signal anomalous activity and indicate potential high risk. It is also essential that the advanced analytics tool be strategically implemented to correlate the data that will lead to anomaly detection and facilitate the interruption of forward motion of a potential insider. These stakeholders should be viewed as partners in the overall effort since these constituents are the owners of an organization's critical data and are policy owners that can help protect assets and improve business assurance. Said another way, these key stakeholder executives are owners in protecting, preserving, and enhancing an organization's reputation.

In summary, the challenges an organization faces in developing a holistic and proactive insider threat program are (1) alignment and support of all key executive stakeholders (risk, IT, HR, legal, finance, etc.); (2) policies and defined business processes aligned to establish baseline job behaviors for personnel; (3) linkage between the organization's cyber security, the policies, processes, and training of personnel in handling confidential information, and the resultant insider threat program; and (4) finally, the technology elements of an insider threat program. Source system integration with an analytics tool is essential in getting indicators to flow from endpoint computers and other source systems to an advanced analytics tool where data are loaded, correlated, alerts generated, and anomalies escalated and investigated.

The book provides a number of different perspectives to consider in developing an insider threat program, from the challenges organizations face to thinking through ownership, privacy, the use of technology for monitoring, as well as strategies for investigating. Additionally, the book will look closely at how an insider threat complements and integrates into a larger cyber security strategy effort as well as provide a perspective on third parties and supply-chain risk. Lastly, given that insider threats are really all about people, examining the importance of employee engagement as a risk mitigation strategy to asset loss will be discussed. Remain secure, vigilant, and resilient!

Ralph Sorrentino
US Chief Confidentiality Officer, Principal Deloitte Consulting LLP

Acknowledgments

This book represents a professional transformation for me across a profession career spanning 30 years of studying the insider threat. It collectively reflects the contributions of family, mentors, and colleagues whose thinking, influence, and guidance have led to the evolution of how to better mitigate the risk of insider threat today. A journey supported by my wife Lisa and my children Bryan and Lauren, and thinking that has evolved as the world has evolved from bricks and mortar to bits and bytes. My entry into the world of the insider would never have happened without my two mentors Drs. Melvin Gravitz and Joe Krofcheck. Their teaching and insights shaped my thinking in the field. Throughout my career, there have been several who contributed to the understanding of insider threat through an operational lens: Drs. Neil Hibler and Richard Ault, who introduced me to understanding the mind of the spy through Project Slammer; Drs. Robert Fein, Chris Hatcher, and Jim Turner, whose mentorship and teaching contributed to my understanding of targeted violence and threat assessment; Drs. Cathleen Civiello, Randy Borum, Russel Palarea, and Kris Mohandie, who as peers helped shape my thinking throughout many years of looking at the insider threat. A special acknowledgement to Dr. Jim Turner, whom I collaborated with on my first book on threat assessment. Additionally, there have been many who have allowed me to think innovatively and explore different aspects of insider threat. Dave Brant, my close friend and former Director of NCIS, who encouraged and supported opportunities for my experiences in counterespionage at NCIS and throughout the government. The special agents with whom I had the privilege to work on cases are too many to list; however, acknowledging Mark Fallon, Bob McFadden, Ralph Blincoe, Tom Betro, Kim Sasaki-Swindle, Steve Corbett, Bryan Vossekuil, Matthew Doherty, Tom Neer, Ali Soufan, Greg Scovel, Mike Dorsey, Mike Prout, Carl Caulk, and Sandy MacIsaac is important for all that I have learned from them. At Deloitte, I began a new phase of the journey. Senior partners Greg Pellegrino, Dan Helfrich, Linda Solomon, Nathan Houser, Sean Morris, Alex Mirkow, Marshall Billingslea, and Jessica Kosmowski have taught me how to modernize the approach into a more robust business solution. My greatest appreciation goes to my partners and team who have developed and contributed to my most recent thinking around mitigating the insider threat and this book that addresses the current challenges of today: Dr. Kwasi Mitchell, my partner and collaborator who compliments my behavioral perspective with a business and technology acumen that helps bring this solution to what it needs to look like today; Borna Emami, who tirelessly challenges all of us to think more innovatively and creatively around risk, and how to incorporate behavior, process, and technology into risk modeling and who with Dr. Mitchell have contributed significantly to this book; John Cassidy, who helped to create the first business assessment for insiders during a time when insider threat was still a high-frequency, low-impact event in the minds of many leaders; and my partners in Cyber Risk Services, Ed Powers, Adnan Amjad, Craig Astrich, James O'Kane, and Deborah Golden, who have helped to bring an integrated perspective to insider threat and incorporate the cyber risk factor, which is essential to any program and solution. I am grateful for my friendship with Doug Thomas who leads the Lockheed Martin program and who has been a role model to all of us in how to take our collective experience and operationalize it into a successful program that is a recognized model in the public and private sector. My appreciation to Ted Almay Deloitte's Chief Security Officer for his insights and support. Also, Kate Swofford, Lacey Gray, Hannah Carlisle, and John Townsley who drove the book to completion through their outstanding editing and management of the project.

This book is a collective effort, with many contributions from many professionals at Deloitte who have delivered many solutions to the government and private sector in helping to stand up and mature insider threat programs. Many of the team members are cited as key co-authors contributors and researchers in the table of contents. This is the next generation who will continue to innovative solutions in an evolving threat environment. I am particularly grateful to Ralph Sorrentino, Deloitte's Chief Confidentiality Officer, who graciously wrote the Foreword and for the leadership and guidance from Chuck Saia, Deloitte's Chief Risk, Regulatory, and Reputation Officer, in supporting the development of the insider threat program at Deloitte. Their actions and leadership in bringing an organization together to collectively collaborate on identifying threats to our business is reflective of the gold standard for organizations in managing and mitigating risk to protect client data, brand, and reputation.

CHAPTER 1

Introduction – Insider Threat Today

INTRODUCTION

The insider threat is not a new phenomenon. Examples of trusted insiders exploiting, sabotaging, and committing acts of violence against those to whom they were outwardly committed are pervasive throughout human history. Recently, the topic of insider threat has received heightened attention as a result of high-profile incidents: Edward Snowden, the leaker of confidential NSA information; Aaron Alexis, the Navy Yard shooter; and many others. These incidents have reminded leaders that threats to their organizations' most precious assets—physical and information security, financial standing, and mission—may come from within. This phenomenon deserves the attention of leadership in all industries so that organizations are equipped to effectively prevent, detect, and respond to emerging threats.

As many organizations are learning, insider threats can have a significant impact on an organization's reputation, operations, finances, employee safety, and shareholder confidence. In Government, insider threats can affect national security, public trust, and public safety. The challenge of doing business today is protecting assets in a global and virtual environment with a workforce that is increasingly tech-savvy and ubiquitously connected to information and technology. Although the United States Federal Government has rolled out policies to achieve an enterprise-wide standard for insider threat mitigation capabilities, the private sector has no such mandates or benchmarks.[1] It is, therefore, difficult for private organizations to assess where they stand relative to peers and to make decisions regarding their insider threat mitigation capabilities.

---

[1] Intelligence and National Security Alliance (INSA), Cyber Council: Insider Threat Task Force. *A Preliminary Examination of Insider Threat Programs in the U.S. Private Sector*. Arlington, VA: INSA, 2013. Web.

Insider Threat. DOI: http://dx.doi.org/10.1016/B978-0-12-802410-2.00001-0

Looking Ahead

Financial volatility and interconnected business have amplified risks to both the private and public sector in today's changing global environment. A new set of organizational competencies is needed to mitigate insider threats as localized or compartmentalized business relationships have given way to distributed, virtual ones. This shift has forced leaders to manage evolving, networked organizations that need to prevent, detect, and recover from a diverse and growing set of threats in the workplace. If organizations successfully address these risks and prioritize insider threat mitigation as an organizational priority that is viewed as shared responsibility, they will likely adapt a balanced and integrated approach to protecting the organization's critical assets: its people, facilities, systems, and data.

Although it may not be realistic to expect that every attempted insider attack will be stopped before damage is inflicted, it is realistic to build resiliency into an organization's infrastructure and develop an early detection capability, thereby minimizing impact. This book takes a risk-based approach to insider threat mitigation that focuses on protecting the organization's critical assets and defining the collective risk tolerance for assets.

This Book

A team of insider threat experts helped to develop this book to assist organizational stakeholders at all levels prepare for and protect their organizations from insider threat. Each chapter addresses different aspects needed to develop a holistic and risk-based insider threat program. This book also provides general information about insider threat mitigation to interested parties in the public, private, and academic sectors. Working with organizations across a broad spectrum of industries to develop holistic insider threat mitigation solutions has allowed the authors to share hands-on knowledge of what is needed to create mature programs. We advocate a holistic approach to insider threat that is two-pronged: engage all programmatic aspects of the organization and address all facets of individuals' interactions with the organization. This book shares what the authors have learned designing, building, and implementing insider threat programs, including the themes and challenges that organizations commonly experience yet rarely disclose in public forums.

This book covers all aspects of an insider threat program and explores key considerations as well as leading practices. Chapters 1–3 survey how the environment has evolved to impact organizations' vulnerabilities to insider threats. Chapters 4, 6, 7, and 13 outline the building blocks for an insider threat program, including, potential risk indicators, risk appetite, and the establishment of a formal program. Chapters 5 and 8–12 explore specific components of insider threat mitigation, including personnel management, data analytics, information security, technology, cybersecurity, supply chain risk, and employee engagement. Chapter 13 examines the last stage of the insider threat life cycle: what organizations should consider when deciding on how to respond to insider threat incidents. Chapters 10 and 14 discuss matters revolving around workplace violence and privacy—two especially sensitive issues that must be tackled throughout the design, build, and implementation of an insider threat program. Finally, Chapter 15 explores the future of the insider, and what organizations can do to put themselves ahead of the curve.

WHAT IS INSIDER THREAT?

Insider attacks take many forms, such as industrial or government-sponsored espionage, workplace violence, fraud, sabotage, or the unauthorized dissemination of trade secrets, intellectual property (IP), or classified information. Organizations face a variety of insider threat challenges—risks posed by employees, contractors, vendors, and business partners who may cause harm.

As a result, the insider threat is often understood differently across disciplines. For example, chief information security officers may view insider threat exclusively through the lens of an employee's activity on an information system. A chief security officer may view insider threat through the lens of suspicious behavior as an employee interfaces with an organization's facilities or tangible assets. These fragmented conceptions of what constitutes an insider threat do not account for the holistic and multifaceted nature of how individuals interact with the organizations they work for, or partner with.

For the purposes of this book, *insider threat* is defined from a holistic and programmatic perspective to encompass the entire enterprise (Figure 1.1). An insider is a person who possesses some combination of knowledge and access that distinguishes his or her relationship with the organization from those of outsiders. An insider can be an employee, contractor, vendor, or, in some cases, a family member of a trusted employee. The insider threat is the potential for an insider to harm an organization by leveraging his or her privileged level of knowledge and/or access. An insider threat is not necessarily driven by malevolent intent: it may also constitute an individual who is complacent or ignorant about security policies and procedures. A lack of training, for example, can goad ignorance or complacency. These dispositions can provide opportunities for others—both insiders and outsiders—to breach physical or virtual security countermeasures. Throughout this book, insider threat drivers will include (1) malicious, (2) complacent, and (3) ignorant.

Organizations often prioritize external threats over insider threats. Attacks by parties with insider knowledge and access are less frequent than attacks by external actors. As a result, organizations often invest less in developing an

How do you define insider threat?

Organizations must define what constitutes an insider, threats to mitigate, and the overall risk tolerance as critical first steps in building an insider threat capability.

Who is an insider threat?	A person who has the potential to harm an organization for which they have inside knowledge or access. An insider threat can have a negative impact on any aspect of an organization, including employee and/or public safety, reputation, operations, finances, national security, and mission continuity.

Types of Insider Incidents

Information Theft	**Workplace Violence**	**Security Compromise**	**Espionage**
Use of insider access to steal or exploit information	Use of violence or threats of violence to influence others and impact the health and safety of the an organization's workforce	Use of access to facilitate and override security countermeasures (e.g., drug and contraband smuggling)	Use of access to obtain sensitive info for exploitation that impacts national or corporate security and public safety
Terrorism	**Physical Property Theft**	**Sabotage**	**Other**
Use of access to commit or facilitate an act of violence as a means of disruption or coercion for political purposes	Use of insider access to steal material items (e.g., goods, equipment, badges)	Intentional destruction of equipment or IT to direct specific harm (e.g., inserting malicious code)	Captures the evolving threat landscape including emerging threats not covered in the previous examples

Insider Threat Drivers

Malicious Intent	**Complacency**	**Ignorance**
Employees who intentionally abuse their privileged access to inflict damage on their organization or co-workers	Employees whose lax approach to policies, procedures, and information security exposes the organization to external risks	Employees whose lack of awareness of organizations security policy, procedures, and protocols exposes the organization to external risks

FIGURE 1.1

Insider Threat can be Defined Broadly as Organizations will Prioritize Risk in Different Ways Based on Mission and Strategic Objectives.

insider threat mitigation program as part of a risk management strategy. It is important, however, for organizations to understand that insiders can assist an external attacker, sometimes unintentionally. For example, an employee or contractor, either ignorant of or complacent toward organizational policy or security threats, may unwittingly download malware onto the network, giving attackers access to IP, personally identifiable information, or sensitive data, such as, customer credit card information.

What Motivates an Insider to Act?

Insider threats exist within every organization because employees, or insiders, comprise the core of an organization's operational plan and are the key drivers of its business objectives. An insider threat may be an employee who, purely by mistake, is likely to act in a way that results in negative consequences for the organization. Such employees may also conduct themselves in a high-risk manner because their organization lacks defined policies, training, or communication. Unlike ignorant or complacent insiders, malicious insiders act in response to a complex set of problems, conflicts, and disputes, or crises both personal and professional in nature.

Malicious insiders may be motivated by money, revenge, validation, or empowerment. They may possess an exaggerated sense of entitlement. Some may operate as spies for a foreign government or steal critical IP for a competitive entity. Attacks by malicious insiders are seldom impulsive acts. A number of case studies have confirmed this by evaluating the precursors or indicators displayed by the insider before taking action (e.g., declining performance, undue access attempts, negative workplace interactions). Employees wishing to harm a current or former employer, business partner, or client—whether by stealing trade secrets, sabotaging information systems, or by opening fire on colleagues—usually plan their actions. Because this behavioral pattern is subtle, it is often difficult to detect and prevent an insider threat simply by observing an insider's behavior. This book will examine how to proactively mitigate threats by developing, correlating, and analyzing a set of potential risk indicators (PRIs) as part of the insider threat mitigation program.

ENVIRONMENTAL DRIVERS

A number of environmental factors contribute to the potential for increased exploitation of information, access, and data by a trusted employee. The first is the increased use of technology and digital information systems, due in part to a generational workforce that has grown up with the internet, personal computers, and other data and communication devices. These tools are part of the daily lives of this generation's members and critical to the way they process information and solve problems. The Internet has also promulgated the expectation of free access to information resources. Combined, these factors lead people to seek solutions that may involve the exploitation of data and critical information, or excessive risk when using organizational resources or handling proprietary information.

"Bricks and Mortar" to "Bits and Bytes"

As technology continues to evolve and many of our daily activities are performed in the virtual space, business has moved from the world of "bricks and mortar" to one of "bits and bytes." This evolution presents a new set of insider threat challenges that increase the need for a holistic insider threat mitigation program.

The Virtual Space

The assets that organizations need to protect, ranging from proprietary information and intellectual property to critical research and development, exist largely in the virtual space. As a result, risks to those assets have taken on new meaning. Information has become a high-risk asset that can be readily extracted and exploited, with negative impacts to brand, market share, reputation, financial loss, national security, and public safety. Furthermore, as business operations have shifted beyond the boundaries of physical space, they have also shifted from a domestic to a global arena. Mitigating threats outside the national boundaries of an organization's home country introduces additional complications such as variations in legal restrictions, language barriers, and scalability of mitigation measures. Ultimately, an insider threat incident in the current environment can affect an organization's productivity and bottom line, entail the loss of valuable information to a competitor or foreign government, or, in the case of workplace violence, the loss of life.

Exfiltration Points

Another challenge that the use of technology and information systems presents to business operations is the proliferation of exfiltration points, that is, outlets for information removal, which have generated new ways critical assets can leave the organization's secure environment. Data is transmitted more quickly and seamlessly than ever before through the use of e-mail, removable media, cloud solutions, and remote devices. Telecommuting and bring your own device (BYOD) programs give employees access to networks and systems through new portals in private settings. The advent of social media allows for near-instantaneous proliferation of data—and once information is released to social networks, there is no getting it back.

With the advent of technology, motivated insiders have a variety of egress points that can be used to exfiltrate sensitive information. Through a review of insider threat cases, an analysis of leading public, private, and academic insider threat practices, and the design, build, and implementation of over a dozen insider threat programs, we have identified the five most common methods insiders use to remove information from the secure environment: e-mail, removable media, transmittal devices (e.g., printers, copiers, faxes, scanners), file transfer protocol, and cloud transmission. A plan to prevent, detect, and respond to each egress point (e.g., USB drives can only be accessed using encrypted removable media that can only be viewed on company computers) should be developed as part of the organization's overarching risk mitigation plan.

Technology and the Insider Threat

These changes in the way business is conducted today increase an organization's vulnerability to insider exploitation. The shift from a world of bricks and mortar to one of bits and bytes brings along a number of new challenges to successfully prevent, detect, and mitigate insider threats while protecting the organization's assets:

- Manipulating records is possible from almost anywhere.
- E-mail-based text searches do not account for other media (e.g., instant messaging, mail attachments, Web postings).

- Physical copies are no longer required.
- Data is more mobile through e-mail and on USB drives, smart phones, etc.
- Telecommuting gives employees off-site access to networks and systems.
- The proliferation of Web-based applications provides global accessibility.
- For enterprise-wide systems and databases, organizations still rely on policies and manual controls to review user administration, provision, segregation of duties, etc.

Although the medium of business has become more virtual, mitigating against an insider attack must still utilize a holistic and balanced approach that considers an individual's behavior within both the virtual and nonvirtual settings. Moreover, we cannot look only at what a person does in the virtual space and ignore what goes on in the world of bricks and mortar. Taking into account this balanced perspective of virtual and nonvirtual behavior, this book will present a comprehensive approach outlining how a broad set of behaviors, events, and attributes can be correlated and used to stop or disrupt an emerging insider threat.

Changing Workplace Demographics

A change in the global workplace demographic is underway. Generation-Y millennials are filling gaps left by retiring Baby Boomers. These generations were raised on the Internet and socially networked through MySpace, Twitter, Facebook, Snapchat, and other social media platforms. They have developed an expectation for constant and immediate access to information, and readily share information as part of a daily pursuit of knowledge, even if it is nonessential to their specific work responsibilities. This new workforce in a context of evolving technology and mobility in the management of information in conducting business will present many new security challenges. These challenges will be further exacerbated as the workplace becomes more networked and provides greater access to information. Some of these new challenges include the following.

Social Media and Validation:
Social media and networking has increased expectations for "connectedness" and validation.

A Technical Workforce:
Raised with the Internet and other technology, Generation-Y (Millennials) have greater levels of technical expertise across the workforce.

Expectations of Ownership:
If they create it, they feel like they own it.

Limited Control:

Less personal constraint in the virtual environment as people feel they are anonymous.

Challenges Managing Information:

Lack of understanding by organizations on approaches to manage information through its life cycle, including information access management.

Information Mobility:

Change in information medium and mobility.

DETECTING THE INSIDER THREAT

During the past few decades, the United States Government has made a significant investment in the study of behavioral and operational risk indicators of espionage, sabotage, and threats to information systems associated with a trusted employee. In the early 1980s, we learned that the most significant risk to national security was associated with an employee on the inside, and not the result of actions conducted by external spies.[2] Subsequently, the United States Government conducted research to enhance law enforcement's investigative and operational capabilities.[3]

Patterns of Behavior

When it comes to the behavior and actions of malicious insiders, the findings from studies are consistent: actions that are taken by perpetrators are not impulsive, and are intentionally pursued over an extended period of time. In incidents where complacency results in a loss of information, employees often feel as if the work that need to be completed is far more critical than following policy and security guidelines. Employees who feel this kind of entitlement and see themselves as above the rules are frequent violators of policy and compliance standards. This includes executives, who can view themselves above the security policies to which the rest of the organization must adhere.

Malicious insiders move along a continuum from idea to action. Regardless of motivation, an insider's plans often percolate for weeks or months before acting. There is no psychological or demographic profile for an insider threat. Rather, the most significant characteristic or potential risk indicator of an

---

[2] Herbig, K.L. *Changes in Espionage by Americans 1947 to 2007* . Rep. no. T 08-05. 05th ed. Vol. TR 08. Monterrey, CA: Defense Personnel Security Research Center, 2008. Print.
[3] Wiskoff, M., and Wood, S. *Americans Who Spied Against Their Country Since World War II*. Publication. 5th ed. Vol. TR 92. Monterrey, CA: Defense Personnel Security Research Center, 1992. Print.

The Malicious Insider: Personality Characteristics

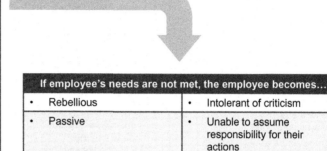

Characteristics of Employees at Risk
• Not impulsive
• No single motive
• History of managing crises ineffectively
• Pattern of frustration, disappointment, and a sense of inadequacy
• Aggrandized view of their abilities and achievements
• Strong sense of entitlement
• Views self above the rules
• Actions seek immediate gratification, validation, and satisfaction

If employee's needs are not met, the employee becomes...	
• Rebellious	• Intolerant of criticism
• Passive	• Unable to assume responsibility for their actions
• Destructive	• Blaming of others
• Complacent	• Minimizing their mistakes or faults
• Self perceived value exceeds performance	• Frustrated by feedback and evaluation/rating/bonus

FIGURE 1.2

Insider Threat Behavioral Indicators.

insider threat is a behavioral pattern: a malicious insider gets an idea, ruminates, and then begins testing if the idea can be executed.

As a result, malicious insiders will often exhibit certain behavior as they move along the idea-to-action continuum, known as potential risk indicators (PRIs) (Figure 1.2). These red flags are observable precursors that are hypothesized to be associated with an insider act. PRIs include changes in attitude or behavior: an insider may grow frustrated or disgruntled, arrive early or stay late at the office, show undue interest in information that does not pertain to his work, try to access sensitive data or a secure facility, irresponsibly handle sensitive information, or use information systems inappropriately. Figure 1.3 outlines some of the causes, effects, and actions that an insider may take.

Sometimes, managers overlook red flag behavior in high-performers out of concern for the bottom line, or fear that action may cause high-performers to defect to a rival firm. When red flags are overlooked, insider threats can fester and grow out of greed. A vigilant workforce, however, is an excellent defense and can usually recognize and report red-flag behavior, no matter how hard insiders may try to cover their tracks.[4] This book will help organizations define PRIs that are relevant to their workforce, and use these to develop a system to proactively detect and mitigate emerging insider threats.

[4] Cappelli, D. *Insider Threat and Computer System Sabotage in Critical Infrastructure Sectors*. Rep. Vol. CERT Program. Pittsburgh, PA: Carnegie Mellon U, 2005. Print.

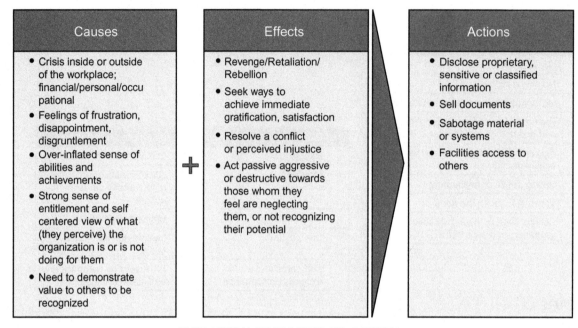

Causes	Effects	Actions
• Crisis inside or outside of the workplace; financial/personal/occupational • Feelings of frustration, disappointment, disgruntlement • Over-inflated sense of abilities and achievements • Strong sense of entitlement and self centered view of what (they perceive) the organization is or is not doing for them • Need to demonstrate value to others to be recognized	• Revenge/Retaliation/Rebellion • Seek ways to achieve immediate gratification, satisfaction • Resolve a conflict or perceived injustice • Act passive aggressive or destructive towards those whom they feel are neglecting them, or not recognizing their potential	• Disclose proprietary, sensitive or classified information • Sell documents • Sabotage material or systems • Facilities access to others

EVOLUTION FROM IDEA TO ACTION

FIGURE 1.3
Causes, Effects, and Actions of a Malicious Insider.

MITIGATING ASSET LOSS: AN INTEGRATED APPROACH

Identifying and mitigating the insider threat requires a group of leaders within an organization committed to protecting assets and looking at the workforce from a holistic perspective. Insider threat mitigation should be viewed as a team sport. An integrated approach is multidisciplinary and leverages multiple resources and tools from within an organization to build a proactive and effective solution. It considers what insiders do—not just who they are—to enable early detection of a potential insider threat. An integrated approach asks: How do individuals' activities in the physical and observable world relate to virtual work spaces, and how do employee's actions in both worlds relate to insider threats?

Accordingly, addressing the insider threat requires the involvement of more than an organization's Information Technology (IT) Group. Physical Security, Privacy, Policy, Human Resources, Legal, Business Units, Information Assurance, Compliance, and Executive Management must also be involved from the start. Similarly, using tools to detect an insider threat is just one component to developing an overall insider threat program. This book discusses in detail why a holistic approach is critical and why looking at behavior in the virtual space alone is insufficient.

Defining Critical Assets

The amount of information that an organization contains is immense, and protecting all of it is nearly impossible. To mitigating asset loss, we recommend leveraging a risk-based methodology to define an organization's critical assets and determine the importance of each. A critical asset (e.g., proprietary information, network infrastructure, financial assets, research and development, PII, source code) is vital to sustain the organization's business operations, mission, and infrastructure, including human, tangible, and intangible resources. An organization should begin with the following questions:

- What data and critical assets are most important to the organization?
- Where does it exist?
- How is it protected?
- Who has access?
- What is the organization's risk appetite, risk tolerance, and risk management plan?

Detection

To detect insiders' intent before they do harm, organizations need to establish a series of potential risk indicators based on the assets they wish to protect. For example, potential risk indicators for a rogue software developer who appears likely to steal his company's source code may include a vengeful attitude, isolation from coworkers, source code system access during off-hours, or poor performance ratings. Employees who believe they are going to lose their jobs may try to steal IP, which could help them land a job with a competitor or start their own company. Heavy equipment manufacturers seeking to safeguard new product designs may keep watch for insiders trying to access or download those plans, traveling to countries where IP theft is prevalent, sending e-mails with large attachments, and/or experiencing financial difficulty.

With potential risk indicators established, companies can then begin to collect and correlate virtual and nonvirtual data related to risk indicators for employees. Virtual data refers to the digital trails employees leave when they log on and off the corporate network, access systems, download or print documents, send e-mail, and use the Web. Nonvirtual data includes information about an individual's role in an organization, performance ratings, compliance with corporate policies, and work habits (such as when they start and stop working, with whom they typically interact, and their physical movement throughout an office).

Other important questions leaders should consider when developing a detection capability as part of an insider threat program include the following:

- How will you develop a holistic program, one that incorporates information from virtual and nonvirtual sources? How will it address contextual factors? (access, clearance, digital identification)
- How does your organization currently define its critical assets, risk tolerance, and priority areas of focus?
- How do you plan to correlate the information collected across siloes and promote cross-functional coordination?
- How does your organization plan to promote information sharing on the topic of insider threat across key offices (e.g., legal, HR, privacy, information technology)? Has the organization considered developing an insider threat working group to meet on a reoccurring basis to tackle insider threat mitigation challenges and issues?
- What are the lessons learned from internal and external cases (e.g., Manning, Snowden, Alexis) as they relate to potential risk indicators, polices, controls, and training that organizations should adopt? How has the analysis of potential risk indicators or precursors displayed by each of these individuals informed the development of insider threat programs?
- How will your organization address the prevention and response to budding insider threats?
- What are some of the key controls that are being administered to prevent and detect insider threats? For example, if an employee e-mails a large attachment with sensitive, proprietary information, would this be captured in a log and, more importantly, would it generate an alert that would trigger human review?
- How does your organization protect individuals' collected data?

Developing a Secure Workforce

A key to prevention and early detection in insider threat mitigation practice is the development of a securely managed workforce. Such an approach takes into account what is known about insider threat, potential risk indicators, and associated triggers that result in asset loss, and aligns them to a series of solutions. These solutions include, for example, refining the vetting and hiring process; establishing a system to report suspicious behavior and activity; providing resources to assist employees who may experience a crisis that leads them to exploit assets as a solution; and augmenting the workforce to function as an early warning system. These are all leading practices associated with mature insider threat mitigation programs.

Some of the most frequent rationalizations offered by violators when queried about their actions are that "no one notices," "physical and information security is lax," "no one will get hurt," and "I made it, so I own it." These sentiments indicate that insiders rarely enter an organization with the intent to commit an insider act, but fall into ignorant or complacent behavior over time, after they are employed and granted access to information.

Insider threat behavior is also influenced by how effectively an organization manages risk in the workforce. As mentioned earlier, insiders are frequently employees who are ignorant or complacent about what needs to be protected, and proper protocol such as not sharing passwords with anyone. In these situations, organizations often lack policies that define expectations for employee behavior in the workplace, specifically when using information systems. Potential risk indicators are not captured and little or no training is available during employee onboarding or on a regular basis. From our cross-industry experience building insider threat programs, policies and communications define behavioral expectations that help create acceptable employee behaviors. Such expectations also assist employees in knowing what kinds of information are most damaging if lost, stolen, or otherwise acquired by others. Moreover, without a set of expectations and rules, it is more difficult to proactively detect changes in the behavior of an employee who is moving along the idea-to-action continuum.

Establishing a Workforce Culture to Mitigate Risk

Competencies exist that identify people who are less likely to pose security risks. As the culture and demography of the workforce transforms, individuals who are selected for positions in sensitive and secure jobs will need to possess core competencies that reflect integrity, self-restraint, and a dedication to the "collaborative cause." Generation Y (millennials) introduce a new type of risk into a secure work environment—based on their need for rapid-fire communication, constant connectivity, and a natural propensity to share information.[5] With sensitivity to the right competencies, however, these generations can be guided to be team-oriented, responsive to constructive criticism, and more likely to express, rather than withhold, frustration—in other words, less likely to disclose classified information. Companies can vet and hire employees with these competencies.

Successfully mitigating insider threats requires addressing vulnerabilities as part of an organization's overall risk management strategy. Risk management strategies often fail to consider the people who control organizations'

---

[5] Garretson, C. Balancing Generation Y Preferences with Security. *Network World*. N.p., 29 Aug. 2007. Web. <www.networkworld.com/news/2007/082907>.

digital information and critical infrastructure. Such strategies may also fail to consider in a reward-to-risk ratio the culture higher-level executives establish by emphasizing achieving revenue targets. In essence, the moral tone of the organization is an important factor. Organizations that overcome risk-spot blindness and understand the variety of actions that can serve as potential risk indicators or precursors to an insider attack establish a better posture for stopping or disrupting emerging insider threats. The Top 10 Tips for Leaders section outlines the strategic considerations for leaders establishing an insider threat program.

TOP 10 TIPS FOR LEADERS

Threats and vulnerabilities define the environment in which an organization operates and dictates the risk management strategy needed to protect the organization's assets. Additionally, leadership's risk appetite and risk tolerance will drive what a organization is willing to do to mitigate the insider threat, and what operating guidelines executives are willing to follow or overlook in the pursuit of greater reward.

Risk appetite is defined as what an organization wants to protect or, conversely, what it does not want to lose. Risk tolerance is the extent to which an organization is willing to take steps to mitigate the threat and protect assets. Risk tolerance can be influenced by a number of factors, including the risk necessary to conduct business. For example, some organizations may not want to conduct background investigations and refuse to monitor the activity of their employees on the company's information systems.

There are ten considerations we believe leaders need to consider as they review the development or the maturity of an insider threat program. These key considerations are relevant to leaders whether they are protecting proprietary information, facilities, and material in the private sector, or safeguarding classified information in the public sector in accordance with Executive Orders.

1   Define The Insider Threats

Don't be surprised if your organization hasn't defined an insider threat. Because only external threats historically have been prioritized by security and IT budgets, the reality is that few organizations have a specific, internal, working definition. An insider can be an employee, contractor, or vendor that commits a malicious, complacent, or ignorant act using his or her trusted and verified access. Defining threats from within your organization and business environment is a critical first step to formulating a program because it informs the size, structure, and scope of the program.

2   Define Your Risk Appetite

As we discussed, it is critical to define your organization's critical assets (e.g., facilities, source code, IP and R&D, and customer information) and the organization's tolerance for loss or damage in those areas. Identify key threats and vulnerabilities in your business and the way you do business. Tailor the development of the program to address these specific needs and threat types, and take into account your organization's unique culture. Carefully consider whether employees might violate the risk/reward guidelines that you have established. These guidelines exist to help executives critically analyze why they are about to violate a guideline so there is an informed decision as to the upside and the downside risk, and not just wishful thinking or greed.

3   Optimize a Broad Set of Stakeholders

An insider threat mitigation program should have one owner but a broad set of invested stakeholders. Establish a cross-disciplinary insider threat working group that can serve as change agents and ensure the proper level of buy-in across departments and stakeholders (e.g., legal, physical security, policy, IT security, human resources, ethics). The working group's support will be critical to building the insider threat mitigation capability and securing the data needed for the program. It should assist in addressing common concerns (e.g., privacy and legal) and support the development of messaging to executives, managers, and the broader employee population.

4   Don't Forget the Fundamentals

The insider threat challenge is not purely a technical one. It is a people-centric problem that requires a holistic and people-centric solution. Organizations should avoid the common pitfall of focusing on a technical solution as the silver bullet. A robust program should include key business processes, policies, technical and nontechnical controls, training, and the organizational change management components needed to promote an environment of security awareness and deterrence.

5   Trust but Verify

Establish routine and random auditing of privileged functions, which is commonly used to identify insider threats across a broad spectrum of threats in a variety of industries. Organizations should trust their workforce but balance that trust with verification to avoid instances of unfettered access and single points of failure. This auditing is particularly essential in areas that are defined as critical and high risk.

6   Look for Precursors

Case studies have shown that insider threats are seldom impulsive acts. Rather, insiders move on a continuum from the idea of committing an insider act to the actual act itself (e.g., fraud, espionage, workplace violence, IT sabotage, and IP and R&D theft). During this process, the individual often displays observable behaviors (e.g., requests undue access, violates policies, and demonstrates disgruntled behavior) that can serve as potential risk indicators for early detection. Programs should aggregate, correlate, and visualize PRIs to serve as an early detection capability.

7   Connect the Dots

By correlating precursors or potential risk indicators captured in virtual and nonvirtual arenas, your organization will gain insights into micro and macro trends regarding the high risk behaviors exhibited across the organization. This can be achieved through the use of an advanced analytics platform that ingests and correlates PRIs from a variety of data sources (e.g., personnel management, SIEM, HR, DLP). This can in turn be used to identify insider threat leads for investigative purposes. It can also shed new light on processes and policies that are either missing or could be improved upon.

8   Stay a Step Ahead

Insiders' methods, tactics, and attempts to cover their tracks will constantly evolve, which means that the insider threat program and the PRIs or precursors that it analyzes should continuously evolve as well. This can be achieved through a feedback mechanism that includes an analysis of ongoing and historical cases and investigations.

9   Set Behavioral Expectations

Define the behavioral expectations of your workforce through clear and consistently enforced policies (e.g., social media, removable media, reporting incidents, bring-your-own-device) that define acceptable behavior and communicate consequences for violating policies. Ensure policies that set behavioral expectations are standard, centrally located, routinely updated, and consistently enforced.

10   One Size Does Not Fit All

Customize training based on physical and network access levels, privilege rights, and job responsibilities. Train the workforce on specific insider threat risks, challenges, and responsibilities for each position (i.e., a data administrator's curriculum should be different from a sales representative's curriculum).

IN SUMMARY

This book highlights a people-centric, technology-enabled approach to iden-tify and mitigate the risk of insider threat. As the workplace becomes more complex and insider threats become more difficult to detect, the tools and detection techniques must become smarter and more capable of adjusting to evolving threats. Having too many security controls can impede the mission. Having too few increases vulnerabilities and leaves the organization exposed. Insider threat programs should strike a proper balance between countering the threat and accomplishing the organization's mission. Quick responses, real-time data feeds, and analysis of behavioral indicators are imperative to stay in front of the insider's exploitative tactics. The goal should be to detect anomalies as early as possible and to investigate leads in order to interrupt the forward motion of the potential insider threats before assets, data, or per-sonnel are compromised.

By focusing on one of the organization's primary asset, *its people*, an organiza-tion can systematically identify and manage the risks associated with insider threat through the support of a cross-organizational team. Traditionally, com-panies have implemented technology solutions and believed that their organ-ization will be secure, but studies have shown the insider threat is still on the rise. Managing people and creating a secure workforce represents the missing link in protecting the organization from the inside.

Because the workforce has evolved to be more mobile and less organization oriented, leadership matters even more than in the past. It is critical today that leaders demonstrate a commitment to an insider threat program and encourage participation by all the key stakeholders on the executive staff or in the C Suite.

KEY TAKEAWAYS

- An insider is a person who possesses some combination of knowledge and access that distinguishes his or her relationship with the organization from those of outsiders.
- To build an insider threat mitigation capability, your organization will need to define the insider and prioritize insider threat risk to focus resources.
- Understanding the three drivers of insider threats is critical to developing mitigation approaches: Insider threats can be malicious (i.e., intended to do harm, with a plan developed in advance), complacent (i.e., with the assumption that the behavior does not have a noticeable impact and that no one is monitoring it), or ignorant (i.e., lacks an understanding of security protocols).

- Malicious insiders move along a continuum from idea to action. Regardless of motivation, an insider's plans often percolate for weeks or months before acting.
- Collecting, correlating, and visualizing potential risk indicators across the organization enables proactive risk detection and mitigation.

CHAPTER 2

Common Challenges to Maturing an Insider Threat Program

INTRODUCTION

The development of an insider threat program will be influenced by what an organization defines as critical to protect, and what it is willing to do to protect those assets. At the same time, an organization must retain a balanced perspective on security and conducting business.

One constant that organizations face that goes beyond the external perimeter of a company or organization is the growing threat from within the organization. The world has evolved over the last 25 years and technology has become a major force in defining a global and virtual environment where business is conducted. Technology has provided a medium where information can be instantaneously accessed and transmitted to include the exfiltration of critical proprietary information from an organization by malicious employees. Because of the growing dependence on technology, there are risks associated with employees beyond those who are malicious. These employees are complacent—an equally dangerous category. Complacent employees are often careless with security practices when working on an organization's systems and may open the door to external attacks by hackers.

Regardless of the advent of technology, an insider threat program is all about *people*. Although technology has increased our capacity to do business, it has also increased the risk of doing business. Business is conducted by people—people who have thoughts, feelings, aspirations, needs and attitudes, and who can be vengeful, passive, aggressive, aggrandized, and ignorant. Although many insider threat programs are dependent on technology as a mechanism to mitigate the risk of information theft, the use of technology to capture and detect anomalous behavior needs to be rooted in an understanding of a person's motivation—essentially what a person does and not who a person is.

Technology can enable an organization to capture the behavior of an employee or contractor who has direct access to their systems, and then monitor behavior to detect anomalies. This provides an organization with an early detection capability that enables the organization to interrupt the forward

Insider Threat. DOI: http://dx.doi.org/10.1016/B978-0-12-802410-2.00002-2

motion of a potential insider threat. Using technology with other key program initiatives (segregation of duties, role based access, training and awareness, vetting) to prevent, detect, and respond to an insider threat can help organizations to move from a reactive to a proactive stance and to protect its critical assets, brand, and reputation.

CHALLENGES FACED BY PROGRAM MANAGERS

As a result of consulting with many clients who are building or maturing insider threat programs, there are several key questions that clients ask about moving a program forward. This chapter will share some common questions that insider threat program managers and key stakeholders ask. The chapter will share insights from working with clients, including leading practices for optimizing programs.

For several decades, insider threat has been a topic of great interest for organizational leaders. National security leaders have historically focused on insider threat as a component of a broader counterintelligence program. For other government and corporate leaders, insider threat was considered a low-frequency, high-impact event that was not treated as a priority because it did not have national security implications. Historically, physical security programs and reactive investigations have been in place to respond to insider threat activity determined by uncovering lost information or a threat of potential violence in the workplace. In the early 1990s, workplace violence programs began to surface in both the government and private sector. Beyond observable behavior and reports of suspicious actions, there was no proactive detection capability and a reactive response to a set of indicators or reported behavior by bystanders was the only method to respond.

In 2011, President Obama signed Executive Order 13587[1] that mandated government agencies stand up insider threat programs to protect classified information. Shortly thereafter, the Defense Security Service (DSS), which is responsible for managing the Defense Industrial Base (DIB), moved forward in drafting additional guidance in the National Industrial Security Program Operation Manual (NISPOM)[2] to guide the DIB, and specifically the cleared contract environment. This has evoked a response from the contractor community to quickly develop an insider threat program, in addition to the cyber

---

[1] Exec. Order No. 13587, 3 C.F.R. 3 (2011). Print. Structural Reforms to Improve the Security of Classified Networks and the Responsible Sharing and Safeguarding of Classified Information
[2] Defense Security Service. "Information on Pending Insider-Threat Program Requirements for Industry." Information on Pending Insider-Threat Program Requirements for Industry (n.d.). Department of Defense. Web.

security programs already designed to secure corporate information systems from an external attack. Interestingly, many companies that have no connection to classified information or government contracts have begun to aggressively stand up insider threat programs to protect their people, facilities, and information. Perhaps the greatest risk that they are looking to mitigate is the risk to their reputation, brand, and market share, should their assets become compromised and impact the confidence of the public in their product, services, or capabilities.

Most recently, there has also been an interest in combining workplace violence programs into a more comprehensive insider threat program. Combining these two major risks is based on today's ability to proactively detect anomalous behavior—whether to protect the workforce from violence or to prevent employees from exfiltrating sensitive and critical corporate data by interrupting the forward motion of potential insiders before they choose to steal or commit a violent act.

The following chapter is organized around specific questions asked by Chief Security, Information, and Risk Officers, as it pertains to developing and maturing insider threat programs. These questions show that organizations are attempting to manage risk and shift from a reactive to a more proactive response.

Are There More Insider Threat Cases Now Than There Have Been in the Past?

One of the more frequently asked questions from leadership is whether there has been a change in the frequency of insider threat incidents. Several surveys suggest that there is a change in the landscape of insider threat activity. A Poneman survey[3] suggests that 59% of workers today who quit or are asked to leave the company take sensitive information with them. One hypothesis is that because of a generational shift, as many Gen Ys enter the workforce, there is a changing perspective around who has ownership of information or assets. Some younger workers believe that if "I developed it and I made it, its mine and I'll keep it." Other data that further illustrates the problem includes a survey by CERT that suggests 97% of employees who were flagged by a supervisor for specific suspicious behavior were not reported and ended up as insider threats.[4] This phenomenon has been a challenge to the security

---

[3] Ponemon Institute, Data loss risks during downsizing, *Rep. Symantec Corporation*, February 23, 2009. Web.
[4] Cappelli, Dawn M., Andrew P. Moore, and Randall F. Trzeciak, *The CERT Guide to Insider Threats: How to Prevent, Detect, and Respond to Information Technology Crimes* (Upper Saddle River, NJ: Addison-Wesley Professional, 2012).

community for many decades. Whether espionage, workplace violence, theft of information, or sabotage, few people report suspicious behavior that they observe in the workplace. There have been many studies to better understand the bystander effect, beginning in 1964 with the Kitty Genovese murder in Kew Gardens NY.[5] More recently, postincident investigations of espionage, workplace violence, and school violence have revealed after the fact that others knew what the perpetrator was planning or felt that the perpetrator's behavior had changed and become odd or strange.[6] Additionally, many organizations do not have a reporting mechanism in place—even if employees did have something to report, there may not be a place to do so or the confidence that it would remain anonymous. Recently, organizations have begun to develop ethics and integrity hotlines that are confidential and could serve as a vehicle to capture suspicious behavior. This is another reason why an organization should proactively monitor its workforce to detect anomalous behavior, given that it may be less likely to be reported.

How Does an Organization Define Insider Threat?

Defining insider threat is the first step to begin to mitigate risk and protect assets. While there are many different definitions for insider threat, it is important that the definition adopted is broad enough to incorporate the risks that the organization has prioritized. Few organizations have a specific internal working definition of "insider threat" (14%). Those who define the term do so broadly.[7] An organization should begin by prioritizing what it is that they want to protect, and what they are willing to do to protect it. The definition should be broad and holistic. It should incorporate multiple aspects of the business. It should also include what an organization is not willing to do given the impact it could have on the way they do business, or on the culture of the organization. For example, an organization should ask: What is not critical to protect? Does doing business in certain foreign countries involve greater risks than in other countries? Are there specific IT security practices, such as access to personal email and use of removal media, that may impede the way business is conducted? These are all decisions that organizational leaders need to consider as they define insider threat for their organization.

---

[5] Gansberg, Martin. 37 Who Saw Murder Didn't Call the Police. *The New York Times*, March 26, 1964. Web.

[6] Fein, Robert, and Bryan Vossekuil, Protective Intelligence and Threat Assessment Investigations: A Guide for State and Local Law Enforcement Officials, Rep. no. NCJ 179981. (Washington DC: National Institute of Justice, 2000). Web.

[7] M. Gelles, Preventing, Mitigating and Managing Insider Threats, Conference Board of Canada, April 2013.

A definition of insider threat that is broad enough to begin the prioritization exercise is as follows: Any person who as access to an organization's information, people, facilities, or material. This might include an employee, a contractor, a vendor, and family members (from many lessons learned in past espionage cases). Some activities in which an insider could engage that are the greatest risk to the organization include workplace violence, espionage, fraud, sabotage, and theft. The list should be specific to the type of business that an organization conducts.

Why Do Insider Threat Programs Need to Look Beyond the Malicious Insider?

There are three specific drivers associated with insider threats: maliciousness, complacency, and ignorance. Historically, the malicious insider has been the main focus for mitigating insider threat. This is someone who has clear, malevolent intent to do damage to information, material, facilities, or people. The more contemporary insider and one that has grown with the continued growth of technology and the new age of business is the complacent insider. This is an individual who is unwitting and not malevolent, but in an interesting way, sees himself/herself above the rules and his/her job as more important than anyone else's and, as a result, believes he/she needs to get that job done within the time frame and will do whatever he/she needs to do to get the job done. This often results in violating rules and controls and, therefore, exposes an organization to tremendous risk. This might include clicking on a phishing email or engaging in behavior that allowed the facilitation of an outsider to gain access to systems, buildings, or people. Finally, the uninformed or ignorant insider is typically the result of an organization's inattention to the insider threat and failure to provide its workforce with the necessary guidance, policy, communications, and training to protect critical assets. In other words, the uninformed individual does not know what they are, and are not, supposed to do. Organizations need to assess how well their policies are defined, assimilated, and enforced, as well as how well communications are pushed to the workforce.

One challenge for a number of organizations has been to gain consensus with all stakeholders (HR, Legal, information security). Insider threat program managers must also take into account the complacent insider—not default to the malicious insider. Often organizations look only for malicious insiders and activity on the virtual systems.

Why Are Insider Threat Related Policies and Training Important?

It is important for training and policies to go beyond foundational principles associated with insider threats, and target the specific risks that exist for key roles.

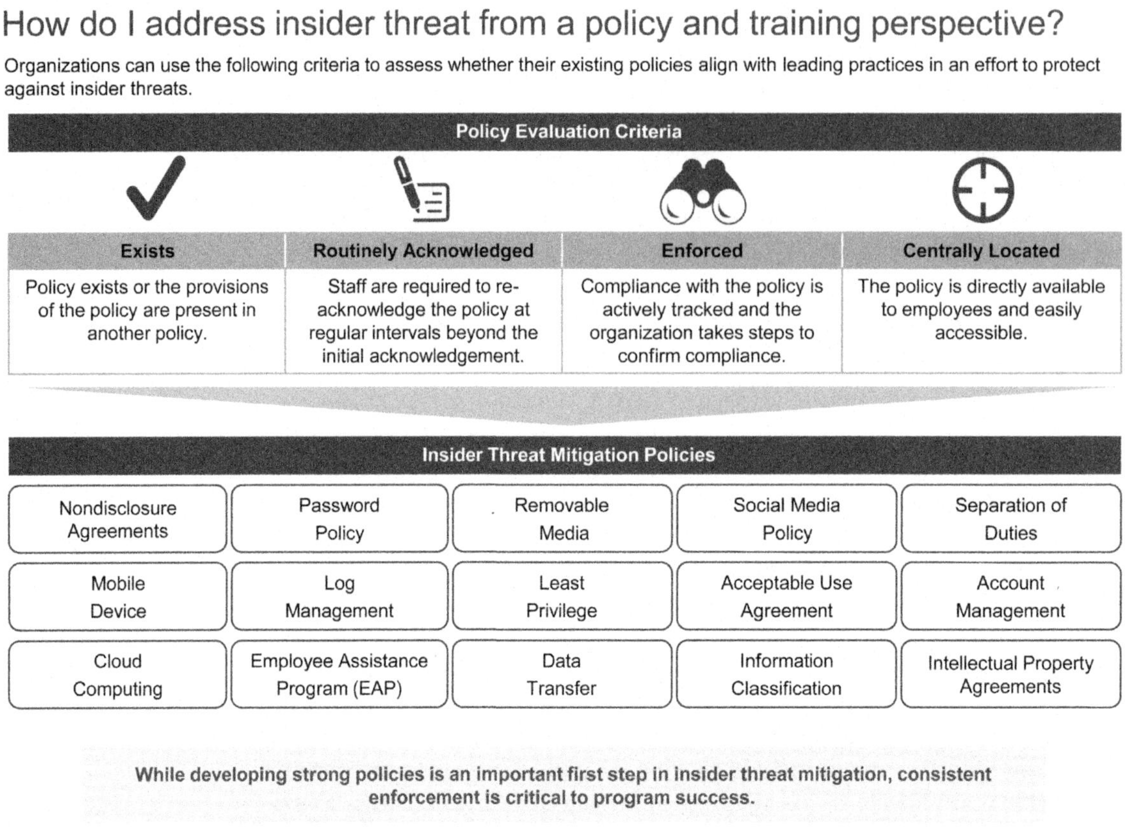

How do I address insider threat from a policy and training perspective?

Organizations can use the following criteria to assess whether their existing policies align with leading practices in an effort to protect against insider threats.

Policy Evaluation Criteria			
Exists	**Routinely Acknowledged**	**Enforced**	**Centrally Located**
Policy exists or the provisions of the policy are present in another policy.	Staff are required to re-acknowledge the policy at regular intervals beyond the initial acknowledgement.	Compliance with the policy is actively tracked and the organization takes steps to confirm compliance.	The policy is directly available to employees and easily accessible.

Insider Threat Mitigation Policies				
Nondisclosure Agreements	Password Policy	Removable Media	Social Media Policy	Separation of Duties
Mobile Device	Log Management	Least Privilege	Acceptable Use Agreement	Account Management
Cloud Computing	Employee Assistance Program (EAP)	Data Transfer	Information Classification	Intellectual Property Agreements

While developing strong policies is an important first step in insider threat mitigation, consistent enforcement is critical to program success.

FIGURE 2.1
Policies to Consider for an Insider Threat Program.

A training for system administrators, for example, should include a specific curriculum targeted to that group. Policies are also important in that they define behavioral expectations for the workforce. The challenge with policy is often around whether the policy clearly articulates what an employee should know about protecting assets. Another common challenge is that policies must be written so they are readily assimilated, acknowledged, and enforced (Figure 2.1).

What Capabilities Differentiate an Industry-Leading Insider Threat Program?

Industry-leading programs have four critical, foundational components: they are (1) coordinated, (2) risk-based, (3) holistic, and (4) proactive. **Coordinated** suggests that the program has one owner, but diverse, invested stakeholders—consistent with an insider threat working group—who can serve as change agents and promote organizational buy-in across departments. **Risk-based** suggests that employee risk levels are based on the collection, correlation, and visualization of potential risk indicators (PRIs), which allows the organization to take a proactive and risk-based approach to mitigating emerging insider threats. **Holistic** includes the development of business processes, policies, technology, controls, training, and organizational change components focused on prevention, detection, and response capabilities. **Proactive** suggests that risk mitigation strategies are developed to allow for proactive threat detection that can stop or disrupt an emerging insider threat. The program's emphasis is on prevention but also includes robust detection and response capabilities.

Advanced program attributes that reflect more mature programs include the following four initiatives: continuous improvement, behavior change, proactive outreach, and return on investment. **Continuous improvement** is incorporated throughout the program's operations through the randomized testing of new PRIs, simulated tests (red teaming) to evaluate detection capabilities, and the development of feedback loops to manage program effectiveness. **Behavior change** is a programmatic goal and includes approaches to improve compliance with business processes and policies through targeted outreach. **Proactive outreach** includes initiatives such as Employee Assistance Programs (EAPs), designed to provide counseling and outreach to individuals that may be at increased risk for committing an insider threat act. **Return on investment** is captured through the quantification of metrics including the number of business processes improvements, policy enhancements, technical control updates, cases initiated, documents retrieved, and law enforcement referrals.

How Do I Escalate and Triage Potential Threats Identified by the Program?

Through the process of lead generation and assessment, individuals are flagged by an advanced analytics tool and assessed for follow-up investigation or identified as a false positive. After identifying that an alert is worthy of further exploration, the next phase of inquiry, review, and validation is pursued. If the individual is not marked as a false positive, it is further reviewed and validated. For threats that need to be further investigated, a case is opened, and the individual's identity is unmasked. The insider threat program drives the first two phases of the Escalation and Triage process using insights from the advanced analytics tool and refers cases requiring an investigative decision to the Insider Threat Working Group (ITWG). During the Triage and Escalation process, the individual's case is further reviewed by the Insider Threat Program and escalated, as necessary. Finally, a course of action is decided on and executed, including contacting the individual, taking corrective action, and/or activating the organization's enhanced monitoring

How do I escalate and triage potential threats identified by the program?

The Escalation and Triage Process Map complements existing escalation processes and provides steps for action when individuals are flagged above a risk score threshold in the advanced analytics tool. The process consists of four additive phases.

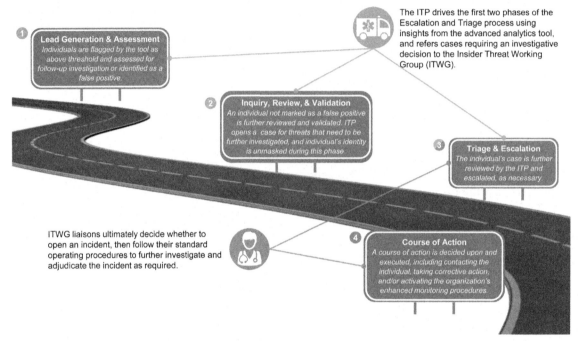

1 Lead Generation & Assessment
Individuals are flagged by the tool as above threshold and assessed for follow-up investigation or identified as a false positive.

2 Inquiry, Review, & Validation
An individual not marked as a false positive is further reviewed and validated. ITP opens a case for threats that need to be further investigated, and individual's identity is unmasked during this phase.

3 Triage & Escalation
The individual's case is further reviewed by the ITP and escalated, as necessary.

4 Course of Action
A course of action is decided upon and executed, including contacting the individual, taking corrective action, and/or activating the organization's enhanced monitoring procedures.

The ITP drives the first two phases of the Escalation and Triage process using insights from the advanced analytics tool, and refers cases requiring an investigative decision to the Insider Threat Working Group (ITWG).

ITWG liaisons ultimately decide whether to open an incident, then follow their standard operating procedures to further investigate and adjudicate the incident as required.

FIGURE 2.2
Escalation and Triage Process.

procedures. ITWG liaisons ultimately decide whether or not to open an incident and follow their standard operating procedures to further investigate and adjudicate the incident as required (Figure 2.2).

How Do I Position an Insider Threat Program to My Workforce?

The following core principles can help leadership proactively address common concerns and effectively communicate the benefits of an insider program to the workforce.

- **Privacy Protection:** Leadership is committed to protecting employee privacy and will continuously strive to improve privacy controls. Routine, semi-annual evaluations of the insider threat program will address evolving threats and reinforce program compliance with legal policy.

- **Employee Wellbeing:** An insider threat program should align to the organization's culture and promote trust among employees and contractors. The Program has built-in mechanisms for employee support, when needed (e.g., Employee Assistance Program).
- **Balanced Approach:** Too many security restrictions can impede an organization's mission and agile workforce, whereas too few increases vulnerabilities. The program must strike a balance between countering the threat and conducting business.
- **Brand Protection:** To protect the business and maintain organization's reputation, an organization should implement technologies, policies, and procedures that go beyond baseline requirements. Employees tend to benefit from a strong brand in the marketplace.
- **Critical Assets:** An insider threat program is designed to protect critical assets like people and data. Without these protections, an organization could be at risk if there is an incident.
- **Risk Based Monitoring:** As the perceived risk of an insider threat incident increases because of the detection of contextual, virtual, and nonvirtual precursors, monitoring should also increase.

How Do I Scale My Insider Threat Program?

This is a key question that people ask about their programs: should I go for an all-in approach, or begin with a pilot, and if so, how should it progress? In most circumstances, a limited pilot is effective. This allows the organization to proof the concept before broad expansion. The pilot can then be expanded geographically or to new business lines to ultimately cover your full workforce. The sheer amount of information that is collected on information systems and personnel can be overwhelming. A limited pilot can help determine what indicators are most relevant. For large organizations or global companies, the development of the insider threat program typically progresses through a series of phases to incrementally scale the program while performing continuous business process improvement. The first phase of developing an insider threat program is running a pilot, which includes

- establishing cross functional ITWG;
- designating the program as a center of excellence by implementing leading practices;
- conducting an organizational assessment based on leading practices;
- developing and implementing evidence-based recommendations for business processes, technology, and policy;
- identifying privacy and legal implications with data collection for threat detection; and
- conducting a proof of concept pilot for the advanced analytics, and evaluating the pilot before expansion.

The second phase is to expand the program geographically. The pilot is expanded across geographic regions to monitor employees and conduct analysis on a regular basis. Key activities include

- implementing recommendations from the first phase of the pilot;
- identifying POCs from additional business lines and subsidiaries to be included in the expansion, and conducting a current state assessment;
- developing communications and training materials to enable expansion to a wider population;
- identifying additional data and data owners to begin ingesting data streams on a continuous basis for analysis; and
- documenting and addressing functionality gaps as analysis is conducted.

The third phase is incremental to full expansion. The program is incrementally expanded to all of the organization's employees, including those who are globally deployed. Key activities include

- scheduling target countries, subsidiaries, and business lines for expansion;
- identifying privacy requirements associated with expanding data collection into different countries;
- developing communication materials, legal documentation, and other materials to facilitate international expansion; and
- identifying any additional data sources, systems of record, and data owners that are required for a wider population.

What are the Skillsets a Leading Program Needs to Have?

Historically we have seen many people who focus on hiring insider threat program analysts with counterintelligence backgrounds, which is perfectly appropriate if you understand the history and the evolution of the insider threat. As the threat has evolved with advent of technology, some of the challenges to analyze the threat have become broader. To optimize an organization's ability to mitigate a complex array of threats and comprehensively discern anomalous activity, there is a need for a more diverse set of skills than in the past.

An effective insider threat program employs staff with a well-rounded set of skills across a variety of organizational functions, including human resources, security, law enforcement, information technology, and counterintelligence. Some of these skillsets will reside within the program and some exist in separate functions that will interact with the program. The following skill sets can enhance an insider threat program:

- **Privacy Specialist:** Provides subject matter expertise for legal issues that organizations must consider when standing up and maintaining a program.

- **Data Scientist:** Correlates and analyzes potential risk indicators to detect anomalous network behavior, and visualizes employee risk trends over time using analytics dashboards.
- **Psychologist:** Provides input on employee attitudes or behaviors and analyzes behavioral indicators.
- **Social Media Expert:** Gathers relevant data from a variety of social media outlets to use for insider threat detection.
- **Policy Specialist:** Provides subject matter expertise on relevant insider threat policies and provides guidance on how to educate and encourage executives, managers, and employees to adhere to policy.

What Data are Needed to Proactively Identify Potential Insiders?

Organizations need to identify the right data and potential risk indicators (PRIs) that reflect what the organization is trying to protect, and what they are willing to do to protect those prioritized assets (Figure 2.3). The challenge becomes understanding what specific data organizations are willing and able to collect. In some instances, the behaviors that make the most sense to monitor will be collected through data that capture the behavior of individual employees. Many organizations struggle with the number of PRIs needed to accurately detect anomalies. The number of indicators can range from 10 to 150. Most successful programs, in Deloitte's experience in standing up insider threat programs, will collect between 20 and 40 indicators on average. A sample selection of foundational potential risk indicators is as follows:

- Large volume of outbound e-mail traffic
- Emails with attachments sent to suspicious recipients
- Transmittal device (e.g., printers, copiers, fax machine) anomalies
- Removable media alerts and anomalies
- Access levels
- Security clearance
- Privilege user rights
- Large collections of files
- Antivirus/malware alerts
- Excessively large downloads
- Access request denials
- Physical access request denials
- Physical access anomalies
- Audit remediation progress
- Noncompliance with training requirements
- Organizational policy violations (e.g., data classification policy, avoiding an e-QIP)
- Expense violations

What data are needed to proactively identify potential insiders?

An insider threat program's ability to detect threats is based on the collection of Potential Risk Indicators (PRIs). The table below includes 25 PRIs, including attributes and behaviors across three key categories: virtual, nonvirtual, and contextual.

Virtual includes behaviors displayed on the network and in the virtual landscape

Nonvirtual includes behaviors displayed off the network

Contextual includes the level of access and role within the organization

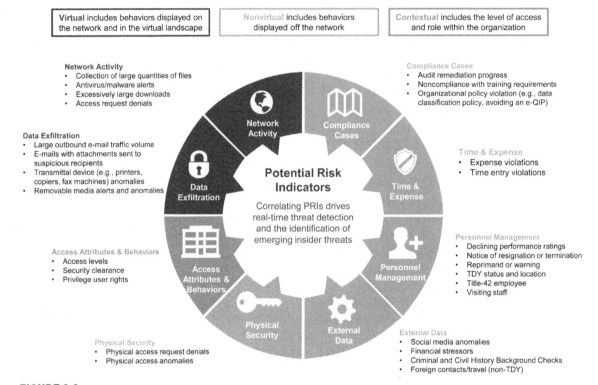

Network Activity
- Collection of large quantities of files
- Antivirus/malware alerts
- Excessively large downloads
- Access request denials

Data Exfiltration
- Large outbound e-mail traffic volume
- E-mails with attachments sent to suspicious recipients
- Transmittal device (e.g., printers, copiers, fax machines) anomalies
- Removable media alerts and anomalies

Access Attributes & Behaviors
- Access levels
- Security clearance
- Privilege user rights

Physical Security
- Physical access request denials
- Physical access anomalies

Potential Risk Indicators

Correlating PRIs drives real-time threat detection and the identification of emerging insider threats

Compliance Cases
- Audit remediation progress
- Noncompliance with training requirements
- Organizational policy violation (e.g., data classification policy, avoiding an e-QIP)

Time & Expense
- Expense violations
- Time entry violations

Personnel Management
- Declining performance ratings
- Notice of resignation or termination
- Reprimand or warning
- TDY status and location
- Title-42 employee
- Visiting staff

External Data
- Social media anomalies
- Financial stressors
- Criminal and Civil History Background Checks
- Foreign contacts/travel (non-TDY)

FIGURE 2.3

Scope of Potential Risk Indicators.

- Time entry violations
- Declining performance ratings
- Notice of resignation or termination
- Reprimands or warnings
- Social media anomalies
- Financial stressors
- Criminal and Civil History background checks
- Foreign contacts and travel

How Do I Evaluate and Select an Advanced Analytics Tool?

Advanced analytics more recently labeled "behavioral analytics" has enabled threat management to take an assertive stand by analyzing risk indicators and data. There are numerous existing capabilities that are fundamentally structured to be insider threat tools. These tools are designed to help identify anomalous behavior early and can collect and integrate vast amounts of data. In many circumstances, an immediate, big data problem can paralyze a program, making it difficult to discern patterns and anomalous behavior. What we contend is that based on a number of key indicators that can be tied to specific activities and actions, you can start winnowing down to more targeted data and establish a fairly robust program with a smaller data set. There are external data sources such as social media, indicators of financial stress, and criminal and civil actions that give more of a complete picture. Several options that can be considered are as follows:

- Procure an advanced analytics capability from an external vendor or run concurrent vendor pilots to compare results. There are many vendors in the marketplace to consider.
- Leverage the organization's existing analytics and visualizations tools to develop and deploy an advanced analytics pilot.
- Combine the two options above as a way to gauge fit. The organization can team up with an external vendor to pilot while building an internal prototype, and then evaluate both through separate trial periods. This approach may be well suited for organizations focused on a broad set of risks or with a complex system architecture.

As vendors are evaluated for alignment with the goals of a program, the following criteria should be considered when evaluating a tool: risk algorithm, visualization capability, scalability, data correlations, end use manipulation, role-based access, automation, cost effectiveness, compatibility, data repository, alerting, and insider threat expertise (Figure 2.4).

What Challenges are Generally Encountered When Standing Up a Program?

Six key challenges are among those encountered when standing up and maturing an insider threat program:

- **Performance management:** Define performance measures to better understand program effectiveness by focusing on metrics beyond law enforcement referrals. Continue to validate the organization's program against market trends. Basing program success solely on the number of incidents referred to legal or law enforcement could lead to oversight of other important indicators of success such as a decrease in nonmalicious incidents.
- **Continuous improvement:** Continuously reevaluate threat indicators to account for changing behaviors and activities driven by demographic shifts within a workforce, such as increased use of collaboration tools and applications. Applying historic patterns to a shifting workforce does not account for new technologies. Emerging trends in data sharing may make internal networks vulnerable.

How do I evaluate and select an advanced analytics tool?

Advanced analytics tools can help organizations correlate high-risk behaviors and identify emerging insider threats across the workforce. The following criteria can help organizations select the right tool for their program.

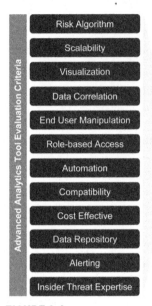

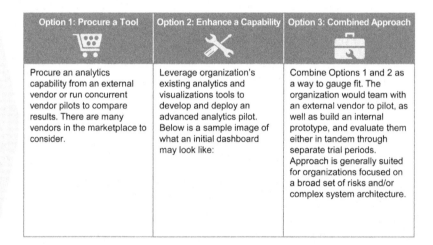

Option 1: Procure a Tool	Option 2: Enhance a Capability	Option 3: Combined Approach
Procure an analytics capability from an external vendor or run concurrent vendor pilots to compare results. There are many vendors in the marketplace to consider.	Leverage organization's existing analytics and visualizations tools to develop and deploy an advanced analytics pilot. Below is a sample image of what an initial dashboard may look like:	Combine Options 1 and 2 as a way to gauge fit. The organization would team with an external vendor to pilot, as well as build an internal prototype, and evaluate them either in tandem through separate trial periods. Approach is generally suited for organizations focused on a broad set of risks and/or complex system architecture.

FIGURE 2.4
Evaluation Criteria for Advanced Analytics Tools.

- **Vendor Management:** Evaluate the insider threat programs of business partners and vendors to determine whether they have adequate controls in place for individuals with access to property and information. An organization's insider threat program is only as strong as its weakest vendor. Failure to properly investigate and clear vendors and partners leaves the organization vulnerable to malicious attacks (see Chapter 10).
- **Career path:** Develop an insider threat career development program to increase retention and the skill levels of analysts. Develop analysts from cross-functional backgrounds to support the identification of different vulnerabilities. Skilled analysts may leave the organization for more lucrative offers, creating a disruption in workflow. There is likely to be significant competition for experienced analysts given the stand-up of public and private sector programs.
- **Risk-based training:** Skilled analysts who leave an organization for more lucrative offers may disrupt workflow. It is likely that there will be significant competition for experienced analysts given the stand-up of public and private sector programs.

- **Security culture:** A one-size-fits-all training program for the entire organization does not properly prepare management to recognize and deter insider threats. Awareness of the insider threat in business operations avoids instilling fear over insider "witch hunts."

How Mature Does My Program Have to Be?

The maturity of an insider threat program is going to depend on what an organization needs to have in place to protect its assets and balance its approach to conducting business. We have defined five stages of maturity for insider threat programs. Many organizations are in Stages 1 and 2 of the maturity model. We made the following findings among 15 of our clients in a variety of industries:

- Federal agencies (excluding intelligence) tend to be in Stages 1 or 2
- Oil, gas, and technology organizations tend to be in Stages 2 or 3
- Finance and intelligence organizations tend to be in Stages 4 or 5

Stage 1: Initial Ad Hoc
- **ITWG:** Purely reactive posture with limited to no coordination
- **Program Foundation:** No standardized threat mitigation processes, training, or policy
- **Advanced Analytics:** PRIs are not collected or standardized

Stage 2: Repeatable and Intuitive
- **ITWG:** Coordination across key functions exists, but not formal or routine
- **Program Foundation:** Limited business processes, policies, formal training, and communication of procedures
- **Advanced Analytics:** Early stages of developing a collection, correlation, and visualization capability

Stage 3: Defined Process
- **ITWG:** Established and periodically meets with the core group of stakeholders
- **Program Foundation:** Baseline business processes, training, and standardized policies are in place; limited communication and enforcement on insider threat mitigation
- **Advanced Analytics:** Initial capability including a limited subset of data and workforce population

Stage 4: Managed and Measurable
- **ITWG:** Meets routinely with executive buy-in to deliver recommendations
- **Program Foundation:** Majority of business processes are in place, including the segregation of duties, least privilege, training, and awareness and physical and logical programs

- **Advanced Analytics:** Virtual, nonvirtual, and contextual risk indicators are collected and analyzed to generate leads
- **Escalation and Triage**: Clear and defined

Stage 5: Optimized

- **ITWG:** Coordinates changes across key functions and serves as agents for change
- **Program Foundation:** Satisfies all leading practices for segregation of duties, least privilege, access control, network controls, physical controls, training, hiring, vetting; built-in continuous improvement mechanisms
- **Advanced Analytics:** Provides the full scope of peer-based and individual baselines, network controls and alerts; routine monitoring
- **Escalation and Triage**: Robust processes that are routinely evaluated and tested

How do You Measure the Return on Investment?

As more organizations seek to establish insider threat capabilities, many program owners struggle to measure and quantify the return on investment from an insider threat program. This is often times a direct result of limited planning to think through key metrics that will resonate with the intended audience and justify the financial investment in the program. In the absence of capturing metrics, the value generated by the program is subject to multiple interpretations and the program may be cut or completely defunded. Consequently, we advise organizations to begin thinking through metrics during the conceptualization phase of the program. This leading practice further ensures that key stakeholders are evaluating and building in processes to capture necessary metrics. The metrics below present a series of program outputs which can be used to assist program owners demonstrate the value of an insider threat program beyond simply detecting a potential malicious, complacent, or ignorant actor. This list is not comprehensive and is subject to change, based on longer term trends. The value is primarily for key leadership situational awareness, and secondarily to program evaluation, trend analysis, and demonstrating the unique value of the insider threat program to the enterprise.

Key Metrics[*]

- **Cases opened:** number and type of cases opened and reviewed by the program
- **Internal requests for information:** number and type of RFIs to organizations stakeholders

---

[*] Note: The metrics listed are limited to outputs from an advanced analytics tool. Additional metrics tracking "programmatic" activity such as number of employees trained are beyond the scope of this list but should be captured as part of the effort to demonstrate ROI for the program.

- **Internal escalation and triage:** number and type of cases escalated and triaged within the organization
- **External escalation and triage:** number and type of referrals to external law enforcement agencies
- **Risk mitigating actions:** number and type of risk mitigating actions (e.g., Employee Assistance Program, enhanced monitoring, employee termination) taken by the program to protect critical assets
- **Documents retrieved:** number of documents prevents from leaving the secure environment
- **Investigation productivity:** average reduction in investigation timelines

A Global Perspective[8]

To stand up an effective insider threat program, it is essential to apply an authoritative independent framework. Such a framework must balance the need for controls such as monitoring, which help protect an organization's assets, with employees' rights to privacy. The Holistic Management of Employee Risk (HoMER) is the premier UK national guidance for managing insider threat and it strikes this balance. It is a framework to improve trust among employees, customers, and shareholders, and is endorsed by the UK Information Commissions, a UK privacy regulator.

Non-technical and written in an accessible, non-academic workbook style, HoMER is for board members and owners of risk. Consistent with other UK national standards, HoMER is principles-based and emphasizes the importance of ethics and core values as essential tramlines for managing employee risk. The guidance sets out principles, policies, procedures, and examples of good practice which help manage insider threat risks in the workplace. The holistic use of targeted security measures and intervention can assist organizations in detecting anomalous and risky workplace behavior, and proactively detect and prevent insider incidents.

KEY TAKEAWAYS

In conclusion, there are a number of key takeaways that program managers should consider when maturing programs.

- **It's a team sport**—Program should have one owner, but a broad set of invested stakeholders that can serve as change agents and promote

---

[8] Centre for the Protection of National Infrastructure. "Holistic Management of Employee Risk (HoMER)." Centre for the Protection of National Infrastructure. CPNI and PA Consulting Group, 20 Sept. 2012. Web

organizational buy-in across departments. This holistic approach allows various aspects of the organization to come together to create the necessary prevention, detection, and response capabilities. One of the consistent findings in mature insider threat programs in the public and private sectors is the extent to which key functions such as legal, privacy, policy, business operations, human resources, physical security, and information technology are engaged. Broad stakeholder engagement is a differentiator and should be a goal of every insider threat program regardless of its current or targeted maturity level.

- **It is a programmatic centric solution not a technologic one—** Implementing a technical solution before establishing the programmatic and foundational components (e.g., business process, policy, and training) can lead to a suboptimal program that lacks the proper mechanisms and capabilities to effectively prevent, detect, and respond to threats. We have seen this common pitfall with a number of programs. Technology can function as a force multiplier, but should be viewed as a single capability in the broader toolset of stopping or disrupting an insider threat. Organizations that implement a technical solution before addressing programmatic requirements often fail to separate the signal from the noise and have to back-track.

- **Prepare before procuring a behavioral analytic—**Insider threat programs should have a behavioral analytics capability. While this capability is foundational, it is only one aspect of an effective program. Sometimes programs have selected a tool without doing the necessary due diligence to include adequately defining critical assets, capturing the organization's risk tolerance, defining PRIs, and creating a structure to organize PRIs. Without preparing for the types of information and how this information will be utilized to detect risk, the tool is likely to flatline and generate little value to the organization.

- **Challenge the status quo—**The proliferation of new technologies has expanded the scope of threats that organizations face. Establishing security protocols and layered defenses to combat these threats requires a proactive and continuous commitment to probe for new vulnerabilities, maintain a state of readiness, and ensure the program regularly improves. Once an insider threat program has been established, organizations should test the controls to identify gaps through the use of red teams and routine penetration testing. Randomized testing of new potential risk indicators (PRIs), simulated tests, audits of detection capabilities (e.g., tests of common data exfiltration points), and development of feedback loops to manage program effectiveness, are all effective methods to reduce blinders and mature a program.

- **Train your managers**—A vigilant manager workforce and a culture of security is a critical aspect of mitigating the insider threat. Organizations must place a concerted effort on training managers to connect with their employees and recognize signs that an employee is stressed and may be going through a crisis. Program managers who interact with staff should be trained to identify the signs of an employee exhibiting elevated risk behavior associated with a complacent, ignorant, or malicious insider threat. Furthermore, there should be clear guidelines on reporting mechanisms, including anonymous reporting.
- **Engage your workforce**—Employee engagement and a security-minded workforce culture is not just about human resources and talent. A productive, innovative, and sustainable workforce that contributes to the growth of the business is a critical factor in the security ecosystem and an important part of an insider threat program. A highly engaged workforce can help mitigate many risks within an organization to include the exploitation of critical assets and prevention of workplace violence. A highly engaged workforce is compliant with policies, procedures, and practices that are meant to protect people, information, material, and facilities.
- Never forget that it is *all about people*.

CHAPTER 3

From Bricks and Mortar to Bits and Bytes

THE TRANSFORMATION FROM BRICKS AND MORTAR TO BITS AND BYTES

"Bricks and mortar" to "bits and bytes" is a useful metaphor to describe the significant way in which information technology has driven changes in the business environment. Information technology has also changed the context of the insider threat: insider behavior is no longer limited to observable actions in a physical context. Rather, the insider threat has spread to a global, virtual context, encompassing activity via an array of technical devices and platforms. In short, as information becomes more transparent, behavior becomes more opaque.

For many years, the insider threat was viewed as a high-impact, low-frequency event. Today, however, the potential for an insider attack has significantly increased as a result of information technology, specifically, the fluidity of information. Theft and sabotage of sensitive information no longer requires physical access to the place where the information is stored.

The "world of bricks and mortar" is the period of time that pre-dates information technology. It is a world characterized by observable behavior and tangible tools used to conduct business: pen and paper, the written word, envelopes, packages, sketches, and diagrams. In this analog world, communication was based on letters and messengers, then later, on telegraphs, radios, and telephones. Communication became faster, but information or material continued to be passed person-to-person, both directly and indirectly. Stealing information meant copying it by hand, or later, by machine, then physically removing it.

Beginning in the late 1980s, information technology began to transform the world of bricks and mortar (Figure 3.1). Communication grounded in digital tools—computers and email, for example—became mainstream. Although information could be managed in larger quantities and with greater speed and expediency, there was still a need to copy and carry information. The

Insider Threat. DOI: http://dx.doi.org/10.1016/B978-0-12-802410-2.00003-4

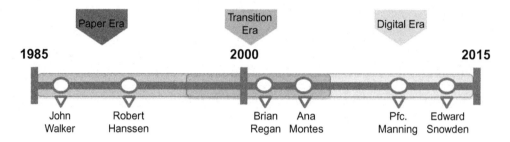

Over the past 30 years, insiders have shifted from extracting paper files to digital data

Deloitte.

FIGURE 3.1

Evolution of Insider from the World of Bricks and Mortar to Bits and Bytes.

development of removable media—floppy and compact discs—allowed large quantities of information to be hidden, carried, and transferred more easily.

At the same time, the shift to information technology gained momentum, many organizations and government agencies became increasingly concerned with harmful insider activity. Known as the Decade of the Spy, the 1980s shifted the attention of leadership from external to internal threats. External agents were recruiting insiders to provide information that, in most cases, compromised national security. Insider threat, and the approach to detecting an insider threat, was synonymous with espionage. Information still had to be physically removed to fall into the hands of foreign intelligence or competitors.

Today's world of "bits and bytes" exists in a virtual space where digital media and computer codes have replaced paper and written information. Through the Internet, large quantities of electronic information can be passed nearly instantaneously over great distances with no more physical effort than a keystroke. Information is stored in the Cloud and accessed using laptop computers and mobile devices that are also used for communication.

Not more than 40 years old, the world of bits and bytes is still in its infancy. Information technology in the last 20 years has revolutionized the way we communicate with each other. The ability to store, transfer, and manage large quantities of information without being physically associated with that information has changed the way we do business. It has also changed the way information is exploited: removing sensitive information by hand has been replaced by its exfiltration in seconds with a keystroke. In the world of bricks and mortar, sabotage meant penetrating a physical barrier or secure site to access material that could be manipulated, destroyed, or redesigned to fail. Today, sabotage can include much more, like using a virus or malware to undermine an organization's information system to disrupt power grids, communication channels, satellite orbits, etc. All this can be achieved without leaving the comfort of one's home or vehicle.

INSIDER THREAT IN A WORLD OF BRICKS AND MORTAR

In the world of bricks and mortar, insider threat behavior was composed of observable actions that could be disguised or clandestinely executed without detection. Exploiting information with the intent to damage an organization often required the physical removal of information, often papers or other material that would be passed on to a foreign intelligence agent or business competitor.

Before information technology, physical security was the main barrier and preventive mechanism of the insider threat. Because insider behavior relied on the physical extraction of information, it was possible for keen observers to recognize suspicious behavior. In Government, security awareness campaigns like "loose lips sink ships" emphasized counterintelligence and protecting sensitive information. The private sector implemented few, if any, measures to prevent intellectual property loss. Instead, most insider threat mitigation efforts focused only on fraud.

Detecting an insider threat required keen observation from other employees, during business and, sometimes, personal hours. Indicators included changes in a person's behavior, the amount of time one spent at the office, what a person carried out of the building, and what a person talked about with coworkers. If detected or reported by others, an investigation or surveillance provided additional insight into the motivation of a potential insider, whether they were disgruntled, frustrated, or in crisis.

Insider activity that was not observed or recognized would generally go undetected. It was very difficult to investigate insider activity unless the insider was caught in the act. Further, detection was not comprehensively considered in an environment where insider acts were almost exclusively associated with spies—a phenomenon that was so infrequent it was not worth investing in a mitigation program. As a result, responses to an insider threat in the world of bricks and mortar were always reactive—the result of something observed firsthand or reported by others.

In the world of bricks and mortar, all behavior was observable by another person (Figure 3.2). Behavior, therefore, was self-monitored by external constraint—the impact that learned social mores and societal values have on an

The Bricks and Mortar Workplace

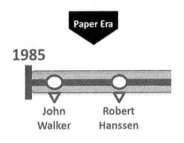

Era Characteristics

Attributes: Physical actions are observable, which leads to external constraints

Behavior: Person-to-person handoffs of hard copy information

Insider programs: Counterintelligence focused and reactive

John Walker (Navy)

Access: Navy Chief Warrant Officer and communications specialist

Rationale: Validation, $500 to $1,000 a week

Exploit: Helped the Soviet Union decipher more than one million encrypted messages

Robert Hanssen (FBI)

Access: Held key counterintelligence positions with high level of access

Rationale: Validation, $1.4 million over 22 years

Exploit: Provided classified intelligence information to the Soviet Union

Deloitte.

FIGURE 3.2
The Bricks and Mortar Workplace.

individual. In many instances, this awareness of being observed keeps people from doing things that are taboo, against the rules, or damaging to their reputations. In other words, the risk of getting caught because someone else notices deters insiders from behaving badly in the first place. External constraint may explain why there were so few instances of insider activities leading up to the advent of the world of bits and bytes. It may also suggest that during this time, individuals in crisis may have been more likely to seek alternative solutions to harming the organizations for personal motivations. Nonetheless, for decades, external constraint interrupted forward motion of potential insider threats if good security practices were implemented to include background checks and for more sensitive access, polygraphs.

TRANSITIONAL PHASE

During the latter part of the 1990s, there was a transition phase that ran for several years depending on your perspective on the evolution of technology (Figure 3.3). This was a period that while classified in the world of bits and

The Transitional Workplace

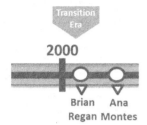

Era Characteristics

Attributes: Unobservable virtual actions avoid external constraints – leaving only internal constraints

Behavior: Download data using removable media

Insider programs: Use physical, behavioral, and some technology indicators

---

Brian Regan (USAF)

Access: Signals intelligence specialist with access to Intelink

Rationale: Needed to sell information to get out of debt

Exploit: Stole 15,000 pages, CD-ROMs, videos

Ana Montes (DIA)

Access: Intelligence research analyst with access to US/Cuba classified information

Rationale: Conflicting ideologies on U.S. foreign relations with Cuba

Exploit: Shared knowledge of classified U.S. military information with Cuban spies

Deloitte.

FIGURE 3.3
The Transitional Phase.

bytes, it was an era post bricks and mortar but pre digital and mobile. This was a period where large quantities of data could be placed on removable media, but such large quantities of data still needed to be hand carried or passed from person to person. It was a period where large quantities of data could be lost but still required interpersonal interaction. In some cases, information was memorized and then documented in a safe and isolated location.

INSIDER THREAT IN A WORLD OF BITS AND BYTES

The salient characteristics of the world of bits and bytes that render it fundamentally different from the world of bricks and mortar are the ability and expectation to connect instantaneously with a degree of anonymity. Today, cyberspace allows individuals to act anonymously. Because behavior cannot be observed in the same manner as it could be before the advent of information technology, societal pressure to behave in a certain way has lifted. Without external constraints, individuals are governed only by internal constraint. Internal constraint is the sense of integrity and morality that impedes behavior, whether or not a person is acting anonymously. Individuals who lack internal constraint are emboldened by a sense of impunity, resulting in potential insider threat.

The Internet has made it possible to conduct business outside an organization's boundaries almost as efficiently and effectively as conducting business strictly within an organization's physical boundaries.[1] As people increasingly conduct personal and business operations in cyberspace, organizations are no longer limited by traditional physical boundaries. Virtual business and personal networks mean that organizations can no longer rely on observant coworkers to interrupt or impede potential insider actions. The insider today can readily extract information from a host of information systems without ever touching it. In the world of bits and bytes, the insider can readily search, find, and download information that is stored outside of his/her physical workspace, has little relevance to his job, and is extracted, in many instances, unbeknownst to anyone (Figure 3.4).

The Bits and Bytes Workplace

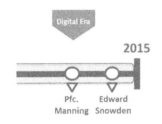

Era Characteristics

2015

Attributes: Tracking of virtual actions create external constraints

Behavior: Machine to machine file transfer to exfiltrate data

Insider programs: Correlate virtual and non-virtual behavior

Pfc. Manning (Army)

Access: Intelligence analyst with access to classified databases

Motivation: Societal frustration

Exploit: Leaked classified information to WikiLeaks

Edward Snowden (Contractor)

Access: Network Administrator with a high level of access to classified information

Motivation: Disagreement with US surveillance and privacy policies

Exploit: Leaked classified information to the media, starting in May 2013

Deloitte.

FIGURE 3.4
The Bits and Bytes Workplace.

---

[1] Palmisano, Samuel J. "The Globally Integrated Enterprise." Foreign Affairs. Council on Foreign Relations, May-June 2006. Web. <https://www.foreignaffairs.com/articles/2006-05-01/globally-integrated-enterprise>.

Same Behavior, Different Context

The shift from bricks and mortar to bits and bytes has shifted the context of the insider threat, but not its associated behavior. Before the advent of information technology, an insider attack meant gaining access or facilitating another person's access to a physical space where he or she was not permitted, then removing information or performing some unauthorized activity, for example, "doctoring the books." Although these actions no longer require physical access, the behavior surrounding these actions is the same for an insider today.

In contrast, the context of an insider attack has changed. As a result of the Internet driving a networking and communications revolution, many business models and processes are leveraging Internet-based technologies. Understanding this cataclysmic shift is paramount to understanding the insider threat and the context in which insider attacks now occur. Today, we are challenged to see what an employee does day-to-day in the office, if an employee even has an office. It is challenging to know when an employee logs on to a computer or mobile device and what they do on different information systems. Moreover, the insider threat continues to be a person-centric problem, but one that exists in a world of technology. Today, methods to prevent, detect, and respond have changed as the context for exploiting information, material, facilities, and people has changed.

Is Insider Activity More Prevalent Now?

Today, destructive insider activity has increased because information is more readily transferable and using the Internet to share and seek information is a societal norm. There have been a number of studies that offer a window into the staggering amount and cost of information that can be removed. Recent surveys reveal the prevalence of IP and research and development (R&D) theft involving separating employees. A study by Cyber Ark software indicated that 90% of IT employees surveyed would consider taking sensitive company data if they were laid off.[2] Another study by the Poneman Institute revealed that 59% of employees who quit, or are asked to leave,[3] take sensitive business with them. Twenty-five percent of employees who were evaluated in a Computer Emergency Response Team (CERT)[4] database of more than 700 cases used e-mail to extract data from their organization.

---

[2] Kenneth C. Laudon and Jane P. Laudon, *Essentials of Business Information Systems*, 7th Edition, Pearson 2010. http://wps.prenhall.com/bp_laudon_essbus_7/0,11885,3149210-,00.html.

[3] "Data Loss Risks During Downsizing." The Ponemon Institute. 2009. <http://www.ponemon.org/local/upload/fckjail/generalcontent/18/file/Data%20Loss%20Risks%20During%20Downsizing%20FINAL%201.pdf>.

[4] Cappelli, Dawn M., Andrew P. Moore, and Randall F. Trzeciak, *The CERT Guide to Insider Threats: How to Prevent, Detect, and Respond to Information Technology Crimes* (Upper Saddle River, NJ: Addison-Wesley Professional, 2012).

The financial impact of insider threat has also been evaluated. According to CERT, the estimated financial impact of IP theft on an organization averaged around $13.5 million in actual loss.[5] An annual estimate by the FBI indicates that losses to companies in the Unites States due to IP theft from both internal and external sources ranges from $200 to $250 billion.[6]

The Workforce in a World of Bits and Bytes

Generation Y and Millennials—people born between the early 1980s and the late 1990s—have a keen ability and proclivity for collecting and sharing information and are comfortable using technology to meet their professional and personal goals (Figure 3.5). According to the Pew Research Center,

Demographic Comparison

Boomers
Ages 45-65

- Respectful of differences and well educated by traditional methods
- Digital immigrants who have learned to adapt to technology
- Work for them defines value
- Driven to overwork; live to work
- Need to assert their individuality but view teams as effective
- Influenced by WII post economic boom

Generation X
Ages 30-45

- Open minded and sensitive to diversity
- Educated by traditional methods supplemented by the Internet
- Digital natives. Comfortable with the internet, prefer, and embrace the internet and technology to help control their lives
- Work to live they will work with others in a team, but also comfortable working alone. Most effective one task at a time
- Influenced by corporate and government failures, increased divorce and violence rates

Generation Y
Ages 21-30

- The most diverse and most educated of all generations
- Influenced by technology referred to as digital natives who are information fluent. Connected 24/7
- Have the ability to multi-task and engage multiple activities simultaneously
- Expect speed and change and have a low tolerance for things that don't make sense. View face time and politics as a waste of time
- Energetic, positive, innovative and creative
- Value teamwork and collaborative efforts. Are responsive to mutual guidance and mentorship
- Thrive on flexibility at work and require the opportunity to pursue new challenges; need "space" to explore
- Will stay when offered ongoing opportunities to grow and learn new things. Loyalty must go both ways   Work to live
- Their lives have been influenced by national disasters and the GWOT

Deloitte.

FIGURE 3.5
Generational Differences.

[5] Cappelli, Dawn M., Andrew P. Moore, and Randall F. Trzeciak, *The CERT Guide to Insider Threats: How to Prevent, Detect, and Respond to Information Technology Crimes* (Upper Saddle River, NJ: Addison-Wesley Professional, 2012).
[6] "Spectresoft 2014 Insider Threat Survey." Spectresoft. 2014. http://downloads.spectorsoft.com/resources/infographic/spectorsoft-2014-insider-threat-survey.pdf.

Generation Y has "grown up with personal computers, cell phones, and the internet, and are now taking their place in a world where the only constant is rapid change."[7] Members of Generation Y are "tech-savvy," expect access to information, and want it with speed and accuracy. They leverage technology to create social networks that embrace open communication.[8] Because members of Generation Y spend their developmental years collaborating on teams in academic and extracurricular settings, they tend to value collaboration and perform well in team-focused work environments.

These traits make them a natural component of a networked workforce, which is connected through information networks to improve business and mission performance.[9] Networked employees have a natural proficiency in activating, arranging, stabilizing, integrating, and managing a network.

Generation Y, however, is not satisfied with the "passive" attributes of information sharing: waiting for data owners to grant access and make data available. Instead, its members proactively obtain information based on their emergent knowledge and solution requirements. This attitude toward information sharing goads increased risk to insider threat because it is at odds with regulations on a secure operating environment.

Mitigating the Insider Threat in the World of Bits and Bytes

With the advent of information technology, business has been propelled into a virtual space where information is more readily accessible and transferable. It is no longer necessary for insiders to physically handle assets or information. As businesses leverage information technology to grow, risk from potential loss of assets increases.

Technology has also enabled organizations to investigate the new threat. Today, we are able to translate virtual and non virtual behavior into data. That data can be monitored, analyzed, and correlated to identify anomalous patterns of activity. Technology may be used to characterize an insider as malicious, complacent, or ignorant, and proactively identify a potential insider before they have committed an insider act. Today, in the world of bits and bytes, organizations can interrupt the forward motion of a potential insider by using detection methods that help identify at-risk behavior.

As organizations continue to enhance monitoring capabilities, they are making the unobservable world of bits and bytes a little less opaque. Information

---

[7] The Pew Research Center, "A Portrait of Generation Next" (2007)
[8] Robin They, "Its 2008: Do You Know Where Your Talent Is?" (2008)
[9] "Center for Network Innovation: Improving Performance Through the Power of Networks

technology has made it possible to observe how employees behave in the virtual space and to allow the return of external constraints to govern behavior when conducting business there. Computer technology alone does not accomplish this, but rather facilitates a platform that helps mitigate asset loss by inhibiting behavior that would otherwise go largely unchecked.

The Insider Threat of Bits and Bytes: A Case Study

John Doe, a 27-year-old contractor at a technology company, works in an IT support center in the United States. For the past three years, John has received declining performance reviews and has been passed over for an anticipated promotion. John has become increasingly disgruntled with his company. After overhearing troubling conversations regarding a work-related dispute, a supervisor becomes concerned that John is disgruntled to the point that he may want to retaliate against the organization, but the supervisor does not know how to report or log this concern.

In the meantime, John begins taking short trips to foreign countries (e.g., China) and interviewing with his company's competitors. John uses his access to look for information to take with him. He avoids setting off alerts while searching through the company's systems. John submits a request to access a sensitive upstream database that is not required for the performance of his duties. His access request is denied but is not evaluated in a broader context. After his access denial, he puts in his two-week notice. In his final two weeks, John is able to obtain project-financing information regarding competitive bids and operations. He uses administrative credentials to change the permission levels on restricted folders to access data with his regular user credentials. He e-mails these data to his personal e-mail address in a series of emails, each below 5 MB. In his exit interview, he expresses that company will "regret how they treated him," referring to his perceived low pay, performance ratings, and negative interactions with his supervisor. Despite this, no action is taken to assess John's network activity after he leaves. Ultimately, John is able to covertly extract approximately 20 MB of highly sensitive business information.

KEY TAKEAWAYS

- "Bricks and mortar" to "bits and bytes" is a useful metaphor to describe the significant way in which information technology has driven change in the business environment. Insider behavior is no longer limited to observable actions in physical space. Instead, the threat has spread to a global, virtual space consisting of actions performed on diverse mobile devices.

- The salient characteristics of the world of bits and bytes that render it fundamentally different from the world of bricks and mortar are the ability and expectation to connect instantaneously with a degree of anonymity.
- The shift from bricks and mortar to bits and bytes has shifted the context of the insider threat, but not its associated behavior.
- Today, insider activity has increased because information is more readily transferable and the population is more comfortable using the Internet to share and seek information.
- Internet-based applications has fundamentally shifted the context in which insider attacks now occur.

CHAPTER 4

Identifying Functional Ownership

INTRODUCTION

Among the initial challenges organizations face when standing up an insider threat program is identifying an owner (i.e., functional area) for the program. Some common questions organizations have at this juncture include the following:

- Which function should "own" the insider threat program?
- What factors should be considered when identifying a program owner?
- Where are insider threat programs commonly located in other organizations?
- What skill sets are necessary for an insider threat program manager and its staff?

This chapter seeks to identify how a program will operate from a governance perspective and, more importantly, provide a concept of operations (CONOP). In many instances, organizations move quickly to identify an owner and select a monitoring tool, without spending enough time developing the framework for the tool to be successful. This chapter contains suggestions, based on Deloitte's experience, to help ensure that the program owner has the structure in place for programmatic success.

PROGRAM LOCATION

Although there is no one-size-fits-all approach to selecting a location for the program, there are a number of general guidelines that organizations should consider as part of the decision-making process. Most importantly, organizations need to recognize that although someone is accountable for the program, a partnership among key organizational stakeholders who can implement the necessary risk mitigation measures should support the program. Examples of such measures are policy changes and updates, communication strategy, training modules, employee lifecycle changes, and information security controls. The following section highlights three key

51

Insider Threat. DOI: http://dx.doi.org/10.1016/B978-0-12-802410-2.00004-6

considerations for organizations based on our experiences developing and implementing insider threat programs.

Executive Support

An organizational function with a direct reporting relationship to the organization's executive leadership (e.g., CEO, Board of Directors, Secretary, Director) should own the insider threat program. Although all new initiatives can benefit from executive-level support, this support is imperative for insider threat programs. Implementing and maturing a new insider program requires cross-functional coordination and broad organizational change, which can lead to conflict. Strong executive commitment helps to ensure that programs can withstand common challenges facing new insider programs, resolve conflicts, and maintain credibility within the organization. The program should have the necessary executive support to help engage resistance to sharing data, changing policy, and mitigating territorial conflicts. This truly becomes a leadership issue for the executive—whether that is the CEO or COO—as it relates to getting the "team" on board with the vision of protecting critical assets and collaborating across different parts of the organization. Lastly, executive support is critical to support the appropriate resource allocation to build a successful program. Necessary resources may include hard dollars for contractor support, analytic solutions, software, or soft dollars for resources within the organization to build, administer, and manage the program. These costs can have a wide range and it is difficult to say how much a program truly costs for a specific organization.

Independence

It is critical that insider threat programs be viewed as independent entities within the broader enterprise. Without this independence, programs potentially risk association with the ownership function and, subsequently, the loss of stakeholders' ability to remain collaborative and flexible to meet changing program requirements. Although program ownership and accountability can be assigned to a specific organizational function, insider threat programs should be designed as a partnership with "shared" resources from functions involved in the insider threat mitigation process (e.g., e-Forensics, Security, Human Resources). Functional representatives can provide input on program strategy and report progress back to their respective functional leadership, helping to gain buy-in and cross-functional alignment to insider threat program goals.

Collaboration

Organizations should assess which function is best suited to collaborate with the stakeholders needed to advance the program. Specifically, program ownership should reside within an organizational function that collaborates across the enterprise as part of its day-to-day operations. A successful program is viewed as a shared responsibility that requires involvement from physical security, information technology, privacy, policy, human resources, legal, business units, information assurance, compliance, and executive management. Organizational functions that operate in a silo will likely encounter difficulties collaborating on insider threat mitigation with other organizational functions. This could cause other functions to resist fully engaging as partners in the process of standing up an insider threat program. Furthermore, such friction can increase territorialism, and likewise, create divisions as roles and responsibilities are not clear. This can result in program that is less holistic than required to mitigate insider threat effectively (e.g., programmatic focus on technology at the expense of behavioral analysis).

DEVELOPING A PROGRAM TO PREVENT, DETECT, AND RESPOND FRAMEWORK

Program Ownership

Holistic, risk-based insider threat programs identify and respond to insider threats throughout the security lifecycle. The "prevent, detect, respond" framework provides a lens through which organizations can assess different functions' core competencies when trying to determine where best to situate their insider threat program. Although no one area "does it all" in the mitigation process, organizations should identify which function is best equipped to carry out respective roles and, where gaps remain, to coordinate with other functions. For the purposes of our functional analysis, we suggest organizations focus on the prevention and detection aspects of the insider threat mitigation process. At a minimum, candidate functions should have:

- **Data Access**: Function should have access to and/or ownership of a significant amount of relevant, real-time data used in insider threat detection including virtual (e.g., system access, download history, DLP alerts, etc.) as well as nonvirtual or behavioral information about the employee population (e.g., work hours, policy compliance, training, job performance data, expense data).
- **Operational Integration**: Function should have a high level of cross-functional outreach as a part of its normal business operations.
- **Credibility**: Function's role and capabilities should align with key insider threat mitigation responsibilities.
- **Privacy**: Function should have the ability to sequester a program from the mainstream organization to help ensure a secure location for insider threat analysis and response.

Functional Assessment in Choosing a Program Owner

Table 4.1 highlights some of the executives commonly tasked with insider threat program oversight, as well as some insights on their function's ability to prevent and detect insider events. Our assessment is intended to provide some core considerations to help guide an organization's decision-making process.

Table 4.1 Key Considerations for Different Program Owners

Executive	Key Considerations
Chief Security Officer (CSO)	Often the central figure in response, but may not have direct access to all the necessary data used to prevent and detect insider activity.
	Since aspects of security are integrated across the enterprise, there is a natural collaboration with other functions as part of daily operations.
	Central role in promoting a culture of security and awareness.
	Responsible for formulating processes, controls, and training to help prevent insider activity.
Inspector General (IG)	Often sequestered with firewalls from the rest of the organization, but understands enterprise-level trends as part of their investigatory role.
	Historically does not "own" data, but collaborates with other functions and can access needed data as part of ongoing investigations at all levels of the enterprise.
Chief Ethics & Compliance Officer	Familiar with challenges associated with running an independent program and has a strong executive voice.
Chief Information Officer (CIO)	Natural role in developing the policy, process, and technology needed to protect critical information, and will be familiar with analytic solutions.
Chief Information Security Officer (CISO)	At risk of becoming too technology-focused and having a less holistic view, given the technical requirements needed to protect modern organizations' data.
	Targeted functional responsibility can make it challenging to engage with broader organization on security issues.
Chief Financial Officer (CFO)	An important role in formulating policies, procedures, and system controls.
	Owner of a significant amount of relevant data, although unlikely to do any real-time, virtual data integration and analytics.
Chief Operations Officer (COO)	Strong executive voice within the organization and well positioned to provide the support needed to resolve conflicts.
	Daily responsibilities include coordinating with many different stakeholders, which enables them to build strong relationships.
Chief Risk Officer (CRO)	A critical role in developing the policies, procedures, and technical controls to protect it, although unlikely to own any enterprise-level data.
	Often direct reporting responsibilities to the Board, and familiarity with operating an independent program.
	Understanding of risk-based approaches with subject matter expertise that is critical to the PDR framework.
Chief Human Resources Officer (CHRO)	Owner of a significant amount of employee lifecycle data, but data often has latency issues and is limited to nonvirtual information.
	Unlikely to garner the same amount of executive-level support as other senior positions with the organization.
	Targeted functional responsibility can make it challenging to engage with broader organization on security issues.

Decisions about where to house insider threat mitigation capabilities within organizations can have a profound impact on the success and viability of the program. Although there is not a one-size-fits-all approach, organizations that fail to give proper consideration to functional areas' access to data, level of executive support, and ability to collaborate risk the effectiveness and credibility of their insider programs. Determining which function is best able to prevent and detect insider threat events enhances the creation of a holistic, risk-based insider threat program that can protect the most critical assets.

Program Design

Organizations must strike the proper balance between countering the threat and accomplishing the organizational business mission when empowering new program owners to oversee the development of a successful insider threat program. Instituting too many security restrictions may impede an organization's ability to conduct business effectively. Instituting too few security restrictions increases vulnerabilities, which may lead to an unacceptable level of risk from insider threats. In order to facilitate proper alignment, the new owners should work closely with the collaborative partners or, in many cases, be referred to as the Insider Threat Working Group (ITWG) to help ensure the programmatic strategy aligns with organizational and functional goals.

The illustration below highlights the cross-functional shared responsibility of implementing various components that drive toward a holistic and risk-based insider threat program. The cross-functional set of stakeholders, or Insider Threat Working Group (ITWG; highlighted in gray in Figure 4.1), should identify lessons learned, establish response procedures, explore vulnerabilities, and discuss trends related to insider threat mitigation. The ITWG is the key program driver for changes in how business is conducted. Its makeup can range from a collaborative partnership that produces recommendations for leadership to a group of true change agents in the organization. The Program Foundation consists of policies and processes that encompass the employee lifecycle—vetting, hiring, training, personnel management, and separation—and prevent and detect insider threats. The Access and Technical Controls of the program include physical and information technology (IT) security controls to mitigate insider threats governed by principles such as least privilege and segregation of duties. The framework culminates in the use of an Advanced Analytics capability able to continuously monitor individual behavior, identify a subset of the population that is at an elevated risk, and identify threats in a proactive manner.

Strategic Framework

As the ITWG drives towards accomplishing its objective to develop the insider program CONOP, develop a governance structure, and implement the executive strategy, members should consider the principles laid out in the following strategic framework (Figure 4.2).

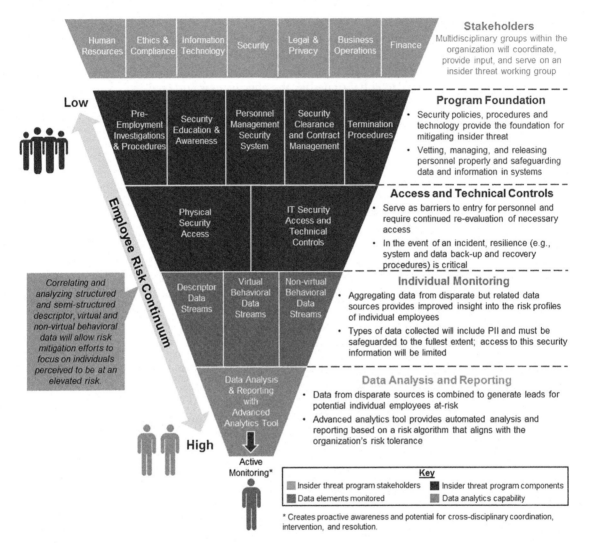

Stakeholders
Multidisciplinary groups within the organization will coordinate, provide input, and serve on an insider threat working group

Program Foundation
- Security policies, procedures and technology provide the foundation for mitigating insider threat
- Vetting, managing, and releasing personnel properly and safeguarding data and information in systems

Access and Technical Controls
- Serve as barriers to entry for personnel and require continued re-evaluation of necessary access
- In the event of an incident, resilience (e.g., system and data back-up and recovery procedures) is critical

Individual Monitoring
- Aggregating data from disparate but related data sources provides improved insight into the risk profiles of individual employees
- Types of data collected will include PII and must be safeguarded to the fullest extent; access to this security information will be limited

Data Analysis and Reporting
- Data from disparate sources is combined to generate leads for potential individual employees at-risk
- Advanced analytics tool provides automated analysis and reporting based on a risk algorithm that aligns with the organization's risk tolerance

Key
Insider threat program stakeholders | Insider threat program components
Data elements monitored | Data analytics capability

* Creates proactive awareness and potential for cross-disciplinary coordination, intervention, and resolution.

FIGURE 4.1
Insider Threat Program Foundation.

Program Assumptions

As the Insider Threat Program begins to develop the CONOP it is important to establish a few common assumptions:

- Modifications to the program are reviewed by the Insider Threat Working Group (ITWG) and approved by Legal and Privacy personnel.
- The program is staffed with existing resources on which it relies to support program initiatives and processes.

Insider Threat Program Strategic Framework

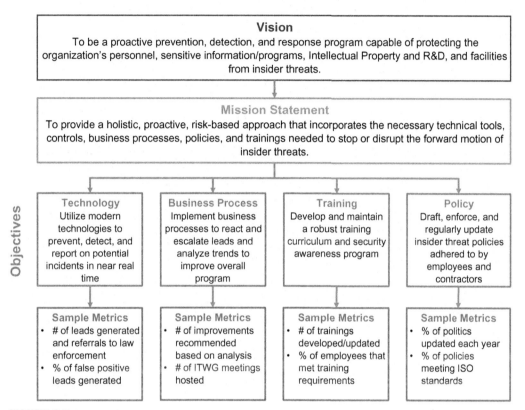

FIGURE 4.2

Insider Threat Strategic Framework.

- The program utilizes an advanced analytics tool to generate leads for potential inquiries and investigations; data needed for inclusion in the advanced analytics tool are available and is shared by functional owners.
- As the program progresses, data collected from the advanced analytics tool to generate leads informs continuous improvements to business processes, trainings, policies, and technology.
- Leads generated from the advanced analytics tool do not imply malevolent action or intention for the individual employee, but rather alerts Company X to investigate the situation further.
- ITWG members continue to serve as change agents and champions for the Insider Threat Program in their respective functional areas.

- Communications regarding the program vary based on a "need to know" basis, level of involvement with the program, and seniority level within the organization.

Program Guiding Principles

The guiding principles below are precepts that inform the program CONOP:

- **Compliance Program**: The program is developed and administered in accordance with privacy requirements, policies, and standards (e.g., Data Privacy Policy, Code of Conduct Policy, and HR Policies and Practices).
- **Legal Program**: Information collected regarding individuals is done in accordance with legal standards, including privacy policy, and with the approval of legal counsel. The program is lawful and abides by the rules and regulations that bind the company. Beyond the United States, the program may be modified to align with the legal policies of the host country, where applicable.
- **Monitoring Policies**: Creates and updates monitoring policies and procedures before institutionalizing an internal monitoring program (e.g., complies with legal requirements and provides disclosures).
- **Notification Procedures**: Employees are informed that their use of information systems or property may be monitored. This is communicated through the acceptable use policy, logon banners, and security awareness training.
- **Consistent Application**: The program has clearly defined criteria and thresholds for conducting inquiries or investigations, referring cases to Security, Ethics, Legal or Human Resources; providing information to civilian law enforcement, government agencies, or requesting civil or criminal judicial process.
- **Secure Processes**: Inquiries and investigations are controlled by a process and systems that provide privacy and confidentiality and are entrusted to a limited group of individuals for resolution. The information handled throughout various aspects of this program may be sensitive, requiring individuals to handle cases with discretion and protection. Privacy and confidentiality protect the integrity of the investigation process.
- **Enterprise-Wide Commitment**: A program should be viewed as a shared responsibility across the enterprise and requires involvement from executives, management, human resources, legal counsel, privacy, global security, physical security, IT, ethics, compliance,

finance, and business operations. Each of these stakeholders is responsible for the success of the program and effective risk management.

Four Program Pillars

The pillars below are the structural and resource divisions of the program. These pillars represent critical workstreams that operate together and in conjunction with other functional areas to accomplish the mission and vision of the program. The pillars serve as guide posts that help to organize the functions and processes of the program. These become the essential building blocks of the program.

- **Technology**: The technology pillar is composed of network controls, insider threat–related systems, and the application of an advanced analytics tool. The culmination of the technology pillar is the advanced analytics tool, which collects, analyzes, and reports on insider threats by correlating data from disparate data sources and systems. Other security-related tools work in conjunction with the advanced analytics tool, including a Security Information and Event Management (SIEM) system, Endpoint Monitoring/Data Loss Prevention (DLP), Data Labeling Tool, and Intrusion Detection System (IDS)
- **Business Process**: The primary business process associated with the program is the escalation process associated with how the organization triages and handles elevated risk behavior and anomalies that may be indicative of an insider threat. This business process drives the proactive insider threat lead generation for the program, including coordination with functional area (HR, Legal, Privacy, Ethics, etc.), specialists for inquiry and investigation processes, and the ITWG for approval and guidance. Additionally, program management and governance business processes led by the ITWG provide cross-functional collaboration, opportunities for enterprise improvements, and risk tolerance discussions to continuously improve the program.
- **Training/Communication**: A component of the program is prevention of insider threats through ongoing security awareness training and communication. Increasing insider threat security awareness serves a twofold purpose: to decrease the potential for unintentional insider incidents and increase communication of potential suspicious activities through the proper channels. A training curriculum and program baselines security knowledge across the enterprise allows for in-depth and role-specific security education on how the workforce may mitigate insider threats.

- **Policy**: An overarching insider threat program policy holds the program together by outlining program rules, regulations, enforcement, governance, and responsibilities for all parties involved. Having clear, transparent, accessible, and consistently enforced policies provide the foundation for an effective insider threat program. Policies should be developed and updated in accordance with existing global policies and with local, state, and federal laws and regulations.

Governance Structure and Roles and Responsibilities

Mitigating insider threats is a shared responsibility that requires collaboration and ongoing coordination across functional areas (e.g., Human Resources, Information Technology, Security, Legal & Privacy, Ethics & Compliance, Business Operations, and Finance). This coordination is achieved through the establishment of the ITWG. This group consists of executives from functional areas that serve as the governing body for the program. The group promotes and enforces collaboration and coordination among functional areas. The ITWG defines critical assets, identifying existing and future capabilities to mitigate risk and vulnerabilities, and serves as agents of change for transitioning to the future state of insider threat mitigation (e.g., in support of corporate business objectives).

The insider threat program establishes a structured process for the approval of potential risk indicators used to evaluate threats in the workplace. This process includes approval by the Legal, Security, Human Resources, Ethics and Compliance, and Privacy executives within the ITWG. The use of data complies with policies is conducted within legal parameters, and reflects the organization's values and ethical principles. Insider threat lead generation to investigate anomalies is operated on a day-to-day basis by a small team of security specialists within Security, and consists of a targeted two Full-time Equivalents (FTEs).[1]

Governance Structure

The program governance structure centers on a cross-functional guidance board, the ITWG. The ITWG reports its findings, progress, and recommendations to the ITESC and GRCC. At the same time, the ITWG receives assistance with functional area–specific requirements from the ITWG workstreams, as well as other functional delegates. Table 4.2 outlines the responsibilities and meeting frequencies of these stakeholders.

---

[1] Industry leaders, including two defense contractors with 65,000 and 75,000 employees, respectively, utilize two FTEs to manage their insider threat mitigation program.

Table 4.2 Roles and Responsibilities of Functional Groups

Group	Responsibilities	Meeting Frequency
ITWG Workstreams/ Delegates	▪ Develop content for functional areas of the program (e.g., Program Policy, Security Awareness Program, Advanced Analytics Tool Implementation) ▪ Develop communication regarding the program ▪ Provide change management processes ▪ Recommend updates to the risk algorithm, weighting, and potential risk indicators based on subject matter knowledge and data analysis as part of the escalation process ▪ Evaluate recent relevant laws, regulations, and court rulings related to data collection processes and insider threat trends ▪ Perform reviews of program components and resolve conflicts	Weekly
ITWG	▪ Validate outputs with informed and committed executives to the program ▪ Attend meetings and come prepared to provide input, address issues, and share knowledge ▪ Coordinate business roll-out ("deployment") of program components ▪ Coordinating sign-offs on risk mitigation processes	Bi-weekly
ITESC	▪ Address roadblocks and properly mitigate risks ▪ Serve as advisors and agents of change for implementing the program ▪ Coordinate sign-offs on risk mitigation processes	Monthly
GRCC	▪ Provide leadership oversight approval and guidance as needed ▪ Coordinate approval of risk mitigation processes	As Needed

Program Communication and Change Management Plan

Once the ITWG develops the communication and change management plan used to inform program stakeholders, including Executive Leadership, and broad supervisory and line-level staff, the change management strategy provides guidance on how to implement the program through clear objectives and process change tailored to each audience. The plan

- defines the program's change management requirements through identification of target audiences, messages, delivery vehicles, and internal team communication process flows
- explains the impacts of the program on the workforce through tailored communications that prepare the workforce to adapt to the changes
- rolls out the program so that it serves as a deterrent for complacent, ignorant, and malicious insider acts
- increases the understanding and responsibilities of the organization's workforce in mitigating insider threats and establishing accountability for employees involved with insider acts

- provides leadership with information that drives the change and promotes support and commitment from the business units on the implementation of projects
- generates the proper level of awareness for each stakeholder, increases buy-in, and reduces resistance to develop a risk-managed culture

The communication and change management plan will be drafted and validated through the corporate communication process with input from the ITWG and approval by the ITESC.

Incident Response Process

Operating manuals assist security analysts with the triage and escalation processes, including recommendations for inquiries and investigations. The program should have criteria and thresholds for conducting investigations, referring cases to internal and external investigators and requesting criminal charges (Figure 4.3). Inquiries should be controlled by a process to allow for privacy and confidentiality. Procedures for investigation and dealing with malicious, complacent, and ignorant insiders are planned, clearly

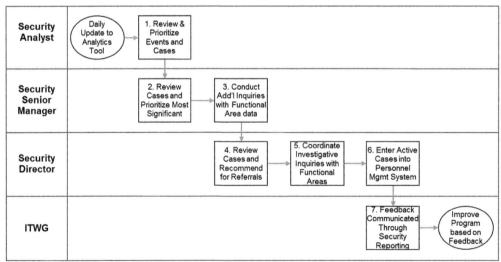

Triage and Escalation Process

Elevated risk employees that are "Cleared As Acceptable" are subject to a review by a security analyst after a predetermined time period or an increase in their risk score. All steps in the escalation process require approval from applicable stakeholders.

FIGURE 4.3

Triage and Escalation Process.

documented, and validated by ITWG participants and the organization's legal counsel. The Incident Response Plan

- outlines the response coordination structure, including whom to involve, who has authority, with whom to coordinate, to whom to report, what actions to take, and what improvements to make;
- includes specific actions to control damage by insiders;
- identifies the circumstances under which those efforts are applicable;
- describes the general process to be followed and the responsibilities of response team members;
- identifies a mediator for communication between the departments involved in response; and
- feeds lessons learned from insider incidents back into the insider incident response plan to inform continual improvement and, as applicable, modifies processes based on postmortem results from prior incidents.

Each business function should have a trusted agent (who also sits on the ITWG) who may coordinate on behalf of that function during time-sensitive incident response. The ITWG identifies functional POCs ahead of time, so they may be contacted in a timely manner when an incident occurs. This process mirrors the current process for coordinating internal investigations between Security, HR, Legal, and Ethics.

Ongoing Updates and Process Improvements

In an effort to have a dynamic and continuously improving insider threat mitigation program, the ITWG meets on a quarterly basis. During these meetings, the ITWG analyzes insider trends and discusses mitigation strategies and improvement opportunities across the businesses. The ITWG prioritizes vulnerabilities and assigns owners for implementing and completing action items to address these issues. As the program progresses from the pilot phase to different regions of the world, specialists from Legal, Privacy, Security, and HR are assigned to each region to monitor that region's business processes, to address specific privacy and legal issues, and to collect potential risk indicators (PRIs).

KEY CHALLENGES

Organizations in both the government and the private sector have confronted numerous challenges when standing up an insider threat mitigation programs. Several of these challenges include are as follows:

- The organization has not established a clear owner, defined insider threat, developed an insider threat response plan, or prioritized insider threat as a critical threat vector. As a result, the organization's critical assets are exposed to a potential malicious, complacent, or insider threats.

- The organization does not collect and correlate technical and nontechnical PRIs for proactive detection of emerging insider threats. As a result, there is increased risk that the organization may fail to stop or disrupt an emerging insider threat as a result of a failure to correlate PRIs.

- The organization lacks a risk-based, targeted monitoring strategy for individuals at increased risk for committing an insider act based on their separation status. As a result, the organization is vulnerable by not reviewing activity of separating personnel who are more likely to commit an insider act.

- Training and security awareness efforts do not sufficiently address the insider threat, and opportunities exist to better educate the workforce on its role in reporting suspicious activity. As a result, supervisors may not be aware of the proper mechanisms for reporting or of suspicious behaviors that should be reported.

- Monitoring and alerting does not exist for common exfiltration methods (e.g., e-mail, File Transfer Protocol [FTP], transmittal devices, removable media, cloud storage). As a result, employees with access can remove data from secure environments as a result of a lack of monitoring on exfiltration methods.

- Insider threat mitigation tripwires (e.g., excessively large downloads, evidence of undue access, unauthorized altering of privileges) are either infrequently monitored or are not adopted into the IT infrastructure. As a result, tripwires targeted at malicious insiders are largely not adopted into the IT infrastructure, thereby increasing risk exposure.

KEY TAKEAWAYS

- There is no one-size-fits-all approach for standing up an insider threat program. The program should sit within an organization, spanning functions depending on the culture and structure of the organization. In all cases, the insider threat program is a partnership with key stakeholders throughout the organization with a single entity that is accountable to the organization's leadership

- The development of a concept of operations (CONOP) is critical to the development and operation of the insider threat program. The CONOP becomes the guiding charter for the program that informs governance, structure, as well as incident response in the, prevent, protect, and respond framework.

CHAPTER 5

Identifying Critical Indicators in Organizational Data

An employee who decides to steal from his employer, sell his customers' personal information, or attack his coworkers does not typically wake up one the morning and decide to harm his organization, customers, or coworkers. Rather, such actions generally unfold over time, beginning with an idea, then leading to preparations, and finally resulting in an act or series of acts that inflict harm on the organization. Although many of the warning signs that such an event might unfold go unnoticed, it is rarely the case that there are no warning signs at all. Rather, insiders tend to move along a continuum from idea to action, leaving behind a trail of behavior and data traces as they do so. Certain changes in personal and workplace behavior can serve as indicators that an employee is in crisis and may pose an increased risk of engaging in harmful behavior. If these potential risk indicators are identified early, insider incidents can be interrupted by supporting at-risk employees with alternative solutions. Training, mentoring, and in some instances referral to an Employee Assistance Program are ways to help an employee feel supported, respected, and valued. In more urgent or serious cases, direct intervention or dismissal may be warranted. If the elevated risk is not detected, however, the employee could potentially harm his or her organization's reputation, customers' privacy, or coworkers' safety.

The key to preventing and detecting insider incidents is to proactively identify the information that indicates that an employee poses an increased risk. The good news is that data abounds in the digital age, and these indicators are often readily available. Today, through data, we are able to capture the behavior we were only able to observe years ago. We are also able to codify behavior in ways that reflect when an employee is moving along the idea-to-action continuum.

Data can reflect behavior in both the nonvirtual space—such as performance, compliance, and physical movements—and virtual space (e.g., websites accessed, information downloaded, e-mails sent). Data captured in the virtual space includes when employees log on, what they download, what files they print, and what files they e-mail to recipients outside of the organization. The

Insider Threat. DOI: http://dx.doi.org/10.1016/B978-0-12-802410-2.00005-8

challenge is that the volume of data produced can be so overwhelming that indicators can often go unnoticed or unprocessed by the organization. The very indicators that indicate that an employee poses an elevated risk to an organization can be drowned out by equally unhelpful "noise." How does an organization separate the signal from the noise? The key to using available data, without being overwhelmed, is to know where to look, what to prioritize, and how to escalate.

POTENTIAL RISK INDICATORS

Potential risk indicators (PRIs) are behaviors that can be used to identify when an employee poses increased or decreased risk compared to peers and his or her own baseline behavior over time. PRIs exist within every organization, but to fully leverage them, stakeholders must identify the PRIs and align them with the organization's critical assets and risk tolerance. Examples of PRIs include declining performance ratings, undue access (probing the system outside of what is needed in the performance of an individuals duties), policy violations, and sending information outside of the secure network through a common egress point (e.g., e-mail, removable media, cloud). Other PRIs may reside outside the organization, but are publicly available. Examples of external PRIs derived from open sources include arrest records, bankruptcy records, and civil litigation that may indicate a possible crisis. Currently, there are privacy concerns about using open-source data, such as social media, in the workplace. Nonetheless, data derived internally, when correctly defined, collected, and correlated, can provide significant insight into an employee and the potential risk they may pose.

PRIs fall into three main categories: contextual indicators, virtual indicators, and nonvirtual indicators (Figure 5.1). In isolation, these indicators may identify

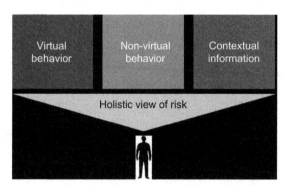

FIGURE 5.1
A Holistic View of Risk.

an emerging insider threat. In aggregate, however, indicators from across these categories can help organizations assess risk and take a thoughtful approach to investigating anomalous behavior before an action is taken. When leveraging PRIs, the main objective is to detect anomalous activity so that the employee can be appropriately engaged, and the threat can be disrupted and investigated.

Contextual Indicators

Information about an individual's role and access within an organization inform how PRIs are leveraged and weighted to mitigate insider threat. Contextual PRIs assume that even though a workforce is dedicated to the same objective, there are many different roles employees play. Moreover, those roles are all unique to the objectives of the organization. Some roles have greater risk associated with them than others, based on an employee's level of access to classified or proprietary information. For example, a data entry clerk will have an inherently lower contextual risk profile than a system administrator that has access to critical data, systems, and network. Contextual indicators tell a story about how an individual interfaces with organizational resources and assets, providing information on how a person fits in the overall management of risk by the organization. It is important for organizations to prioritize enterprise-wide risk and then assess which positions pose the greatest risk. Contextual indicators can help understand this.

Contextual indicators (Table 5.1) primarily focus on the sensitivity of information an individual has access to and the unfettered ability to access it. Individuals with high levels of contextual risk could be at any level of an organization, based on their physical access, virtual access, and ability to work unsupervised or remotely. For example, an executive could pose a high level of contextual risk, based on his knowledge of sensitive business decisions and access to information throughout an organization. A relatively junior employee, like a junior systems administrator, could pose an equally high risk, based on his often privileged access to critical IT infrastructure that acts as the bedrock of business operations. By understanding the assets that would do the most harm to an organization if compromised, organizations can begin to address contextual risk and develop appropriate mitigation strategies. System administrators, for example, can be equipped with two accounts,

Table 5.1 Contextual Potential Risk Indicators	
Indicator Type	**Potential Risk Indicator**
Contextual	■ Clearance Level ■ Access to highly sensitive documents ■ Access to classified materials within multiple agencies

one for everyday work and one for making changes to the systems they manage. While some organizations have put the two-person rule in place, it requires each system administrator to have another administrator with them when making changes to the system or accessing sensitive information. By removing the single point of failure by using the two person rule, the organization reduces the likelihood that a single motivated insider can cause damage. This level of checks and balances are critical for building resiliency and mitigating insider threats.

In 2011, Dr. Stewart David Nozette pled guilty to attempted espionage when he was apprehended after passing classified government documents to undercover FBI agents who posed as Israeli intelligence.[1] Prior to his arrest, Dr. Nozette held high-level government security clearance and was frequently granted access to classified research and development information relating to national defense technology. In the course of his work, Dr. Nozette had access to highly sensitive information while working at the White House, U.S. Department of Energy, and the Defense Advanced Research Projects Agency (DARPA). The information Dr. Nozette attempted to pass to the undercover agents would have compromised the development of new intelligence collection technology that was in a prototype stage at the time of Nozette's arrest. Nozette used a thumb drive to remove the Top Secret information and printed hard copies of the sensitive documents and transported them in a manila envelope. Contextual factors and indicators (e.g., clearance level, access to highly sensitive documents, access to highly classified agencies and offices) can contribute to detecting insider threat incidents similar to Nozette's. Individuals with elevated access pose an inherently higher risk, given the sensitivity of information and materials they have access to. As a result, elevated access should be regularly evaluated and individuals with higher access should face additional scrutiny to protect the critical assets that are at risk of compromise.

Virtual Indicators

An individual's virtual behavior is reflected in a digital trail, created each time an individual accesses or uses an organization's systems, networks, or devices. This digital trail, sometimes referred to as digital exhaust, makes virtual indicators the most readily accessible category of PRIs for most organizations. Virtual indicators are valuable because they capture an employee's behavior on the computer—behavior that would otherwise not be observed. Although

---

[1] U.S. Department of Justice, "Noted Scientist Pleads Guilty to Attempted Espionage," September 7, 2011, accessed online: http://www.fbi.gov/washingtondc/press-releases/2011/ noted-scientist-pleads-guilty-to-attempted-espionage.

contextual indicators provide a sense of who an individual is, virtual indicators help organizations understand what an individual does with a computer. Monitoring an individual's actions could reveal anomalous activity indicating an insider action, regardless of whether those actions are witting or unwittingly committed. Although few indicators can show if an employee poses an immediate threat to an organization, virtual indicators paired with information about employee access and non-virtual behaviors can provide an early detection mechanism.

Virtual behavior (Table 5.2) is captured in a set of PRIs directly aligned to an organization's IT systems that may indicate an individual's proclivity to commit a malicious or complacent insider act. The virtual data organizations use for detecting insider threats vary, but are generally focused on uncovering data exfiltration, sabotage, and fraud. Indicators that point to data exfiltration (see Table 5.3) may include undue interest in network sites that are outside an employee's scope, excessively large downloads or e-mail attachments, and attachments e-mailed to personal accounts. Indicators that point to sabotage include system access at uncommon times and the introduction of foreign data transmittal devices (e.g., USB drives).

Table 5.2 Virtual Potential Risk Indicators	
Indicator Type	**Potential Risk Indicator**
Virtual	▪ Web crawler download and use on classified system ▪ Anomalous encryption activity ▪ Use of USB on classified system ▪ System log changes

Table 5.3 Most Common Methods of Data Exfiltration
▪ E-mail ▪ Removable media ▪ Transmittal devices (e.g., printers, copiers, faxes, scanners) ▪ File transfer protocol ▪ Cloud transmission

The virtual behavior an organization cares about most will depend on the assets it defines as most sensitive and seeks to protect. These behaviors of interest can vary across industries and organizations, depending on the type of information or assets of concern. The presence of anomalous behavior alone, however, rarely warrants grave concern. Instead, in order to understand, correlate, and interpret virtual data in a way that is meaningful for gauging the potential risk, organizations must first have a baseline against which to compare that behavior. A baseline can represent an individual's

Table 5.4 When is it Appropriate to Use an Individual or Peer Baseline?

Individual Baseline	Peer Baseline
• Employee holds unique role within the organization • Role involves repetitive tasks, a regular schedule, without significant variation • Individual baselines look at behaviors over an extended period of time by capturing what is normal for an individual so that anomalies (excessively large download) can be identified. An individual baseline compares an individual's behavior to what he or she commonly does in order to identify anomalous behavior.	• There are a number of employees with similar roles in the organization • An individual's behavior can be dynamic, but there are trends in work for the peer group • Peer baselines look at behaviors over an extended period of time by capturing what is normal for an individual compared to that of his or her peers. If it is common for an individual peers to access the building at 9 am (i.e., the baseline), and an individual accesses the building at 4 am, this would generate a peer based anomaly.

historical behavior, or can represent the expected behavior of an individual, based on aggregating information of individuals in peer groups with the same role or function (i.e., peer baseline). Once a baseline is established using historical data, anomalies in new data will be more apparent, helping organizations to focus on potentially at-risk behavior (Table 5.4).

As details about the actions of Edward Snowden emerge, it is clear he carried out one of the largest leaks of classified information in U.S. history. In the months before leaking classified documents about top-secret NSA programs, Snowden displayed a number of virtual potential risk indicators: between March and May of 2013, he downloaded a web crawler to use within a classified system; he encrypted files to hide the transfer of classified data[2]; he used USB drives to remove classified documents[3]; and changed system logs to cover his tracks.[4] Virtual behavioral indicators may have helped to identify this anomalous behavior. Further, to help combat these types of virtual actions, organizations can establish a set of IT controls, like alerts on data alterations, routine log monitoring, or leveraging data loss prevention tools to flag suspicious use of common egress points such as e-mail, removable

---

[2] Sanger, David E., Schmitt, Eric. "Snowden Used Low-Cost Tool to Best N.S.A." The New York Times. February 8, 2014. http://www.nytimes.com/2014/02/09/us/snowden-used-low-cost-tool-to-best-nsa. html?_r=0.

[3] Dilanian, Ken. "Officials: Edward Snowden Took NSA Secrets on Thumb Drive." Los Angeles Times. June 13, 2013. http://articles.latimes.com/2013/jun/13/news/ la-pn-snowden-nsa-secrets-thumb-drive-20130613.

[4] Higgins, Kelly Jackson. "How Did Snowden Do It?" InformationWeek. November 13, 2013. http:// www.darkreading.com/attacks-breaches/how-did-snowden-do-it/d/d-id/1140877?page_number=1.

media, cloud storage, file transfer protocol and transmittal devices (printers, copiers, scanners, and fax machines).

Nonvirtual Indicators

Although virtual indicators help organizations understand what individuals are doing on systems and networks, they cannot account for an individual's offline behavior. Nonvirtual indicators provide a complementary view of an individual's behavior to give a more holistic picture and to provide an additional warning sign of the potential risk associated with an individual.

Nonvirtual indicators include information on an individual's activity in the workplace, in the physical sphere, and prior to joining an organization (Table 5.5). This data could range from background checks, trends in performance ratings, compliance with expense reporting, security requirements and other policies, reports of threatening behavior at work, to social media. As many nonvirtual indicators include information not strictly internal to an organization, this is an area in which indicators vary widely from organization to organization. The type of data an organization is willing to use to detect anomalous behavior may vary, depending on the organization's culture, risk appetite, and privacy concerns. In parts of the financial industry, for example, employees may sign releases permitting companies to use internal and external data. Other industries do not perceive any risk associated with their employees and thus are at elevated risk for insider threat event.

Table 5.5 Nonvirtual Potential Risk Indicators	
Indicator Type	Potential Risk Indicator
Nonvirtual	■ History of reprimands ■ Past recommendation for discharge ■ Social media posts that disparage employer ■ Odd work hours

Chelsea Manning, the high-profile source of the Wikileaks Department of Defense leaks in 2011, demonstrated a number of anomalous nonvirtual PRIs during her three-year career in the Army. In 2007, Manning was sent to the discharge unit as a result of conduct issues stemming from her retaliations to the rampant bullying she faced in basic training.[5] In 2010, Manning was recommended for discharge by an Army psychiatrist after a confrontation with a supervisor and other emotionally erratic behavior. The supervisor, Army Specialist Jihrleah Showman, later recalled that Manning worked

---

[5] Guardian Films. "Bradley Manning: Fellow Soldier Recalls 'Scared, Bullied Kid.'" The Guardian. May 28, 2011. http://www.theguardian.com/world/2011/may/28/bradley-manning-video-transcript-wikileaks.

at odd times and kept to herself, leading Showman to inform her superiors that Manning was exhibiting suspicious, "spy-like behavior." Manning also voiced dissatisfaction with life and the Army over social media.[6] Although nonvirtual indicators such as those exhibited by Manning are difficult to collect and correlate, they could have indicated that Manning posed an escalating risk.

TRANSLATING KNOWLEDGE ABOUT INSIDERS INTO ORGANIZATIONAL DATA

Developing PRIs should not be an abstract process. Instead, an organization's PRIs should directly result from a comprehensive assessment of real risks facing the organization from business processes, security practices, and external threats to the organization by competitors and foreign governments. PRIs are simply a conversion of an individual's behavior into data that is or can be routinely aggregated by an organization. When PRIs are aggregated, correlated and visualized it provides the organization with an early detection mechanism that can lead to an inquiry or investigation.

When understanding how organizational data can be used to prevent, detect, and respond to emerging insider threats, it is important to examine cases and scenarios based on organizations that have previously had insider threat incidents. Using historical insider threat cases, it is possible to extrapolate scenarios in which a pattern of behavior emerged before the insider incident. Organizations can use these scenarios to stress test their own systems and processes to see how an insider could remove data, sabotage systems, or harm coworkers. Based on an understanding of how these known cases impacted other organizations, insider threat program managers and working groups can use these scenarios to develop mitigation strategies to support prevention. These case scenarios can help to shape specific use cases that can more specifically define prioritized threats and risk indicators used to detect anomalous behavior that is of the greatest concern to an organization.

A sample scenario is presented here to illustrate the ways organizational data can be used to identify an individual who poses a high risk of insider threat. References throughout the scenario identify PRIs, listed in the table that follows, which could help the organization to prevent or detect a similar insider incident to the one represented below.

---

[6] Serrano, Richard A. "Manning's Supervisor Describes Brawl, Suspicions He Was a Spy." Los Angeles Times. July 19, 2013. http://articles.latimes.com/2013/jul/19/nation/la-na-manning-trial-20130720.

NOTIONAL EXFILTRATION USE CASE

John Doe works for a major, multinational company and is based in an IT service center in India (1). His primary duties are focused on operations and maintenance of a series of major databases containing personnel data, corporate finance data, and corporate communication (i.e., e-mail) records. To facilitate his ability to perform maintenance on the systems and support users, he is able to reset passwords, add new accounts, change permission levels, and use administrator credentials to access the databases (2).

John has been employed by the company for more than 10 years, but over the past three years, he exhibited declining performance quality, which has resulted in declining performance reviews (3). As a result of his low ratings, John's career progression and salary have stagnated. He has become increasingly dissatisfied and makes snide comments to his coworkers. His supervisor becomes concerned that John is so disgruntled that he may retaliate against the organization (4).

John begins interviewing with major competitors of his current company, often taking short trips to nearby foreign countries (e.g., Bangladesh) (5). To support his attempts to find a new job, John uses his access to sensitive databases to log in to systems after regular business hours (6) and to look for information that he can use as leverage with a new employer. Because of his access and the lack of rules in the Security Information and Event Management (SIEM) system, no alerts are generated and no advanced monitoring is conducted on his network activity, enabling John's anomalous searches through these databases to go undetected. To deepen his search for valuable information, John submits a request to access a more sensitive database, which is not required in the performance of his duties (7). His access request is denied but is not evaluated in a broader context.

John puts in his two weeks' notice (8) after securing an offer with a competitor who expressed interest in some of the data to which John claims to have access. In his final two weeks, John accesses the databases under his responsibility with the intention of copying and removing the sensitive data he had previously explored. He uses administrative credentials (9) to change the permission levels on restricted folders (10) so he can access data with his non-admin ID without generating access-denied alerts. The data from these databases are exported and e-mailed to his personal e-mail address in a series of e-mails, each below the company's current data limit of 5 MB (11).

John leaves the company as scheduled, and goes through a standard exit interview. In the interview, he expresses that the organization will "regret how they treated him," referring to his perceived low pay, performance ratings, and negative interactions with his supervisor (12). Despite this, no action is taken to assess his network activity.

(#) PRIs correspond with Potential Risk Indicators outlined in Table 5.6.

Table 5.6 describes each of the PRIs that the company in the scenario above could have used to recognize the elevated level of risk John posed. Because PRIs should be drawn from real-world experience, each of the indicators is supported by a real historical case, showing the potential for that indicator to highlight potential risks.

Table 5.6 Examples of Contextual, Virtual, and Non-virtual PRIs

#	Data Type	Potential Risk Indicator	Description	Case Example
1	Contextual	Located in foreign location with high degree of competition	Employees located in foreign locations with known industrial espionage pose an elevated risk for committing a malicious or complacent insider act driven by foreign governments or competitor organizations looking to steal intellectual property, bypass research and development, or harm a company's headquarter country.	In 2013, a guard at a U.S. consulate in China, Bryan Underwood, pleaded guilty to attempting to sell classified photographs, documents, and information about the consulate to China's Ministry of State Security (MSS).[1]
2	Contextual	High-level system access	Individuals with high levels of system access pose a higher risk, given the critical nature of the systems and information to which they have access. Moreover, roles that provide privileged access (e.g., systems administrators) pose a greater risk because of their ability to access systems through the "back end" or through other accounts.	Terry Childs, a former system administrator for the city of San Francisco, used his access to change network passwords to the FiberWAN system that managed most of the network activity for the city government. When his supervisor requested the passwords, Childs refused, resulting in a 12-day lockout and $900,000 spent to recover access to the system.[2]
3	Nonvirtual	Declining Performance	Declining performance can indicate that an individual is becoming disengaged, disillusioned, or disgruntled with an organization. Declining performance may be a precursor to an insider threat incident.	In 2010, Michael Mitchell was sentenced to prison for information theft. Mitchell, who was fired from his job due to poor performance, kept and passed along a number of trade secrets from his employer to a rival Korean company, with whom he entered into a consulting agreement.[3]
4	Nonvirtual	Alarming Supervisor Feedback	Peers or supervisors represent an important source of nonvirtual indicators, given their position to observe what coworkers say and do. Incidents like threatening another coworker provide insight into an individual's current mindset/opinion of the organization.	On September 16, 2013, Aaron Alexis killed 12 people at the Washington Navy yard, where he was a subcontractor. Years earlier, while in the Navy Reserve, Alexis was cited eight times for misconduct, ranging from traffic violations to insubordination and disorderly conduct."[4]
5	Nonvirtual	Anomalous Foreign Travel	Unexplained foreign travel could raise the risk of an individual being in contact with foreign entities that wish to steal trade secrets or harm an organization in, or inflict damage on, its headquarter country.	In 2006, an employee took a leave from her company and began working for a Chinese telecommunications firm. When she returned to work at her company, she purchased a ticket to China. The employee spent two days downloading hundreds of thousands of documents and, during a random security check at an airport, was found with more than 1,000 proprietary documents in her luggage.

(Continued)

Table 5.6 Examples of Contextual, Virtual, and Non-virtual PRIs (Continued)

#	Data Type	Potential Risk Indicator	Description	Case Example
6	Virtual	Anomalous Login Times	Employees who access databases or systems at anomalous hours may be attempting to conduct activity (e.g., exfiltration) at times where there are few other employees nearby to see the activity or to avoid a productivity loss associated with removing data during the work day.	At Chelsea Manning's court-martial hearing, Army specialist Jihrleah Showman testified that "clues were everywhere—a combination of odd behavior, nervousness, and stealth. Manning worked long hours, stayed late and kept to herself inside their offices."[5]
7	Virtual	Access Request Denials	If an employee receives a larger than normal number of access denials, it may indicate that they are attempting to access systems and information that are not necessary for their role.	An unusual number of access denials could indicate an unusual interest in matters outside the scope of an employee's duties – a primary potential indicator identified by the FBI[6]
8	Nonvirtual	Separation Notice Delivered	Employees have a higher risk portfolio immediately upon submitting notice of voluntary separation. The time between submitting notice and ultimate separation is the period of particularly high risk for data exfiltration.	In 2014, a start-up filed a lawsuit against its former COO who left the company to join a rival. The lawsuit claims the employee downloaded files (including company e-mails, contacts, and documents) to his personal Dropbox account and brought the information to his new employer.
9	Virtual	Use of Administrative ID	Administrative credentials enable users to access more sensitive parts of an organization's systems and conduct activities that can facilitate or support data exfiltration. A user's activities using administrative credentials should be closely monitored for anomalies and suspicious activity.	A financial services employee, used his systems administrator access to put a "logic bomb" in the company's network that was scheduled to delete all the company's files in every branch. About a month after he left the company, his "logic bomb" caused around 2,000 company servers to go down resulting in more than $3 million in damages.
10	Virtual	Altering Permission Levels	For users with administrative rights, altering permission levels on folders may indicate an individual's attempt to circumvent technical controls and gain access to more sensitive or previously restricted areas of the network.	Antoine Deltour was given access to sensitive tax files that were not required to perform his job while working at PwC. While copying training documents, Deltour discovered tax ruling files that outlined a method large corporations used to lower their taxes. He copied over 28,000 documents from internal systems that outlined this tax practice and subsequently leaked the files to the media. Deltour admitted that although he should not have had access to the files, he did not breach any virtual security to obtain them.[7]

(Continued)

Table 5.6 Examples of Contextual, Virtual, and Non-virtual PRIs (Continued)

#	Data Type	Potential Risk Indicator	Description	Case Example
11	Virtual	E-mail Traffic to External Accounts	E-mail is a primary mechanism for data exfiltration and is particularly high-risk when employees send e-mails to their personal accounts. A high volume of e-mails with large attachments can be indicative of data exfiltration and attempts to circumvent data limits placed on e-mails.	An engineer at an automotive company, found an assignment working with motor control systems of hybrid vehicles. Using this position, the employee allegedly thousands of sensitive documents—some of which she sent over her e-mail account—to share with her husband, who secretly ran a hybrid technology company and exploited the information she provided to win new business.
12	Nonvirtual	Exit Interview Feedback	Threats or suspicious statements made in an exit interview could indicate ill-will toward an employer, which could have already manifested itself in the employee's actions over his final weeks of employment. These types of statements, or indications that an employee is going to a competitor, should prompt a review of that individual's activity prior to departure, and increased monitoring for data exfiltration, sabotage, or other malicious activity following the individual's departure.	The FBI cites disgruntlement to the point of wanting to retaliate against the organization and allegiance to another company as two significant personal factors that increase the chances someone will spy against their employer.[8]

[1]U.S. Department of Justice, "Former U.S. Consulate Guard Sentenced to Nine Years in Prison for Attempting to Communicate National Defense Information to China," March 2013. http://www.fbi.gov/washingtondc/press-releases/2013/former-u.s.-consulate-guard-sentenced-to-nine-years-in-prison-for-attempting-to-communicate-national-defense-information-to-china.
[2]Robert McMillan, "Network Admin Terry Childs Gets 4-Year Sentence," August 2010. http://www.networkworld.com/article/2215761/lan-wan/network-admin-terry-childs-gets-4-year-sentence.html.
[3]Federal Bureau of Investigation, "The Insider Threat: An Introduction to Detecting and Deterring an Insider Spy." http://www.fbi.gov/about-us/investigate/counterintelligence/the-insider-threat.
[4]U.S. House of Representatives, Committee on Oversight and Government Reform, "Slipping Through the cracks: How the D.C. Navy Yard Shooting Exposes Flaws in the Federal Security Clearance Process," February 2014. http://oversight.house.gov/wp-content/uploads/2014/02/Aaron-Alexis-Report-FINAL.pdf.
[5]Richard Serrano, "Manning's Supervisor Describes Brawl, Suspicions He Was A Spy," LA Times, July 2013. http://articles.latimes.com/2013/jul/19/nation/la-na-manning-trial-20130720.
[6]Federal Bureau of Investigation, "The Insider Threat: An introduction to detecting and deterring an insider spy," accessed online (April 20, 2015): http://www.fbi.gov/about-us/investigate/counterintelligence/the-insider-threat.
[7]Lara Marlowe, "Luxleaks: Former PwC Employee Admits He Took Files," The Irish Times, December 2014. http://www.irishtimes.com/business/economy/luxleaks-former-pwc-employee-admits-he-took-files-1.2038226.
[8]Federal Bureau of Investigation, "The Insider Threat: An Introduction to Detecting and Deterring an Insider Spy," accessed online (April 20, 2015): http://www.fbi.gov/about-us/investigate/counterintelligence/the-insider-threat.

IDENTIFYING CRITICAL INDICATORS THROUGHOUT THE ORGANIZATION

Organizations are swimming in data about their employees, but it generally exists in a number of disparate locations, offices, and systems. This makes it essential to get key offices from across the organization involved in insider threat mitigation efforts—a security division will not be effective on its own. Instead, offices including HR, legal counsel, information technology, and security need to work together to identify and supply critical indicators and balance security with employee privacy. These offices should become members of an Insider Threat Working Group, which helps drive an Insider Threat program. These stakeholders not only own critical data but are also responsible for implementing mitigation strategies. Those organizations that are successful in building a broad coalition of stakeholders across the organizaiton will be most effective at mitigating insider threats. The following stakeholder divisions of an organization are key to the success of the insider threat program.

Human Resources divisions have access to a number of important, but sensitive, data points. Ensuring HR buy-in for insider threat mitigation is essential, as the data housed within HR will often require the greatest amount of coordination to share in a responsible way. HR divisions generally house contextual data, including initial background check results and employee status, level, and tenure. HR is also one of the main sources of nonvirtual behavioral indicators, including performance ratings, HR violations, and supervisor/coworkers' complaints. HR is also involved during the employee separation process—a critical time in which many known insider threat attacks occur.[7] Often, an organization's *legal* division can be a helpful partner in defining the parameters around the use of this data.

In most cases, *information technology (IT)* divisions own all virtual behavior data, as they house the digital trails left by employees conducting their daily business. These digital trails provide a rich set of data that can be used to establish baselines. IT offices may maintain data on network access patterns, e-mail patterns (including size of attachments, recipient domains, etc.), user rights, system logs, and access denials. If an organization employs a data loss prevention (DLP) tool, IT would also have access to information associated with trying to remove data from the network or an employee's work computer. IT must be especially attentive to privileged users—many of whom may work for IT—as their high-level systems access makes them at greater risk of engaging in harmful insider behavior.

---

[7] Andrew P. Moore, Michael Hanley, and David Mundie, "A Pattern for Increased Monitoring for Intellectual Property Theft by Departing Insiders," Software Engineering Institute, April 2012.

Security divisions tend to house data about employees' offline, or nonvirtual, behavior. Potential indicators a security office may own are badging trends—for base-lining both time and location patterns—security violations, background investigation data, and unauthorized access attempts. Security may also house important contextual data, including physical access rights. Other holders of nonvirtual behavior include *finance* and *compliance* divisions, which may track when employees trend downward on compliance issues manually, or in separate systems.

Although the stakeholders listed here represent key offices that should be engaged to stand up to any insider threat mitigation effort, there are many other stakeholder groups organizations should consider leveraging. The exact configuration and involvement of offices will depend on each organization's specific concerns, the data collected by each office, and by the organization's willingness to use that data in an attempt to prevent, detect, and mitigate insider threats.

KEY CHALLENGES

There are a number of key challenges that must be considered and actively managed in order to successfully leverage organizational data to identify critical indicators:

- **Get buy-in from across the organization**—As illustrated in the previous section, data lives in various offices spread all over organizations. It is critical to get those data-owning offices onboard and engaged early on to pave the way for information-sharing in a responsible and proactive way, rather than in a rushed, reactive way when an insider incident is imminent or in progress. It is critical to engage the CEO or organizational leadership and encourage full participation and cooperation.
- **Clean and managed data**—A byproduct of critical information housed in many offices throughout an organization is that data likely resides in different systems and exist in different formats. The data may also vary in consistency and quality. It is important to take the time to make the data manageable, so it can be used by a data analytic tool supporting insider threat mitigation.
- **Understand Perceptions**—Employees may see an organization's data collection efforts as an effort to play "Big Brother." As such, it is important to not be secretive about a program, especially if it is common knowledge among employees. Instead, focus on ensuring that employees understand the importance of a program as a way of protecting them, their customers, their organization, its brand and public reputation, and its most sensitive information. Effective

communication of the purpose of the program and its existence can also serve as a deterrent for common insider acts such as data exfiltration.

- **Understand legal challenges**—It is important to understand both federal and state employment and privacy laws, to ensure that insider threat mitigation efforts do not inadvertently use data illegally. For instance, organizations should understand protected classes, for example, the Federal protected classes of race, religion, age, and gender. This kind of data cannot be used as grounds for terminating employment.[8] It is critical that organizations work with their legal counsel to ensure their efforts do not conflict with federal or state law.

Moreover, to be successful, organizations need to understand the contextual, virtual, and nonvirtual data available, and the challenges an organization may face in using that data to identify employees who pose the greatest risk to an organization.

KEY TAKEAWAYS

- Potential risk indicators (PRIs) reflect behavior that can be used to identify when an employee poses an increased or decreased risk compared to peers and his or her own baseline behavior over time. There are three categories of PRIs: contextual indicators, virtual indicators, and nonvirtual indicators.
- Human resources, information technology, legal counsel, security, and other groups within an organization must work together to identify and supply critical indicators and balance employee privacy. Those organizations that are successful in building a diverse approach to insider threat mitigation will be most effective at establishing behavioral baselines and detecting anomalous behavior.
- The true value of proactive identifying anomalous behavior will enable organization to interrupt forward motion and, in many instances, proactively prevent damage to an organization's assets.

---

[8] U.S. Equal Employment Opportunity Commission website, "Laws Enforced by EEOC," accessed April 2015. http://www.eeoc.gov/laws/statutes/.

CHAPTER 6

Establishing an Organizational Risk Appetite

RISK TOLERANCE DEFINED

> Risk Tolerance: The level of risk an organization is willing to accept around a specific objective.[1]

The underpinning of any insider threat mitigation program is the organization's determination of its risk tolerance. It should be noted that not all risk can be mitigated, only managed to a tolerable level. Establishing an organization's risk tolerance is a multistage process that requires stakeholders to ask difficult questions about what they care about and where to devote resources. Determining risk tolerance is a necessary precursor to tailoring the insider threat program to address the specific needs, threat types, and unique culture of the organization. Most importantly, organizations have to determine what it is that they need to protect and what they are willing to do in the way they conduct business to achieve the necessary risk mitigation around a potential insider threat. To do this, an organization should follow a five-step process:

1. **Identify key stakeholders.** Before an organization can begin evaluating its tolerance for loss of key assets, it must first identify the stakeholders that need to be involved in the conversation to arrive at a comprehensive definition of insider threat. Stakeholder buy-in from across all areas of the organization is critical to establishing a comprehensive approach to insider threat mitigation. Common representatives include stakeholders from physical security, IT, privacy, policy, human resources, legal, business units, information, compliance, assurance, and executive management.
2. **Prioritize critical assets.** Key stakeholders must prioritize assets and determine the extent to which the organization is willing to go to mitigate loss or damage to those assets (e.g., facilities, source code, intellectual property, customer information, systems, infrastructure, and people). The stakeholders' tolerance for loss or damage in different

---

[1] Institute of Management Accountants, Enterprise Risk Management: Frameworks, Elements, and Integration, (2011), p26.

Insider Threat. DOI: http://dx.doi.org/10.1016/B978-0-12-802410-2.00006-X

areas will inform the cost and administrative burden the organization is willing to incur to protect different assets, as well as the security protocols and parameters it operates under.

3. **Define insider threat in the context of the organization.** Once critical assets have been identified and prioritized, stakeholders have the information they need to determine what insider threat means to them. In the context of the organization's specific business operations, certain threats (e.g., theft of IP) generate more concern and thus warrant more resources to mitigate because of the nature of critical assets they have determined need protection. A completely virtual organization will invest little in mitigating physical threats, whereas a construction company might invest a significant proportion of its insider threat mitigation budget into physical security controls.

4. **Determine data to collect.** The data collected as part of an insider threat mitigation program should reflect an employee's or contractor's behavior in both the virtual and nonvirtual work space in relation to the critical assets they can access or affect. This often includes data on the organization's workforce and the organization's overall approach to workforce management as well as its information security and compliance posture.

5. **Select appropriate controls.** The types of controls an organization implements should be based on the potential impact of various destructive insider behaviors, such as theft of R&D, espionage, sabotage, workplace violence, or fraud, on its critical assets in accordance with its determined risk tolerance. For example, an organization may monitor certain positions more vigorously than others, introduce additional authentication processes for certain systems, or establish more stringent rules for certain job functions. Some controls may require too high an administrative or financial burden in relation to the value/risk of the asset in question, requiring stakeholders to use a risk-based approach to achieve an appropriate balance. Having too many security controls or countermeasures can impede the mission and impact an agile workforce. Having too few increases vulnerabilities and leaves the organization exposed. Controls should strike the proper balance between countering the threat and conducting business.

Gathering Key Stakeholders a Critical First Step in Defining and Prioritizing Risk Tolerance

Before categorizing assets and corresponding tolerance for loss, key executive stakeholders from across the business enterprise must be engaged. This group will be responsible for defining risk tolerance, critical assets, and the path forward for developing and implementing a comprehensive program that prevents, detects, and responds to insider threats. It is important that critical functions

Table 6.1 Key Stakeholders*
Function
Business Operations
Finance
Human Resources
Information Security
IT Security
Legal/Ethics/Privacy
Physical Security
Policy

Public Affairs
  – Information Assurance
  – Compliance
  – Executive Management

List of possible key stakeholders for an insider threat program; stakeholders will depend on an organization's structure, and therefore this list is not all inclusive.

within an organization are represented in insider threat discussions in order to provide an enterprise-wide view of critical assets, vulnerabilities, and risks. An insider threat program should also have a designated owner or program manager, but mitigating insider threats is a shared responsibility that requires collaboration and ongoing coordination across functional areas, including human resources, information technology, and compliance (see Table 6.1).

Establishing a governance structure that enables stakeholders to regularly communicate regarding insider threat activities and issues is essential. In many cases, chartering an official insider threat working group empowers individuals to take responsibility for the development of an insider threat program and provides a structure for sharing relevant information and securing buy-in from across the organization. Membership of the working group should overlap with the stakeholders that played a role in prioritizing the organization's critical assets.

A holistic insider threat program requires diverse input and perspective because individual behaviors associated with increased insider threat risk are often tracked by different functions within an organization. A common pitfall of insider threat programs is the tendency to involve stakeholders with a background in information technology or cybersecurity to the exclusion of other key areas of the organization. These stakeholders may have a siloed or skewed conception of what critical assets an organization should spend its resources protecting. Together, cross-functional stakeholders can develop a balanced approach to which assets are most critical and where the organization is most vulnerable. These perspectives are essential for stimulating an important dialogue about what should be protected and how investments are spent.

DEFINING YOUR ORGANIZATION'S CRITICAL ASSETS

An asset is an item of value owned.[2]

Critical assets are those tangible and intangible assets that are vital to sustain the organization's business operations, achieve mission goals, and maintain its infrastructure. What constitutes a critical assets depends on the values, resources, and business needs of the organization, but some examples are facilities, credentials, source code, intellectual property, research and development, financial assets, customer information, and workforce safety. Although industries prioritize their assets differently, general trends do exist. The greatest priority for organizations is protecting their people, which includes protecting facilities from attack and sabotage, and then the secondary concern is safeguarding products and reputation from sabotage. Organizations that have already instituted a data classification policy will be more mature in their ability to effectively and efficiently identify critical assets. Table 6.2 lays out some information types that are commonly held as critical to organizational integrity and operations, thus often qualifying as critical assets.

At present, Federal agencies are required by law to categorize their information and information systems according to:

> the potential impact on an organization should certain events occur
> which jeopardize the information and information systems needed by the
> organization to accomplish its assigned mission, protect its assets, fulfill
> its legal responsibilities, maintain its day-to-day functions, and protect
> individuals.[3]

In defining critical assets, private sector organizations should conduct a similar exercise, and perhaps even expand it to include all assets. Another leading practice when establishing risk tolerance is to consider how critical assets, when in the wrong hands, can lead to different insider threat incidents, including:

- Inconvenience, distress, or damage to standing or reputation
- Financial loss or organization liability
- Harm to organizational programs or interests
- Unauthorized release of sensitive information
- Public safety and national security
- Civil or criminal violations[4]

---

[2] Merriam-Webster Dictionary, http://www.merriam-webster.com/dictionary/asset (March 1, 2015).

[3] Federal Information Processing Standards Publication 199: "Standards for Security Categorization of Federal Information and Information Systems," February 2004. http://csrc.nist.gov/publications/fips/fips199/FIPS-PUB-199-final.pdf.

[4] OMB M-04-04 E-Authentication Guidance for Federal Agencies (April 3, 2015).

Table 6.2 Common Insider Information Types

Information Type	Definition	Examples
Personally Identifiable Information (PII)	Information that may directly or indirectly identify an individual or that relates to an identifiable person	Government identifiers (SSN), credit card and bank account numbers, address, date of birth, personnel number, compensation, demographic data, photograph or video identifiable to an individual
Protected Health Information (PHI)	Information transmitted or maintained in any form or media by a HIPAA-covered entity that identifies an individual or with respect or relates to health condition, records, or payments	Medical treatment and diagnostic records, health insurance records, health payment records, smoking status
Financial Information	Information about an entity's financial records	Financial and salary information such as financial statements (10 K), tax, audit, and investments data
Competitive Intelligence	Information about an entity's products, customers or competitors, or any aspect of the competitive environment	Trade secrets, source code, merger and acquisition information, products, markets, pricing, or business plans
Customer Information	Information about customers	Usage rates, pricing, sales pipeline, marketing information, payment information, contract information
Intellectual Property (IP) and Research and Development (R&D)	Creations of the mind for which exclusive rights are recognized	Methodologies, products, services information, tools, templates, organizational assessments, business processes, and software
Sensitive Information	Privileged or proprietary information that could cause serious harm to an entity if compromised; proprietary information is information owned by an entity or information in which an entity has a protectable interest	Information varies by organization, but can include forensic investigation, fraud investigation, restructuring or bankruptcy, e-mail communications, system testing results, security controls, IT infrastructure, and network security capabilities

Defining organizational assets is not challenging in and of itself, but prioritizing critical assets according to organizational risk tolerance can be far more difficult. Understanding the effects of different insider threat incidents, including the above mentioned list, proves extremely useful when determining critical assets. Stakeholders may be hesitant to articulate their tolerance for protecting different types of assets. However, organizations routinely exhibit their tolerance on employee actions in everyday business operations. For example, many employees are required to report their total number of hours worked on a daily or weekly basis. Most organizations tolerate an acceptable level of negligence, recognizing that employees may occasionally forget to submit their timesheets. But what if an employee fails to submit his or her time with far greater frequency? At a certain point, the organization will no longer tolerate the employee's disregard for policy and will intervene. Organizations can apply a similar strategy towards prioritizing critical assets by identifying the behavioral infractions of an insider that can be tolerated and those that cannot. For example, an employee publicizing a sales cycle diagram is much less damaging than publicizing a strategic investment approach with associated budgets. As a general rule, the more sensitive an asset, the lower the tolerance for risk for potential loss or damage to that asset should be.

DETERMINING THE THREAT INSIDERS POSE TO YOUR CRITICAL ASSETS

After identifying cross-functional representation within the insider threat governance structure, stakeholders should move forward and define what an insider threat is in their organizational context. For example, a large oil corporation will define insider threat very differently than a burgeoning tech start-up. Very few organizations have built insider threat into the enterprise risk mitigation strategy. Roughly 14% of organizations actually have a working definition of insider threat.[5] The nuances of what an insider threat means to a certain set of stakeholders will vary. Examples of potentially dangerous insider characteristics can include:

- An employee who has reached the tipping point and sees no way out
- Betrayal of trust motivated by money, self-grandeur, or revenge
- A person who has access (knowingly or unknowingly) to information that can harm the organization
- An individual whose placement and access within an organization, coupled with motivation to do harm, poses a risk to the organization's operations
- An individual who views himself as above the rules and who will do whatever it takes to get the job done, exposing the organization to considerable external risk
- An individual who has no knowledge or awareness of organizational policies or procedures for information systems, workforce safety, and asset security
- An individual who believes because they developed IP, they own it whether they stay or leave the organization

The key to level-setting a discussion on characteristics of potential insider threat is to aggregate and identify recurring themes, or gaps, that everyone can agree upon. Getting all stakeholders on the same page regarding what insider threat means to the organization is critical when discussing tolerance for loss of critical assets. Individuals need to understand the potential impact of insider incidents to begin to prioritize which assets are more indispensable

---

[5] "Preventing, Mitigating, and Managing Insider Threats," The Conference Board of Canada, 4/12/2013

Table 6.3 Common Insider Threat Types

Threat Type	Description	Examples
Information Theft	Use of insider access to steal, exploit, or exfiltrate information that is not suitable for public consumption	A scientist sends valuable information on research and development efforts to his personal computer, which is hacked by an outside party
Physical Property Theft	Use of insider access to steal material items	A construction worker loading valuable copper wire into his personal vehicle on site and selling it for a profit
Espionage	Use of insider access to obtain sensitive information for exploitation that impacts national security and public safety	A government official sells confidential documents to a foreign government
Fraud	Wrongful or criminal deception intended to result in financial or personal gain	A database administrator modifies data without authorization on the pretense of fixing corrupt data for personal gain
Security Compromise	Use of access to override security countermeasures	An employee at the IT service desk obtains the passwords of employees whose computers are in need of repair to access sensitive information
Workplace Violence	Use of violence or threats of violence to influence the behaviors of others	A disgruntled employee brings a weapon to work to intimidate and scare coworkers
Sabotage	Intentional destruction of resources or damage to reputation and business operations	A maintenance worker inserts a removable media device with malware into a server to bring down the system

than others. This exercise often leads to the development of use cases that reflect a prioritized set of incidents.

Next, stakeholders should build upon areas of mutual understanding by identifying the different types of threats that drive insider activity and have the potential to impact the organization. Table 6.3 reviews common insider threat types pertaining to organizations across a diverse set of industries. This list is not exhaustive.

Prioritizing relevant threats may seem daunting at first, but it is important to narrow an organization's focus in an efficient and effective manner. To begin understanding organizational focus areas, stakeholders should ask themselves the following question:

What is the one threat that is unacceptable to have happen?

Answers to this question will vary, but the list of threats will decrease. Using this refined list, stakeholders should prioritize the threats by answering the following question:

If you had to choose the one thing that your organization would get the most benefit out of addressing in the next six months, does your response to the first question change?

Using the Deloitte Greenhouse Approach to Establish Insider Threat Programs

The Deloitte Greenhouse provides an innovative environment that changes the way organizations solve business challenges. Day long lab sessions provide an opportunity for key stakeholders to coalesce around a shared understanding of insider threats, key assets, and existing vulnerabilities. The activities below provide a series of additive activities that will inform risk tolerance.

Act I	Where is the organization today? | Build a shared understanding of the insider problem and the current state capabilities	
	Identify the Threat	Align on a shared definition of insider threat and build a shared understanding of the top threats facing the organization
	Assess the Landscape	Review the initial findings from surveys and interviews to understand what the firm believes to be the most critical assets and vulnerabilities

Act II	Where are the greatest challenges? | Identify priority insider areas of concern and assess risk tolerance.	
	Targeting Time and Energy	Identify critical assets and assess relative risk tolerance across the portfolio of critical assets to identify those that merit the greatest security and resilience to the insider threats identified in the previous discussion.
	Challenges	Explore initial findings on vulnerabilities using stories/use cases mapped to the employee lifecycle.
	Prioritizing Challenges	Compare and overlay critical assets to determine which priority assets are at risk.

Act III	Where decisions does the organization need to make? | Frame key decisions to be made around priority challenges/vulnerabilities	
	Challenge Deep Dive	Deep dive on each priority challenge to frame the decisions that must be made develop recommendations. Deep dive will include a focus on: impact to business, culture, timing, implementation, next steps, etc.
	Roadmap	Building on the outputs of the deep dive, develop a roadmap, bucketing all challenges into the short, medium, and long term. Identify key next steps coming out of the lab.

FIGURE 6.1

Deloitte Lab.

Taking the steps to prioritize efforts around two or three specific threats helps an organization take a more tactical approach to insider threat mitigation and positions stakeholders to move forward with defining critical assets. The Deloitte Greenhouse works with clients to identify these critical components (Figure 6.1).

BALANCING SECURITY INVESTMENTS AND TOLERANCE FOR LOSS

It is important to balance an evaluation of tolerance for critical asset loss with the level of investment the organization is willing to make to protect those critical assets. An abundance of security restrictions and control may results in unreasonable financial and logistical burdens. However, too few countermeasures can obviously expose the organization to the insider threats the organization has determined constitute the greatest risk to its critical assets. Stakeholders must strike an appropriate balance between efficiency and security. Figure 6.2 provides a framework for evaluating the current level of security and risk tolerance for organizational assets. Think of risk tolerance, the Y-axis, as a spectrum of an organization's willingness to accept the loss of an asset, ranging from low for critical assets to high for less essential assets. In other words, a business has low risk tolerance for an asset when its compromise would produce material harm or damage to reputation, operation, or infrastructure. Conversely, an organization has high risk tolerance for loss of an asset that it deems less valuable. High-risk and low-risk assets will vary by industry. The X-axis in Figure 6.2 is an organization's security and resource investment to protect its critical assets, including technical controls, existing policies, processes, and trainings utilized to protect assets.

Organizations can use this matrix to define their risk tolerance for critical assets and evaluate their current state of protection against insider threats. The matrix can also stimulate meaningful dialogue on which vulnerabilities merit further investment to protect. It also provides a platform for a dialogue

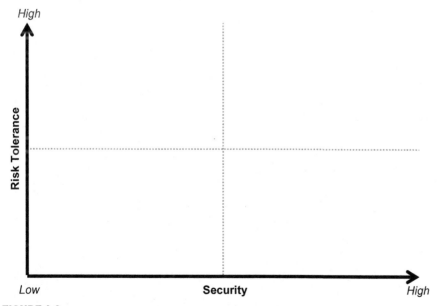

FIGURE 6.2
Risk Tolerance and Security Investment Matrix.

around what the organization is not willing to do based on culture and business objectives that supersede lower-risk assets.

The location of assets within the matrix will inform how the organization's insider threat program should be structured and the level of investment required to protect those items deemed most critical. Figure 6.2 outlines key characteristics for assets classified in each of the four quadrants.

Figure 6.3 is a sample tolerance matrix filled out. In this example, an organization demonstrates a medium tolerance for loss of assets (top right quadrant), but currently employs a high level of security to protect the asset itself. This demonstrates a potentially inefficient investment, especially because there are a number of assets for which the organization has a lower risk tolerance (lower left quadrant), but that are less protected against insider threats. Conversely, Figure 6.3 also shows a high level of investment in security for assets the organization has defined as having a low tolerance for loss. This may indicate an area that has adequate safeguards in place, and is not in need of additional security measures.

Using a matrix to evaluate the security-to-tolerance dynamic allows organizations to determine where additional investments should be made, based on its tolerance for loss of different assets. For example, organizational financials are categorized below as "low tolerance," and few security measures

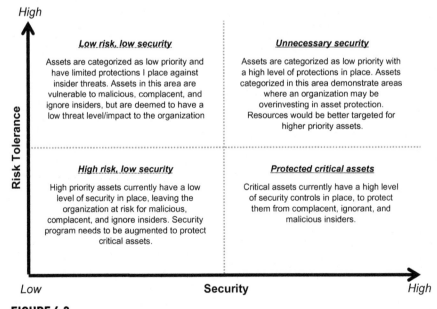

FIGURE 6.3
Risk Tolerance and Security Investment Matrix Defined.

are in place to protect such information. This demonstrates an efficient investment: if the organization were to employ security measures such as restricting access to financial information or implementing a data classification tool, productivity could be negatively affected because it would be more difficult to access and transmit information across the organization. In addition, reduction in access privileges and increased oversight may have an impact on organizational culture, as staff would have to adjust to new policies and procedures, and be educated on the importance and need for insider threat programs.

The matrix-style asset classification in Figure 6.4 helps organizations strike a balance between efficiency and security for their insider threat programs.

Table 6.4 organizes sample critical assets by industry and identifies some corresponding considerations for decision makers.

Figure 6.5 captures an ideal state for asset prioritization and organizational security investments. The matrix illustrates efficient application of resources to protect those assets most critical to the organization. Assets with the lowest tolerance for loss are assigned the greatest investment in security (bottom right quadrant), whereas the assets with the highest tolerance for loss are afforded limited security (top left quadrant).

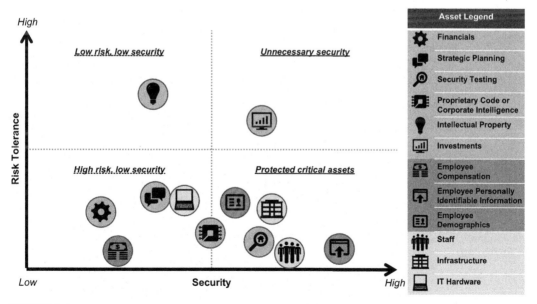

FIGURE 6.4
Sample Risk Tolerance and Security Investment Matrix.

RE-EVALUATING ASSET PRIORITIZATION

Identifying and prioritizing critical assets is an essential step in determining risk tolerance and increasing an organization's ability to prevent, detect, and respond to insider threats. As the business world continues to change, however, with increasingly flexible workplaces and large shifts in the generational composition of the workforce, insider threat challenges will continue to evolve. Continuous evaluation of risk tolerance by organizations' leaders provides an enterprise with options to reinvest resources and address changing

Table 6.4 Key Considerations for Organizations Across Industries

Industry	Sample Critical Assets	Key Considerations and Questions
Energy and Utilities	■ Protection of key energy infrastructure from malicious intent, fraud, or theft	■ The latest sensory technology, like Distributed Acoustic Sensing (DAS) can pinpoint leaks, but an improved culture of safety makes the difference in identifying real threats among false alarms
Federal Government	■ Protection of employees' physical safety and key infrastructure critical to national security ■ Maintaining integrity of access to classified information	■ Are federal and contract staff at risk of workplace violence? ■ Are clearance levels appropriate for the level of access to national security data?
Financial Services	■ Protection of individual and institutional financial assets ■ Securing proprietary information and practices, such as software or code for trading	■ Threat to financial assets can be the customer or clients themselves ■ In a competitive industry with frequent turnover, departing employees may pose a threat to proprietary materials
Health Care	■ Protection of personally identifiable information according to HIPAA	■ Where are the weak links for healthcare providers? Are hospitals, labs, and urgent care professionals securing patient information properly with secure transmissions?
Research and Development	■ Security of defense and aerospace technologies that are vulnerable to corporate espionage and foreign government intelligence	■ Are leading businesses equipped to combat attacks by foreign governments or terrorists to the firewalls and systems protecting technology critical to national security?
Telecommunication, Media and Technology	■ Protection of over 1B smart phone users' data ■ Securing copyrighted and in-progress publications before release, like movies, albums, and books	■ What controls are in place to protect users of digital data from image or message theft? ■ What role does executive leadership play in proactively combatting loss of copyrighted material to hackers or insiders?

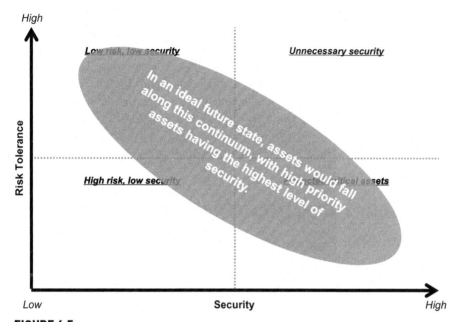

FIGURE 6.5
Future State Matrix.

priorities before new vulnerabilities emerge. See Chapter 16 for more about emerging insider threat patterns.

IN SUMMARY

Bringing the right stakeholders to the table is critical to ensuring a holistic review of critical assets and current security measures. Through this prioritization exercise, an organization establishes the foundation of its insider threat program by building a shared understanding around the following:

1. What does insider threat mean to the organization?
2. Where does our organization stand in terms of insider threat?
3. Where should we focus our investment in insider threat to achieve the greatest value for our organization?

CASE STUDY 1: FINANCIAL SERVICES FIRM

The Financial Services industry has influence over trillions of dollars of private, institutional, and sovereign wealth across the world. The manner in which its professionals and customers access and transmit sensitive financial data and conduct business every day puts data at risk for exposure to loss.

Although complacent or ignorant insiders pose a definite risk to the integrity of the financial industry's security, malicious intent can pose grave consequences. Consider, for example, the arena of highly specialized trading in the global stock exchange. The use of proprietary algorithms and program code is a growing tradecraft among leading investment banks. The turnover among computer engineers who design these instruments between competing banks is high, and, as New York Times Bestselling author Michael Lewis explains in *Flash Boys*, the stakes are high. Banks have prosecuted former employees alleged to have stolen proprietary trading algorithms on their way to other firms.[6]

CASE STUDY 2: HEALTH CARE PROVIDER

Health care providers face stringent regulations for securing patient privacy as dictated by the terms of the Health Insurance Portability and Accountability Act (HIPAA). Willful and negligent loss of patient data is a violation of federal law and carries fines up to and including $50,000 per incident, according to the American Medical Association (AMA).[7] In an age of increased use of digital clinical tools and electronic medical records, several million health professionals and their patients are at risk of ignorant, complacent, or malicious disclosure of patient data. These organizations should ask, "Do our patients and staff know how to securely transmit medical information?"

CASE STUDY 3: TELECOMMUNICATIONS, MEDIA, AND TECHNOLOGY

Telecommunications, Media, and Technology (TMT) businesses operate in a market where more than one billion smart phones will be purchased in 2015.[8] The digital signature of billions of smart phone users is tremendous, as is the volume of data users view and read. What happens when wireless providers, cable companies, and entertainment publishers face willful leaks of private or copyrighted material? What kinds of data loss are acceptable or unavoidable?

---

[6] Lewis, Michael. *Flash Boys: A Wall Street Revolt*. New York: W.W. Norton, 2014. Print.

[7] American Medical Association. 'HIPAA Violations and Enforcement'. http://www.ama-assn.org/ama/pub/physician-resources/solutions-managing-your-practice/coding-billing-insurance/hipaahealth-insurance-portability-accountability-act/hipaa-violations-enforcement.page. Accessed 28 February 2015.

[8] Deloitte TMT Predictions 2015. "A billion smartphone upgrades."

KEY TAKEAWAYS

- Risk tolerance informs the types of assets that need to be protected and the extent to which the organization is willing to take measures to protect them.
- Before categorizing key assets and corresponding tolerance for loss, key stakeholders from across the business enterprise must be engaged. An insider threat program should have a designated owner or program manager, but mitigating insider threats is a shared responsibility that requires collaboration and ongoing coordination across functional areas, including human resources, information technology, and compliance.
- Critical assets are those tangible, intangible, and human entities that are vital to sustain the organization's business operations, achieve mission goals, and maintain its infrastructure. Examples of critical assets include facilities, source code, intellectual property, research and development, customer information, and workforce safety.

CHAPTER 7

Risk Management Using Data Analytics

INTRODUCTION TO ADVANCED ANALYTICS

In this chapter, we will introduce how organizations can collect information or potential risk indicators (PRIs) that can be used to proactively identify emerging insider threats. As organizations move to adopt an improved prevention, detection, and response posture, an advanced analytics capability is a core building block. The tool, which will be discussed at length in this chapter, is a core component of a holistic and risk-based insider threat program. This chapter will provide readers with the following:

- An overview of advanced analytics
- Key advantages associated with the design, build, and implementation of a tool
- How organizations can use analytics to proactively detect threats through use cases
- Selecting the right tool
- The future of advanced analytics

As we have noted throughout the book, insider threats are rarely impulsive. Rather, individuals follow a path from idea to action. Given the advancements of behavioral detection capabilities, we are able to capture this trail of behavior in the form of PRIs. PRIs include an action, event, or condition that precedes an insider act and is hypothesized to be associated with the act. These PRIs are organized into contextual, virtual, and nonvirtual categories. The observable precursors contribute to increased risk and can allow the organization to identify those individuals that might be at elevated risk for a malicious, complacent, or ignorant insider act. Advanced analytics is defined as the technical ability to collect disparate sources of data or PRIs from a variety of system sources (e.g., HR, physical security, network data, ethics data), correlate that information to identify patterns of at-risk behavior, and visualize the data to allow for further inquiry based on predefined risk tolerances. Figure 7.1 outlines the factors that inhibit preventative PRI correlation.

Insider Threat. DOI: http://dx.doi.org/10.1016/B978-0-12-802410-2.00007-1

Organization's often fail to correlate PRIs until
after an incident has taken place. This is largely
attributed to the following factors:

- A historical emphasis on external threats
- A trust without verification approach
- Lack of process and technology to do so
- Risk mitigation strategies that do not
  include insider threats
- Cultures that trust without verification

FIGURE 7.1
Factors Impacting Organizational Failure to Correlate PRIs.

Growing Consensus

Advanced analytics technology is a market that is relatively nascent and grow-ing quickly. To mitigate insider threats, companies are increasingly looking at methods to monitor work habits and behaviors from a variety of sources. There is consensus across leading public, private, and academic leading practices that a detection capability that correlates PRIs is needed to proac-tively detect emerging insider threats. Recent studies and guidance from the National Institute of Standard and Technology (NIST) and various other pri-vate and public institutions have validated the prevalence of PRIs in insider threat cases.[1] Furthermore, they have emphasized the importance of corre-lating these precursors to help identify threats proactively. The studies and standards below represent a sampling of recent publications that supports the need for an advanced analytics capability.

- A study conducted at Stanford University revealed that 97% of insider threat cases involved employees whose behavior was flagged by supervisors as suspicious, but was not followed up on by the organization.[2]
- According to a 2013 report by the Ponemon Institute, fifty-nine percent of employees who quit or are asked to leave take sensitive business with them.[3]

---

[1] "Overview." Cybersecurity Framework. National Institute of Standards and Technology, 12 Nov. 2013. Web. <http://www.nist.gov/cyberframework/>
[2] Zegart, Amy. "Insider Threats and Organizational Root Causes: The 2009 Fort Hood Terrorist Attack." Parameters 45.2 (2015): n. pag. Print.
[3] Ponemon Institute. 2013 Cost of Data Breach Study: Global Analysis. 2013.

- Ninety-two percent of insider threat cases studied in a paper by the Computer Emergency Readiness Team (CERT) were preceded by a negative work-related event such as a termination, dispute with a supervisor, or a demotion/transfer.[4]
- According to CSO Magazine's 2012 Cybersecurity Watch Survey, organizations that experienced cybercrime by an insider in the previous 12 months reported that 51 percent of those insiders violated IT security policies and 19 percent were flagged by a manager for behavior/performance issues.[5]

Furthermore, as outlined by NIST, there is compelling evidence to show that some types of insider activity–driven behavior is often preceded by non-technical behaviors in the workplace (e.g., ongoing patterns of disgruntled behavior and conflicts with coworkers, performance issues); therefore, human resources records are especially important in this effort.

GUIDING PRINCIPLES

Before running through sample use cases and illustrating how the detection aspect of an insider threat program functions, it is important to provide background on the overall risk management approach. One of the questions often asked by clients is what are the precepts or fundamental tenets that guide our approach to risk management and threat detection? Listed below are the guiding principles that should be communicated to the insider threat working group (ITWG) and can be used to develop an effective and risk-based insider threat detection capability.

- **Threat Prioritization:** Not all threats have the same risks, vulnerabilities, and consequence levels. Based on factors such as intent and capability, consequence, and vulnerability, certain threats will have an elevated risk level and will be the focus of risk mitigation efforts.
- **Anomaly Detection:** Identification of emerging insider threats is based on associated indicators, not absolutes. The risk algorithm is designed to identify anomalies that are subject to human review rather than predict an insider act.
- **The Power of Correlation:** The ability to aggregate a holistic set of PRIs and correlate them over time will allow the organization to identify patterns of behavior that may be indicative of an emerging threat.

---

[4] Cappelli, Dawn M., Andrew P. Moore, and Randall F. Trzeciak, *The CERT Guide to Insider Threats: How to Prevent, Detect, and Respond to Information Technology Crimes* (Upper Saddle River, NJ: Addison-Wesley Professional, 2012).

[5] "2012 Cybersecurity Watch Survey." CSO Magazine. 2012.

- **Risk-Managed Security:** The objective of the advanced analytics tool is to support risk-based programs that mitigate vulnerabilities to threats and their potential impacts, thereby reducing risk to an acceptable level. Risk will never equal zero. The key is to manage residual risk.
- **Detection as Part of The Solution:** Because insider threats are people-centric challenges, it requires more than just technology to address the problem set. Organizations should view an advanced analytics tool as a part and parcel of the solution and not the solution itself.
- **Risk-Based Monitoring:** As the perceived risk of an insider increases, because of the detection of contextual, virtual, and nonvirtual precursors, the amount of technical and behavioral monitoring should proportionately increase.
- **Resilient, Risk-Resistant Infrastructure:** Although eliminating all risk is not feasible, organizations should build resilience into their infrastructure, business processes and controls to reduce the overall impact. An advanced analytics solution is a critical step in this process.
- **Balanced Approach:** Having too many PRIs can generate an influx of false positives and having too few increases vulnerabilities and leaves the enterprise exposed. Programs should strike the right balance.

These guiding principles can and should inform the development of an threat detection capability, however, all organizations should go through the exercise of defining guiding principles with the necessary stakeholders.

ADVANCED ANALYTICS IN MOTION

In the previous section, we discussed what is meant by an advanced analytics capability, what role PRIs play in detection, and which basic risk management principles should inform the development of an advanced analytics tool. In this section, we will provide additional details on how the technology can be used to detect an emerging insider threat, and walk through a sample use case.

In order to highlight the application of an advanced analytics tool and demonstrate how this capability fits into the prevent, detect, and response framework, we must first provide an example of the types of indicators that are often displayed by an insider (see Chapter 5 for additional details). PRIs are displayed across three primary categories that organizations should pursue:

- **Contextual Descriptors:** Includes the level of access and role within the organization (e.g., user access permission levels, security clearance level, and privileged rights).
- **Virtual Behaviors:** Includes behaviors displayed on the network and in the virtual landscape (e.g., data accessed, websites visited, e-mail activity).
- **Nonvirtual Behaviors:** Includes behaviors displayed off the network (e.g., suspicious incident reports, complaints, unexplained absences, foreign travel).

Within each of these categories, there is a subset of PRIs that organizations are most likely already collecting. In the list below, you will find six sample PRIs across each of the three categories identified. These PRIs are correlated with sabotage, workplace violence, and the theft of information:

- Attempts to bypass security controls
- Requests for higher level of access without need
- Reprimands (access revocation, suspensions, transfers)
- Disgruntlement toward employees or organization
- Historically poor performance evaluations
- Undue interest in work areas not relevant to role or job function

Although this data exists in different locations, an advantage of the tool's correlation capability includes the combining of virtual, nonvirtual, and contextual information into a single centralized location that allows the organization to "connect the dots" proactively and decide the proper mitigating steps before an event. This ability to correlate and generate insights by bringing disparate but related PRIs together is the essence of the advanced analytics capability. It should be noted that the unit of measure for the capability is the individual; all PRIs are associated with an individual.

Use Case

The example in Figure 7.2 highlights a notional use case scenario and demonstrates the PRIs that are displayed before the act. In the absence of efforts to correlate these PRIs and the necessary network controls, the organization is left to detect the theft after the act.

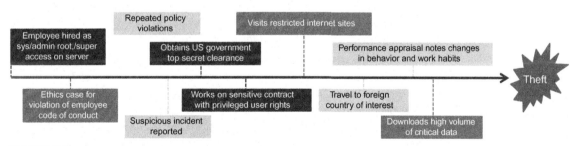

FIGURE 7.2
PRIs Displayed by an Insider.

The Solution

One of the primary challenges faced by organizations looking to manage risk within their unique operating environment is the need for additional context associated with alerts. This is where traditional Security Information and Event Management System (SIEM) has tremendous ingest power but pose challenges with providing context (e.g., who, what, where, when, and why) associated with an alert. An advanced analytics tool is able to correlate a diverse set of PRIs and provide the organization with a means to prioritize alerts. Consider, for example, a situation where two employees are acquiring large amounts of data on their laptops. Employee X has put in his notice and has displayed a number of additional indicators. Employee Y on the other hand has recently been promoted and accepted new job responsibilities that require her to download large amounts of information. A correctly tuned analytics engine would prioritize monitoring employee X and autosuppress employee Y. This can be achieved through both machine learning as well as the review of an analyst that is able to obtain additional contextual information.

To illustrate how an analytical tool works, we will provide an example of an actual use case and demonstrate how PRIs would be collected, correlated, and visualized within the advanced analytics tool.

> John Doe is an Senior Manager based in the New York office of a financial services firm, and works on Mergers and Acquisitions with access to highly sensitive and proprietary information. He has been employed with the organization for six years.
>
> John is noticeably unhappy and his performance is declining. He received negative ratings for two consecutive years and is placed on a performance watch list mid-year. Furthermore, he complains to his colleagues about minimal pay increases and becomes visibly disgruntled. John has several outbursts targeted at junior staff on his team, and colleagues have overheard him yelling at staff.
>
> John Doe also becomes non-compliant on expense and independence requirements and is issued a formal reprimanded. He begins to look for new jobs and researches competitors on his firm-issued laptop.
>
> After putting in his two weeks' notice, John starts printing all of his documents related to pricing strategies, including pricing models and non-public M&A data. Since he was unsuccessful in finding a job, he is determined to set up his own boutique financial services firm and decides to leverage this information to get a head start. In total, he exfiltrates over 500 MBs of information, including sensitive firm and client information.

In the example above, there were eight PRIs displayed that covered the virtual, nonvirtual, and contextual PRI categories (as illustrated in Figure 7.3). With an advanced analytics tool, the insider's risk levels would have exceeded the normal threshold when he put in his notice and would have generated an incremental increase in risk for each subsequent event. This allows the organization to proactively make a determination about how to mitigate risk.

Lead generation

Potential risk indicator	PRI category
Senior job level	Contextual
Sensitive market offering	Contextual
Volume of critical/sensitive information accessed	Virtual
Poor performance	Contextual
Time and expense non-compliance	Non-virtual
Upcoming separation	Non-virtual
High volume of documents printed	Virtual
Key words detected in files printed	Contextual

FIGURE 7.3

Use Case Potential Risk Indicators.

Visualization

To further illustrate how an advanced analytics tool would collect and correlate the PRIs, we have included a sample dashboard in Figure 7.4 that is similar to the visualization capabilities we have built for clients in a number of industries. In the example below, an analyst is able to see a central view of the behaviors that have contributed to the increased risk displayed by the insider. The employee in question demonstrates a pattern of behavior that is hypothesized to be associated with theft. The analyst is able to drill down and see each of the contributing factors that drive the risk score. Consequently, the organization can focus its time, energy, and resources on the insider and ignore background noise. The visual below is broken into five sections:

Section 1: Highlights the as-of date and provides the risk levels used on the dashboard
Section 2: Includes a narrative description of the worker, including his location, tenure, and risk score
Section 3: Provides the change in risk score over the past seven months
Section 4: Summary view of the eight PRI categories and which ones contributed to the risk score
Section 5: Details on how each of the eight categories contributed to the risk score

Advantages

The advantages of advanced analytics outlined below highlight feedback from program owners and experience in the course of building insider threat programs in the marketplace.

- **Proactive Threat Mitigation:** Through the correlation of disparate but related events and individual attributes (access levels, user privilege

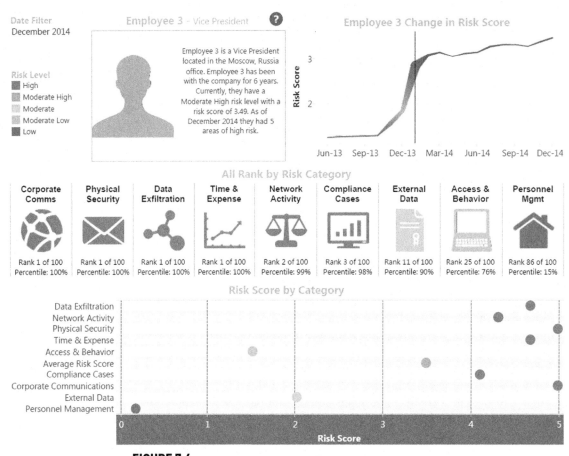

FIGURE 7.4

Correlation of Potential Risk Indicators Visualized in a Dashboard.

rights), an advanced analytics tool provides the ability to "connect the dots" before an event.

- **Tailor Detection Capabilities:** Tailored approach to risk management that is customized to the organization's unique risk tolerance and threat environment.
- **Productivity Enhancer:** Reduce the amount of time needed to collect data and serve as a productivity enhancer; instead of spending 80% of the time trying to get the data and 20% analyzing it, organizations with this capability can spend 80% analyzing it and 20% trying to obtain it.
- **Risk-based Approach:** Target limited investigative resources to focus on areas of elevated risk.

- **Improved Visibility:** Update leadership on areas needing new controls, policy enforcement, or business processes improvement using data-driven analysis.
- **Detect Anomalies:** Improve security and workforce operations through baseline and trend analysis highlighting areas where there may need to be additional policies, controls, or business processes.

SELECTING THE RIGHT TOOL

There are a number of functional requirements that should be considered when evaluating the right advanced analytics tool for your organization. These requirements can be used to evaluate vendor suitability and ensure that the organization selects a tool that aligns to the types of data planned for ingestion (structured vs. unstructured or internal vs. external) and the level of analytical rigor that will be conducted (e.g., peer- and behavior-based anomaly detection through baselines). The requirements outlined below in Table 7.1 include functional requirements for an advanced analytics tool; we have used these common requirements with clients in a variety of industries to hone in on a single tool that fits their respective needs. It should be noted that while these requirements are universal, there will be additions and modifications to this list based on your unique needs. Requirements should be communicated with the ITWG, include input from key stakeholders that will be involved in the prevention, detection, and response to insider threats (e.g., IT and Security) and should be used to evaluate prospective vendors.

Table 7.1 Advanced Analytics Evaluation Criteria

Evaluation Criteria	Definitions
Risk Algorithm	Capable of developing a risk calculation through the use of customized business rules. Generate predefined scoring outcomes based on conditional statements and weighting to emphasize key drivers of risk.
Data Correlation	Perform correlation techniques on a variety of data sources, including contextual data (e.g., security clearance and user access levels) virtual data (e.g., network, security, application, etc.) and nonvirtual data (e.g., people on the HR radar, ethics cases, security incident, etc.).
Automation	Automatic updates to model outputs and visualization based on newly available information (e.g., incoming information about an employee that results in a change in risk level). Provide a level of dynamic adjustments to the model outputs based on newly available information.

(Continued)

Table 7.1 Advanced Analytics Evaluation Criteria (Continued)

Evaluation Criteria	Definitions
Data Repository	Capable of accumulating and analyzing large amounts of incoming and historical data. Provide a repository of employee data that can be analyzed over an extended period of time.
Scalability	Capable of being rolled out on a scale that includes thousands of employees and potentially hundreds of data sources from disparate systems. Able to meet the big data challenges, including data velocity, variety, and volume.
End User Manipulation	Capable of manipulating business rules and risk thresholds by personnel without programming or technical expertise. Allow point and click updates of model drivers (e.g., business rules, weights) and a global user interface for client operability.
Compatibility	Integrates with other tools to address gaps (i.e., data-cleansing solutions or other tangential products such as visualization providers if visualization capability is not satisfactory).
Alerting	Capable of generating risk alerts based on incoming info (e.g., events and descriptors) through automated alerts to stakeholders through e-mail or other workflow processes.
Visualization	Capable of providing a dashboard to display key information including risk levels (e.g., red, yellow, green), recent alerts, and visibility into business rules used to determine risk scores. Drill-down capability should provide clarity into why a certain risk score is generated or a lead is recommended.
Role Based Access	Sensitive data within the tool can be masked to users, user permission levels can be developed and enforced, and logs generated for system activity. Alerts can be generated to authorize certain actions (i.e., manipulating data) to ensure segregation of duties.
Cost Effective	Cost should be analyzed across a variety of tools. The prototype and full-scale rollout should be competitively priced relative to other tool alternatives.
Insider Threat Expertise	Vendor understands the theoretical problems surrounding insider threat and the practical implications involved with developing, deploying, and implementing an analytics tool for an insider threat mitigation program.
Security	Capable of providing key security measures such as data masking, log generation and separation of duties (key procedures in the tool such as unmasking an individual require supervisory approval).

Selection criteria should be created and validated in conjunction with the ITWG and other stakeholders.

BUSINESS RULE APPROACH AND DEVELOPMENT

The advanced analytics tool should be built upon an array of business rules (i.e., conditional if–then statements) that measure a PRI and assign a predetermined risk score. A sample business rule commonly developed to mitigate data theft is as follows: if an individual is separating from the organization and has demonstrated one or more policy violations while with the organization, conduct a scan of network activity and common exfiltration ports (i.e., e-mail and USB). It is recommended that approximately 25–30 business rules be programmed within the tool during the initial pilot phase. Business rules may be expanded as proof of concept is affirmed.

The purpose of using business rules is to define the boundary between acceptable and unacceptable business activity, normal and anomalous behavior, and low versus high risk behavior. The rules engine composed of the if–then statements, weights, and risk score designations provides the rationale behind model outputs. Rules are based on risk mitigation leading practices, regulation, and guidance and are motivated by business and security objectives shaped by members of the ITWG. The cost of rule enforcement is balanced against business risks and against business opportunities that might otherwise be lost. There is one cohesive body of rules, constantly evolving and enforced consistently across relevant areas of business activity. To promote consistency, exceptions to rules are expressed by other rules. The ability to update rules is fundamental to improving the rule engine's adaptability and ability to detect anomalies, identify risk accurately, and drive toward effective insider threat lead generation. Additionally, more discriminating rules may be added, so that over time the system becomes smarter.

The methodology for managing rules is designed to obtain proper validation from personnel within the organization prior to implementing business rules. The methodology spans from discovery to ongoing rule analysis by using an agile and iterative approach. Activities fall into the four steps outlined below:

1. **Business Rule Discovery and Refinement:** Includes designated ITWG members working with system developers to evaluate existing rules and capture suggestions on new rules for consideration. The cross-functional and multidisciplinary ITWG members meet on a recurring basis to examine the business rule engine and modify and adjust the scoring methodology according to the organization's risk threshold, priorities, and the need to manage false positives.
2. **Business Rule Validation:** Designated personnel on the ITWG across legal, ethics, and privacy sign off on new business rules and PRIs. Business rule validation is a recurring agenda item for ITWG discussions and a means to improve the scoring methodology and recalibrate false positives.

3. **Business Rule Design, Authoring, and Deployment:** Includes the programing and development of new rules as well as the modification and existing rules based on direction from the ITWG.
4. **Business Rule Analysis:** Includes reports on false positives and the recalibration of rules to provide manageable and timely outputs of risk levels associated with internal threats. Rule analysis factors in business process changes and operational shifts that may impact the utility of business rules.

When developing business rules, there are three key steps that need to be taken. To begin, an organization needs to work with stakeholders to develop an algorithm framework to include weighting, risk indicators, and risk designations (i.e., what constitutes high, medium, and low risk) based on prioritized threats and critical assets identified in Phase 1. Once the model is firing within the pilot, facilitate conversations to identify adjustments to the algorithm and ensure the necessary stakeholders buy in. This should include individuals from investigations, e-forensics, physical security, and IT. The output of these discussions should be shared with the broader ITWG. In order to stay ahead of the evolving threat landscape, the model should be evaluated on an as-needed basis or, at a minimum, quarterly. This ensures that the correct indicators are evaluated, weights are correct, and risk scores reflect the perceived risk. It also ensures that false positives are managed and that the algorithm is able to continuously improve (i.e., learn from incidents within the organization and externally).

ADVANCED ANALYTICS SECURITY

The advanced analytics tool should include a number of security precautions to protect privacy and prevent sabotage, including masked data, user permission levels, logging and alerting, segregation of duties, and acceptable use agreements.

- **Masked data:** Sensitive data within the tool is masked to insider threat program analysts. Employee names are replaced with a unique identifier to protect the identities of the workforce and maintain objectivity.
- **User permission levels:** User permission levels are developed and enforced to maintain role-based access.
- **Logging and Alerting:** Logs are generated and subject to random and routine review.
- **Segregation of Duties:** Segregation of duties is enforced through the development of an operating manual that requires critical changes to go through an approval process.
- **Acceptable Use Agreements:** Develop acceptable use agreement for personnel with access to the tool and users with privilege rights (system administrators).

SECURITY ANALYTICS AS A BUSINESS ENABLER

In today's highly virtual and interconnected work environment, examples of data breaches and the failures of security programs pervade the news. As a result, many organizations have renewed their focus on security in order to protect critical assets, proprietary information, and client data; to improve security operations; and to avoid the consequences of an insufficient risk mitigation strategy. At the same time, businesses are expected to act faster and do more with fewer resources. Greater focus on security may also be viewed as coming at the expense of investing in operations. Security programs are often seen as having little or no impact on improving business operations.

It is possible, however, for a well-designed security program to complement business operations in addition to protecting an organization's critical assets. There are three significant, cross-functional advantages an organization's security program can offer beyond its traditional scope. This model, based on experience developing over a two dozen security programs in the commercial and Federal sectors, has the potential to improve an organization's bottom line and augment business operations.

As we have established, an effective insider threat detection capability is based on the collection, correlation, and visualization of PRIs displayed by the workforce. These activity-driven events and observable precursors contribute to risk and can be used to proactively identify emerging threats within an organization. In addition to providing clarity on an organization's insider threat risk, PRIs can provide new insights into business operations. Specifically, PRIs have the potential to augment business operations in at least three ways (as illustrated in Figure 7.5): observe trends in workforce behavior and information flow, identify policy gaps, and detect inefficient business processes. In these ways, analyzing PRIs through the lens of business efficiency and effectiveness supports data-driven decision making to improve productivity, business processes, and policy.

Aggregate Data to Enhance Productivity

As security programs move to collect PRI data, many are considering the use of technical systems or advanced analytics capabilities to help centralize at-risk behavior from across an organization. As we have noted, advanced analytical systems serve as mass aggregators of PRIs, affording security programs a single, centralized view and the ability to better detect emerging insider threats. This centralization enables a security program to "connect the dots" before a malicious, complacent, or ignorant insider act takes place. This aggregated security data, however, is also a valuable resource for other constituencies within the organization, such as business operations.

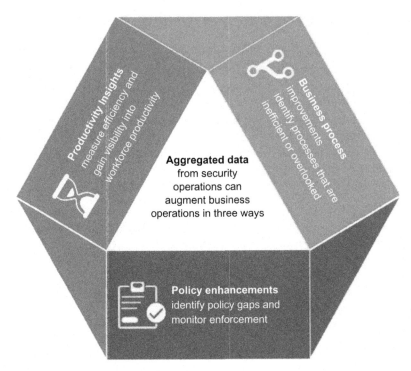

Productivity Insights
measure efficiency and
gain visibility into
workforce productivity

Business process
improvements
identify processes that are
inefficient or overlooked

Aggregated data
from security
operations can
augment business
operations in three ways

Policy enhancements
identify policy gaps and
monitor enforcement

FIGURE 7.5
Analytics Advantages.

Historically, business operations have not analyzed data collected and used primarily for mitigating security threats. However, this data has the potential to reveal valuable information. Tracking time spent on processes that may reveal hidden bottlenecks, measuring policy violations may unearth flaws in communications or a lack of buy-in, and monitoring technology usage may provide detailed information on how time is spent online or on a network. Parsing this data with business operations in mind may reveal opportunities to improve workforce productivity.

Policy Enhancements

Monitoring PRIs as part of a security program can provide new insights on policy adherence, for instance, on compliance with data classification procedures; and the appropriate use of e-mail, social media, and electronic devices. Policy gaps are discovered by comparing policy objectives—the behavioral expectations of the organization—and the actual behavior exhibited by the workforce. "Shortcuts," such as e-mailing sensitive documents to a personal e-mail address, or sending e-mail attachments rather than a secure USB, not only undermine the organization's security but it can reveal opportunities to improve how the organization designs and communicates its behavioral expectations. Prevalent and persistent shortcuts may suggest a lack of policy enforcement, poor awareness, or overly onerous policies that hinder productivity. For example, though the collection of expense-related data and an analysis of substantiated policy violations, organizations have identified policy gaps and areas where additional controls needed to be developed. A proper balance is key: too many policies may impede business, and too few may generate vulnerabilities. Data collected as part of a security program can help to maintain the necessary balance.

Business Processes Enhancements

Centralizing the collection of PRIs into a single repository also enables an organization to identify business processes that are repetitive or lack governance. Identifying these areas of improvements can lead to new opportunities that may otherwise have gone unnoticed. For example, an organization that began collecting PRIs realized that the intake process for creating, substantiating, and closing ethics cases was inconsistent, and that cases were being prematurely opened and closed without adhering to organizational guidelines. This inconsistency impacted overall caseload, and in turn the number of employees thought necessary to manage the intake of ethics cases. The organization renewed and reintroduced its guidelines to address the process gap and to ensure proper oversight. This procedural and governance gap would have otherwise gone undetected, had the organization's ethics component not provided data to its security function.

At a time when accountability is a primary leadership responsibility, a strong security program not only provides leaders with a mechanism for early detection, prevention, and response but also an opportunity to improve workforce productivity, policy, and business processes. As the workplace becomes more complex, and security threats more difficult to uncover, detection tools and techniques will adapt to keep pace with evolving threats. As technology advances, the types of data utilized will also advance, positioning security programs as a growing contributor to organizational objectives that extends beyond the security realm. This evolution toward the collection of new types of data will yield new sources of information with the potential to provide targeted, data-driven improvements throughout an organization.

KEY TAKEAWAYS

- A technical solution is only one portion of the insider threat solution. Organizations should complement an analytical capability with the proper business processes, governance structure, policies, and training.

- Although detection is needed as part of a robust insider threat program, focus should be placed on preventing insider acts.
- When selecting an advanced analytics capability, the organization should evaluate tools based on their ability to collect, correlate, and visualize potential risk indicators.
- When deploying an analytics capability, the organization should ingest a wide variety of indicators capturing behavior on the network, off the network, and contextual descriptors such as access and clearance levels.
- A phased and piloted approach to tool deployment is recommended. This allows the organization to proof the concept before broader expansion.
- As the perceived risk of an insider increases, as a result of detection of behavioral or technical precursors, the amount of technical and behavioral monitoring should also increase.
- Technology and workplace practices will continue to evolve, bringing with them new threats. The analytical program should be part of a routine, semi-annual evaluation to ensure risk is being properly identified and escalated.
- Emerging threats identified through the analytics capability are not absolute, should be corroborated through multiple channels and feed into the organization's existing escalation and triage process.
- Insider threat programs can have a wide range of advantages that extend beyond security, including the improvement of organizational efficiency and effectiveness.

CHAPTER 8

Information Security and Technology Integration

INTRODUCTION

As discussed in previous chapters, insider threat is not just an information technology (IT) issue. At its heart, insider threat is a people-centric challenge. There are psychological and behavioral elements that must be incorporated in order to achieve a truly holistic and effective insider threat mitigation capability. Despite this, with today's IT systems, insider threat mitigation is often regarded as residing in the purview of an organization's IT and information security professionals. Why is this perspective so pervasive and what does it mean for building an insider threat program?

An organization's technical environment, to include computers, software, networks, and associated policies and process, is central to both facilitating and mitigating harmful insider activity. What distinguishes an outsider from an insider is a combination of knowledge and access. Because IT is the primary means by which individuals gain and exchange knowledge and are provisioned access, it is increasingly important for organizations to conduct comprehensive assessments of their IT programs and assets. As part of the assessment process, organizations should identify potential insider threat vulnerabilities as well as opportunities to leverage existing systems and processes to prevent, detect, and mitigate insider threat. Very few organizations incorporate insider threat into their enterprise risk mitigation strategies.

In today's world of increasing external threats to an organization's information systems, and countless dollars budgeted toward cyber security and the resilience of an organization's virtual assets, the complacent insider requires an equal share of attention. The tie between insider threat mitigation and strong information security practices is evident. To mitigate harmful insider acts, an organization must leverage appropriate existing controls to maintain the confidentiality, integrity, and availability of its data in accordance with its external risk assessments.[1] Capitalizing on existing capabilities to integrate the

---

[1] Definitions of confidentiality, availability, and integrity available at 44 U.S. Sec. 3542 (2011) Print.

Insider Threat. DOI: http://dx.doi.org/10.1016/B978-0-12-802410-2.00008-3

processes and technologies that support information security with an insider threat mitigation program is a key opportunity.

Security controls, and their associated technical solutions, should be selected and employed with the goal of supporting the insider threat program's essential capabilities. Stakeholders that understand the organization's risk tolerance should be engaged in the review of any documentation for systems and networks to determine when to leverage existing controls and when to institute new ones. Notably, all insider threat programs should uphold the main tenets of insider threat mitigation—namely, least privilege and segregation of duties. The rule of least privilege calls for individuals to only have access to those resources needed to fulfill his or her organizational duties. Segregation of duties prevents a single point of failure by establishing controls to support dual-approval and a division of responsibilities or entitlements to prevent individuals from being able to inflict harm on an organization by themselves. For example, systems administrators are subject to a two-person rule when making changes to a system, or are required to have two accounts, one for general business and the other for work specifically involving information systems.[2]

The integration of information security as a key pillar of an insider threat program is natural and intuitive. Although information security and insider threat programs in some instances exist independently within an organization, the connection is critical: both programs are designed to protect the organization's assets, one external the other internal. Furthermore, information security practices include the creation and management of the most real-time information an organization has regarding the actions of its employees. Despite this association, one program should not subsume the other, as information security is not the absolute answer to the insider threat problem, nor is information security the only component of an insider threat program. Virtual behavior is, after all, only part of insider threat detection and, thus, only one part of the equation for a holistic insider threat program.

Leveraging the traditional domains of information security—administrative, technical, and physical controls—can help an organization build powerful processes, tools, and insight to help mitigate insider threats (Figure 8.1).[3] This chapter expounds details and considerations for implementing a suite of reinforcing controls. Together, these controls constitute essential components

---

[2] Greenberg, Andy. "NSA Implementing 'Two-Person' Rule to Stop the Next Edward Snowden," *Forbes*, 06/18/2013. Online. http://www.forbes.com/sites/andygreenberg/2013/06/18/nsa-director-says-agency-implementing-two-person-rule-to-stop-the-next-edward-snowden/.

[3] National Institute for Standards and Technology (NIST), Special Publication 800-53 Revision 4, 2013.

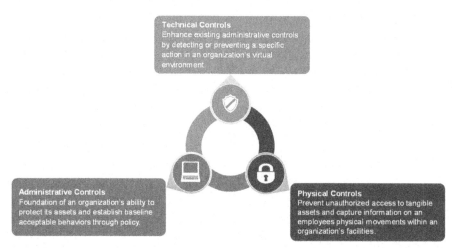

Technical Controls
Enhance existing administrative controls by detecting or preventing a specific action in an organization's virtual environment.

Administrative Controls
Foundation of an organization's ability to protect its assets and establish baseline acceptable behaviors through policy.

Physical Controls
Prevent unauthorized access to tangible assets and capture information on an employees physical movements within an organization's facilities.

FIGURE 8.1

A Holistic Approach to Insider Threat Mitigation Consisting of Complementing Administrative, Physical, and Technical Controls.

of an organization's insider threat mitigation capability and serve as a complement to the aggregation, correlation, and visualization of data elements through advanced analytics, as discussed in previous chapters.

ADMINISTRATIVE AND PROCEDURAL CONTROLS

Strong administrative controls are the foundation of implementing a technology-enabled insider threat program. Administrative controls are most often internal policies, which come in many forms. They can range from change-control processes for an organization's information systems, to defining a recertification process and period for user privileges, to acceptable use of personal devices on an organization's network. In total, these administrative controls establish the organization's baseline for acceptable virtual behavior. When integrated with technical and physical controls, this baseline allows the organization's insider threat program to more easily detect anomalous user behavior, a potential indicator of insider threat. In setting up strong administrative controls, the organization establishes a benchmark from which it can measure possible insider threat activity. For example, an individual circumventing an established administrative control that requires certain files to be encrypted before transmission signals a possible insider threat—the individual has violated the organization's information security expectations. Administrative controls, such as the example above, are upheld in practice by technical and physical controls.

Although not officially designed for the detection and mitigation of insider threats, administrative controls can be tailored for that purpose. In doing so, an organization faces three main challenges: (1) effectively shifting the organization's culture to align to new administrative controls, (2) identifying not only the controls that support the insider threat mission but also the ones that may subvert it, and (3) communicating clear expectations to employees at all levels of the organization on a regular and routine basis. Each of these challenges must be appropriately addressed for organizations to develop effective and efficient insider threat programs.

Improving the IT Culture Through Administrative Controls

Most organizations have a multitude of established internal policies that govern everything from documenting employee time and expense to the acceptable use of social media in the work place. During the transition from the world of bricks and mortar to the world of bits and bytes in the late 1990s and early 2000s, there was a surge in organizational interest in information security. In response to the shift to a virtual and global business environment, organizations started employing large enterprise networks that, in many cases, had poor accompanying documentation and were susceptible to the most basic forms of IT exploitation and attack.

As a result, a wide range of internal policies and administrative controls were developed to help prevent outside attackers, or "hackers," from compromising valuable assets. A "new normal" was developed across the IT domain. The rise of anonymous hackers around the globe led organizations to build virtual walls around their systems and information consisting of administrative policies to limit employee privileges and access, and standards for appropriate behavior when interacting with the external, virtual world. Access and activity within an organization by trusted employees, however, was rarely regulated.

The emphasis on insider threat in recent years has shifted the paradigm of thinking within the IT community. Norms of previous decades, such as "keep everyone else out and everything is fine," are proving false and costly. Trusted employees are increasingly causing significant damage to their organizations, both maliciously and through complacency and negligence born of an inclusive culture of sharing and unfettered access to information.

Much like before, a cultural shift among IT users and professionals is required to counter the insider threat. This change must be driven by new and revised internal policies and communications that establish limits on individuals' behavior within the IT environment and by continuous monitoring to mitigate risk. New concepts, like limiting social media use in the workplace and restricting access to certain information or systems, may be met with resistance, but are critical to an effective insider threat program. To be successful, these changes should be rooted in executive-level guidance that clearly articulates new expectations for the organization's employees. Organizations must also develop more robust communication strategies for IT security, controls, and policy and incorporate this critical messaging into role-specific training for personnel.

Building-In Versus Bolting-On

During the nascence of information security, the need for expedient solutions often resulted in various IT disciplines—infrastructure, networking, software development, and security—to operate independently of each other. Software developers would design a release then pass it off to the infrastructure team for implementation. Typically, IT security professionals designed a range of controls after the design and implementation phases that attempted to balance the need for access and functionality with the need to secure the organization's assets from outside attack. This fractionalized development led to what has been termed "bolted-on" security controls, meaning that each new piece of software or hardware to the IT enterprise received its own set of security controls with limited consideration for how it affected the enterprise.[4]

Although this ad hoc approach to security addressed the immediate problem of securing the organization's information through rapidly implemented technical controls, like firewall exemptions and password protection, it made it nearly impossible to develop effective administrative controls and issue governing policies. The retroactive establishment of controls and security measures often contradicted established policies—the need to "get it done" overrode the need to follow protocol. These problems were compounded by the IT landscape, which evolves rapidly in comparison to the methodical and relatively slow process of developing and publishing new policies and executive guidance.

To alleviate this, the IT community adopted deliberate, coordinated change management procedures. With proper change management, IT disciplines worked together to design a holistic solution that addressed security from inception. This enabled executive management to participate in the effort, to simultaneously develop or adjust internal policies, and to implement administrative controls. The end result was a more effective, efficient, and secure IT enterprise.

As an insider threat program matures, organizations must eliminate conflicting guidance and leverage existing administrative controls by integrating the insider threat program into existing information security processes. To accomplish this, an organization must conduct a top–down review of its established

---

[4] Jacobson, Doug; Rursch, Julie. "The Bolt-On Information Security Trend Needs to End," *Information Security*, October 2012.

administrative controls and associated policies regarding employees' virtual actions. Controls and policies should be evaluated to determine a baseline for expected behavior and how compliance with that baseline can be measured. Throughout this review, it is important to identify gaps in administrative controls that may undermine efforts to mitigate insider threat. For instance, a company may have an existing policy allowing telework with the established administrative control that it must be carried out on a company-provided computer. To better support the insider threat program, however, additional controls, like requiring the use of a virtual private network (VPN), should be layered on top of this policy to limit the information that may be accessed remotely.

Through collaboration with information security professionals to adapt and improve established administrative controls, insider threat program stakeholders can leverage the existing information security program. It must be emphasized, however, that IT or information security are not the absolute solution for an insider threat problem. Virtual behavior is only one aspect of a holistic insider threat program, but it provides a key source of information and layer of protection.

Training

IT training is an area of administrative controls that is particularly well-suited for integration into the broader insider threat program. Prior to granting access to IT assets, many organizations require training to promote employee awareness of information security issues and the acceptable use of the organization's IT systems. In the past, this training, if it existed at all, has been very generic, with the same message delivered across the entire workforce. As business has evolved into a more complex technology-driven environment, organizations have recognized that different roles have different risks and vulnerabilities associated with them, and thus training should be tailored to those specific roles.

Employee training, either virtual or in-person, presents a significant opportunity for insider threat program stakeholders to integrate insider threat themes into required IT trainings. Information security training should include mainstays like warnings against password sharing, external file sharing, and whitelisting/blacklisting software and devices. The organization can also use employee training to establish a foundation for monitoring virtual behavior. Because IT training typically outlines acceptable and unacceptable use of IT assets, organizations can leverage this type of training to convey the baseline for what types of activity will be monitored by the insider threat program.[5]

---

[5] Silowash, George, et al. "Common Sense Guide to Mitigating Insider Threats, 4th Edition," Software Engineering Institute, 2012.

Administrative controls are a valuable way to integrate an organization's IT and information security practices with the insider threat program. By integrating with existing administrative controls, the insider threat program aligns itself with an established process that limits employee behavior and communicates those limits to employees.

TECHNICAL CONTROLS

Technical controls are the tactical application of administrative controls. Constituting a variety of technologies and implementations, they share the specific goal of detecting or preventing a specific action in an organization's virtual environment. In the information security landscape, technical controls are designed either to prevent access to an organization's IT assets from outside its network, like with a firewall, or to detect unauthorized insiders attempting to enter a company's IT systems, like with a network intrusion detection (NID) tool.

Although it is difficult to catalog all of an organization's technical controls, the tools that are most useful to the insider threat program should be identified first. These existing controls typically have the capacity to identify individuals within the system and track their actions, which fall within one of two categories: identity and access management (IAM) and user activity monitoring (UAM). No single tool, piece of software, or hardware will effectively detect all behaviors that are indicative of an insider threat. Rather, a suite of tools must be deployed for effective detection and mitigation.

Once existing relevant controls have been cataloged, the insider threat program and the information security group should work together to evaluate the controls in order to determine how each can be used for the purpose of identifying and mitigating potential insider threats. If necessary, controls may need to be adapted in one of two ways: (1) externally facing controls will be reoriented to collect internal user information or (2) internally facing controls will be optimized to meet the insider threat needs of the organization. The effective collaboration between insider threat program stakeholders and the information security group is the key to successfully integrating existing technical controls into an insider threat program. We have included a series of common controls used by insider threat programs. In addition to implementing these controls, organizations should capture how data is logged, what alerts are generated and if personnel are routinely reviewing anomalies.

- Mine on key words through e-discovery (e-mail, IM)
- Identify excessively large downloads (e.g., e-rooms)
- Generate flags for suspicious e-mails with attachments
- Monitor data exfiltration via removable media

- Monitor data exfiltration via printers/scanners/copiers/fax machines
- Establish baseline network behavior in order to detect anomalies
- Restrict access to prohibited websites
- Document failed access attempts beyond user access levels
- Prohibit file transfers to file sharing websites
- Conduct outlier analysis (e.g., bandwidth consumed)
- Run hard drive scans

Identity and Access Management

An IAM capability is fundamental to any data protection program. At its core, IAM creates an identity link between the employee at the keyboard and his or her actions in the virtual environment through a suite of technical controls and associated implementation structure. This virtual identity is composed of a set of assigned attributes, such as, an individual's name, department, and access rights that ensure that users only have the access needed to fulfill their job functions (e.g., least privilege). For example, a financial clerk in the billing department would be denied access to research and development schematics in the engineering department. By managing the financial clerk's digital identity, an IAM system can determine that access to the R&D schematics is incongruous with the employee's work needs.

The goal of an IAM system is nonrepudiation: an insider threat program analyst should be able to look at a particular virtual event and determine with certainty which employees are responsible for specific actions.[6] An organization should leverage the existing technical controls that comprise an IAM solution to prevent, detect, and respond to behaviors associated with potential insider threats. An IAM solution can be used to enforce administrative controls that are designed to prevent insiders from accidentally or maliciously accessing and damaging IT systems. For example, an IAM system uses multi-factor authentication to increase the assurance of the user's identity, in support of the administrative controls that constitute the foundation of an organization's access regime. IAM is critical to upholding segregation of duties; for example, when some sensitive actions require administrative divisions, such as dual approval, to prevent employees from amassing too many privileges.

By integrating information provided through IAM technical controls with the insider threat mitigation capability, possible attacks can be prevented. Thus, detecting violations of an organization's access regime can aid in identifying a possible insider threat. Furthermore, this integration can capture PRIs to assist in analyzing an insider's behavioral pattern. IAM is a powerful

---

[6] Deloitte LLP. "A Perfect Storm: How High-Profile Data Breaches Expose Critical Flaws in the Way We Manage Sensitive Data," March 2011. Online.

capability that enables technical controls for both the information security and insider threat programs. It can be difficult, if not impossible, to identify and resolve virtual risk indicators without a robust IAM capability.

User Activity Monitoring (UAM)

UAM is developing into an important capability within both information security and insider threat mitigation disciplines. At its core, UAM involves fusing information collected from across an organization's deployed technical controls in an effort to provide a holistic view of an employee's virtual behavior.[7] UAM combines alert information collected from multiple technical controls, like an enterprise content filter or data loss prevention (DLP) tool, with identity information from the organization's IAM controls. By doing so, UAM establishes a pattern for each employee or subsection of the employee population. An insider threat program can leverage this capability as a source of data to input into the advanced analytics tool.

PHYSICAL CONTROLS

A comprehensive, holistic approach to information security utilizes physical controls in conjunction with administrative and technical controls. Physical controls are used to prevent or detect unauthorized access to assets within an organization's facilities. For instance, if an individual gains unwarranted access to a protected physical space, he or she can potentially inflict considerable damage on critical IT assets, such as servers, mainframes, and workstations. Regardless of an employee's intent, the integration of appropriate physical controls can be used to both detect and deter incidents that can have profound effects on both information security and critical business operations. By integrating the physical controls deployed for information security with an organization's larger insider threat mitigation capability, stakeholders are better equipped to prevent insider threats by detecting behavior indicative of an individual moving on the ideation-to-action continuum in the physical realm.

Preventive Physical Controls

Traditional physical controls, like door locks and chain-link fencing, are not intuitive parts of an organization's information security program because they are not always enabled by technology. A poll of organizations' IT departments, however, would likely reveal that very few, if any, leave doors to AV closets or server rooms unsecured. Physical controls that limit access to sensitive areas

---

[7] Narcisi, Gina. "User Activity Monitoring Is Just as Critical as Asset Monitoring." *TechTarget*, November 2014. Online.

or information support an organization's insider threat program. IT-enabled physical access control system (PACS) are becoming the industry standard, and are standard for the Federal Government. By limiting a trusted employee's physical access to sensitive resources, the same physical controls prevent an insider's ability to carry out malicious or negligent activities.

Integrating existing physical controls into the organization's insider threat program introduces an extra level of complexity to the program. Because insiders require some authorized access to sensitive areas and information to perform their jobs, stakeholders must evaluate the effectiveness of the physical controls restricting them. Basic measures like locking a door or requiring a passcode to enter an area are fundamental controls for preventing insider threat actions, but they become ineffective if every insider in the organization has a key, or the passcode is common knowledge.

Detective Physical Controls

Video surveillance, guard force, notification systems, physical access control system (PACS), fire alarms, bollards, locks, and other physical security measures not only protect against external threats but also serve as strong, often visible, deterrents to complacent and malicious insiders. Many physical security measures, however, act as little more than deterrents if they are not supported by proper monitoring practices. User monitoring should be expanded to the physical space to prevent, detect, and mitigate the insider threat. Physical controls capable of capturing information and building a picture of an employee's behavior over time are important to a robust insider threat mitigation capability. An organization should leverage its physical monitoring capabilities to enforce access rules and detect possible violations or suspicious behavior in real time.

By integrating technology-enabled physical controls, such as locks operated by proximity cards, an organization gains the ability not only to prevent insider threat actions but to collect point-in-time information about a potential insider threat actor's behavior, such as what time period was a user in a facility? The key to integrating physical controls capable of informing a holistic view of individual insiders is to review existing physical controls and utilize those capable of providing useful information, for example, building entry timestamps. When used in this manner, physical controls serve as a powerful tool capable of virtualizing employees' physical behavior.

FUTURE OF SECURITY CONTROLS

The nature of logical and physical controls is transforming. Industry is developing identity authentication solutions that leverage biometrics (e.g., retinal scan, fingerprints) to achieve the highest assurance of an individual's identity for access purposes. In a few years' time, this could be industry standard, rendering usernames, passwords, and basic proximity cards obsolete. Forward-leaning organizations should consult in-house counsel regarding legal implications of leveraging personal identifiable information (PII) for access control systems. The advent of biometrics presents an extraordinary opportunity for an organization to enhance its ability to proactively mitigate the insider threat by improving the connection between digital identities and access to both virtual and tangible resources.[8]

CONCLUSION

With the recent increase in attention paid to information security, many private and public sector organizations possess advanced capabilities for protecting their technical environments from outside intruders like hackers and intellectual property thieves. These organizations are developing and implementing progressive administrative, technical, and physical controls to enhance security in the face of external threats. Simultaneously, the need for organizations to protect assets from insiders is crystalizing. Organizations should capitalize on existing information security capabilities and integrate administrative, technical, and physical controls into insider threat mitigation programs. Technology is a key enabler to a robust insider threat program, and an organization's information security stakeholders should be considered key partners.

KEY TAKEAWAYS

- Administrative IT and information security controls are the foundation of an organization's ability to protect its resources.
- Identity and access management as well as user activity monitoring are important sets of technical controls for effective and holistic insider threat mitigation.
- Technical controls are designed either to prevent access to an organization's IT assets from outside its network, or to detect unauthorized users attempting to enter a company's IT systems. The key to integrating existing technical controls into an insider threat program is to identify and leverage both externally and internally facing controls for insider threat mitigation purposes.
- Existing physical controls, prevention controls, and detection controls should be leveraged to complement and inform an organization's insider threat program.

---

[8] "Sandia Exploring Ephemeral Biometrics for Insider Threat Monitoring." https://gcn.com/blogs/pulse/2014/06/ephemeral-biometrics.aspx. GCN, 5 June 2014. Web. <http://gcn.com/blogs/pulse/2014/06/ephemeral-biometrics.aspx.>.

CHAPTER 9

Robust Cyber Risk Management

CYBER RISK MANAGEMENT AND BUSINESS PERFORMANCE

The cyber-related aspects of insider threats and their connections to broader business risk are driving managers' demands for more robust cyber risk management and risk-informed decision making. Cyber risk incidents typically involve system outages, lost intellectual property, and damaged corporate reputation. Many times, such incidents are caused by highly targeted attacks conducted by intelligent adversaries who seek to achieve malicious goals; in some instances, those attacks can be facilitated by witting or malicious insiders and unwitting or complacent insiders as referred to in in previous chapters. Therefore, a necessary business assumption dictates that cyber-attacks driven by malicious intent will occur, including attacks initiated or enabled by organization insiders as well as attacks unwittingly facilitated by employees who either are lax or ignorant of policies and security practices. Although traditional security controls, preventive measures, and compliance initiatives continue to consume a large percentage of organizations' investment in cyber risk management, investment levels are likely to continue or increase, given that malicious actors, especially those motivated by financial gain, tend to operate on a cost/reward basis. Investment in cyber defenses ought to be at a high enough level to raise an adversary's perceptions of risk and level of effort relative to the value of what they perceive as a gain.

Thus, managing cyber risk should no longer be viewed as a necessary evil but an essential aspect of not only enabling, but optimizing business performance. An organization's mission and business growth strategies largely determine the types of cyber risks an organization faces. When the inherent links between business performance, innovation, and cyber risk are considered, it becomes clear that protecting everything, while perhaps not impossible, is economically impractical and will likely impede important strategic initiatives. In the pace of today's climate, organizations cannot afford to slow innovation simply because organizations cannot be perfectly secured. But neither can they innovate without appropriate regard for the inherent risks

125

Insider Threat. DOI: http://dx.doi.org/10.1016/B978-0-12-802410-2.00009-5

that they generate. Given this state of affairs, how should organizations reverse the growing gap between cyber risk investments and risk management effectiveness?

ROBUST MINDSETS: SECURE, VIGILANT, RESILIENT

Given that organizations cannot prevent all cyber incidents, the traditional discipline of security, isolated from a more comprehensive risk-based approach, is not enough to protect against cyber-threats. Moreover, improving cyber risk management is not always about spending more money, and it is also not just about buying the latest risk management technologies and tools. To be effective, robust cyber risk management programs require effective managerial cognition, judgment, and decision making, each of which are key drivers of successful risk management system dynamics. Systemic factors such as management's perceived risk, desired levels of risk management investment, risk detection capabilities, and trust of personnel dynamically interact and can create feedback loops that either reinforce risk mitigation capabilities, or produce and expose organizations to insider threat vulnerabilities. Reducing such vulnerabilities to the emergence of insider threats involves improving risk information acquisition, risk information management, and targeted training of personnel in judgment and decision making.[1]

As business models and ecosystems become more complex and interdependent, managers tasked with mitigating cyber risk will be measured not only by how much uncertainty they can eliminate but also by how much uncertainty they can tolerate and still advise on business direction. The emerging challenge is to assemble what is now known about management mindsets[2] and operationalize such concepts in ways that foster the development and execution of effective cyber risk management strategies and policies.

When crafting robust risk assessment and management strategies, collecting, analyzing, and understanding risk data is not enough. Robust cyber risk assessment and management is a way of conducting business: it comes from being acutely aware of what is happening, and requires an understanding of the perceptions and beliefs of involved stakeholders and how these beliefs drive actions that influence risk management decisions. Managers tend to value insights into real-life risks which, by nature, are systemic and dynamic.

---

[1] Martinez-Moyano, I.J. et al. Modeling the Emergence of Insider Threat Vulnerabilities. *Proceedings of the 2006 Winter Simulation Conference*. 2006.

[2] In decision theory and general systems theory, a mindset is a set of assumptions, methods, or notations held by one or more people or groups of people. This set can be so established that it creates incentives within individuals and groups to continue current behaviors, choices, or tools.

Managers also choose between risk policies, not risk events or consequences. Robust risk analysis and thinking focuses on improving these choices, and recognizes that efforts to measure and determine event and consequence probabilities may be too uncertain to quantify.[3] So, rather than try to assess risks based on probability judgments about what damage insiders may inflict (e.g., through expert judgments of threat, vulnerability, and consequence scores), it may be more practical and fruitful to focus on risk investments that effectively manage/target defenses. This approach starts with informing and adapting management's various mindsets toward a more systemic and inter-dependent view of cyber risk and business performance.

One robust cyber risk management mindset now emerging can be character-ized by the following three quality attributes: secure, vigilant, and resilient. *Secure* means to invest in cost-justified security controls to protect an organi-zation's most important assets. Secure aligns closely with the concept of pre-vent specific to insider threats. *Vigilant* means to put forth greater effort on gaining more insight into threats. This would be consistent to how we have defined detect in previous chapters. Specifically, the detection of anoma-lous behavior of a potential insider, whether that insider is malicious, com-placent, or ignorant. *Resilient* means to seek to respond more effectively to reduce potential threat impacts. This aligns to the response phase in the insider threat framework we have described earlier in this book. Robust cyber risk programs and management mindsets are characterized not only by these three attributes individually but also by how they are structured to inter-act collectively and align with the insider threat program. Each attribute is described in more detail below.

Secure

Robust cyber risk management programs ensure that business processes oper-ate and perform in a secure manner. Secure organizations seek to establish risk-prioritized controls to protect against known and emerging threats, and to comply with standards and regulations. Secure business performance means balancing the costs, convenience, business needs, and risk tolerance levels to allow an organization to protect its valuable resources from internal and external threats, and to allow it to take advantage of the dynamic busi-ness and technology opportunities in the market.

Being secure means focusing protection around the risk-sensitive assets at the heart of an organization's mission, that both the organization and adversar-ies are likely to agree are most valuable. Among the most important elements are critical infrastructure, applications, data, and specialized control systems.

---

[3] Cox, L.A. "Confronting Deep Uncertainties in Risk Analysis." *Risk Analysis* 32.10 (2012): 1607–1629. Web.

These are not isolated components. They are a part of larger services and transaction chains, so it is essential to address weak points along the end-to-end business process, with the awareness that insiders, vendors, and trusted partners at any point can be the source of errors or intentional actions that lead to incidents.

Many organizations can do significantly better by instilling better discipline in some basic areas. One is data tracking and classification. Many organizations don't know where their sensitive data actually resides, either internal or external to the organization. Efforts should also be taken to streamline and control access wherever possible. Another common and closely related area of weakness is asset management. Large organizations generate enormous change on a daily basis: new users, new devices, new applications, and supporting changes to the underlying infrastructure. If security controls are not adjusted to keep pace, technology and process gaps can emerge and leave organizations exposed for days, months, or even years.

Vigilant

Robust cyber risk management programs working to be vigilant seek to establish situational risk and threat awareness and understanding across their environments by building capabilities that work to detect violations and anomalies. In an era of ever-changing threats and consumerization of IT, being vigilant means proactively protecting intellectual property, managing brand risk, and enhancing trust with key partners and stakeholders.

Vigilance begins with establishing a solid picture of what organizations need to defend against. There are discernable threat trends across entire industry sectors. Knowing the landscape within an organization's industry is an important starting point that needs to be supplemented with an understanding of an organization's specific business risks. This set of activities is a broad exercise to examine who seeks to harm an organization, what motivates them, and how they're likely to operate. By carefully plotting the motives and profiles of adversaries, and considering the potential for accidental damage by well-intentioned customers, partners, or employees, cyber risk strategists can begin to anticipate what might occur and, accordingly, inform the design of detection systems.

Resilient

Robust cyber risk management programs working to be resilient establish the ability to handle critical incidents, quickly return to normal operations, and repair damage to the organization. Being resilient allows an organization's operations to rapidly adapt and respond to internal or external dynamic changes—opportunities, demands, disruptions, or threats—and continue operations with limited impact to the business.

Technical teams typically handle many day-to-day, fairly routine security events. Some incidents, however, may become serious business crises and can affect an organization's broader mission. Being resilient means having the capacity to rapidly contain the damage and mobilize the diverse resources needed to limit impact, for example, to direct costs, business disruption, reputation, and brand damage.

Decisive action becomes difficult if response to cyber incidents is viewed primarily as a technical function. Decisive action includes, for example, determining if components of operations should be taken off line, what to report to authorities, and how to collaborate with law enforcement. By exclusively adhering to a technical view, organizations also run the risk of being less nimble in resuming normal operations and less able to manage the perceptions of the public and other stakeholders, such as customers, investors, and regulators.

Although resilience requires investment in traditional technology-based redundancy and disaster recovery capabilities, the bigger resilience picture includes a complete set of crisis management capabilities. Beyond IT, resilience should involve various business and department leaders, and decision makers from legal, risk, human relations, and communications functions. It requires a playbook that addresses all of these entities, designed in advance by considering how threat scenarios that impact critical assets and processes could play out. Playbooks and policies must be written, but it is equally important to rehearse them through cyber war-gaming and simulations that bring together business and technology teams. Staging simulations creates better organizational awareness and understanding of threats, improves cyber judgment, and plants the seeds of "muscle memory" that help teams respond flexibly and instinctively to envisioned scenarios and to unforeseen situations. Finally, incident response and crisis management must feed continuous improvement processes. Resilient organizations take the time to absorb important lessons and to modify the secure and vigilant aspects of the program to emerge stronger than before.

Embedded in the secure, vigilant, resilient mindset framework is a simple heuristic containing three components that represent for managers a subsystem for thinking about risk (see Figure 9.1). These three interacting components form a cognitive architecture: *learning* represents an organization's ability to proactively create, update, and fuse information learned from key risk indicators; *reasoning* represents an organization's ability to apply updated risk knowledge in a manner based on sound evidence and reasoning principles; *decision making* represents an organization's ability to evaluate decisions and execute on decision options that integrate cyber risk and business performance concerns.

FIGURE 9.1
Robust Mindset: Secure, Vigilant, Resilient, and Cognitive Architecture.

Stakeholders do not choose between "risks"; rather, they seek to weigh the trade-offs between the costs, benefits, and risks associated with multiple decision options. Overall, the robust cyber risk management mindset and program quality attributes of secure, vigilant, and resilient offer managers a baseline framework for systemically and dynamically thinking and reasoning about how to manage an organization's cyber risks. This approach views cyber risk management holistically as an overall system, rather than as specific parts, outcomes, or events. Adopting a robust cyber risk mindset allows management to better understand, judge, and decide the various dimensions of cyber risk problems such as malicious and complacent insiders.

INSIDER THREAT: A DYNAMIC, MULTILEVEL PROBLEM

The insider threat problem presents different challenges to organizations attempting to go beyond traditional IT risk management and establish a robust cyber risk management program. Programs will encounter difficulties if they do not account for the individual and group dynamics associated with targeted threats that are characterized by planning, learning, and adaptive replanning by intelligent adversaries. When considering the cyber and business risk problem of insider threat, a robust secure, vigilant, resilient mindset can help managers adopt a systemic point of view and, as a result, work to logically generate, consider, and exercise risk mitigation options.

Cyber risk managers should move beyond representing attacker actions as random events. By their nature, malicious actors' actions represent intelligent,

Table 9.1 Robust Cyber Risk View of Insider Threat

Robust Cyber Risk Program Attributes: Secure, Vigilant, Resilient			
Insider Threat System Levels	Simple Cognitive Architecture		
	Learn	Reason	Decide
Individual **Group** **Organization**	Support multi-level system monitoring (technology and management controls).	Formulate decision options and judgement logic and rationale.	Balance costs, benefits, and risks. Choose best decision option.

goal-directed choices that are responsive to information about defenses and the likelihood of the success or failure of attempted actions. As mentioned previously, insider activity moves along a continuum from idea to action and therefore subject to detection. This dynamic adversary/defender problem is also characterized by high levels of uncertainty, incomplete and imperfect information, incomplete and delayed feedback, a low base rate of events, and the balancing of an organization's need to trust but verify insider actions. This latter attribute relates to managers' risk appetites and tolerances. Decisions about appropriate risk tolerance levels are based on human judgments and perceptions about four possible outcomes: a *true positive*, the risk is detected; a *true negative*, a normal transaction is observed; a *false positive*, a false alarm is raised; and a *false negative*, an unobserved risk is neglected.

In general, insider threats arise from dynamic processes and are best combated by managers who craft and enact policies that recognize system level dynamics. By applying a robust cyber risk management approach and simple cognitive architecture, managers' decisions regarding cyber risk tolerance and the problem of insider threat can be structured and analyzed according to three dynamic system levels: *individual, group,* and *organization* (see Table 9.1).

BUILDING ROBUST MENTAL MODELS AND COLLECTIVE MINDSETS

A key foundation of robust cyber risk programs is risk operations. Frontline workers involved in risk operations routinely make judgments about what events may be both insider and outsider threats to an organization. Managers and executives can use the secure, vigilant, resilient mindset to foster a risk-aware culture by working to influence the risk beliefs, values, behaviors, and decision outcomes of individuals and groups throughout their organizations. Beyond managers and executives, other risk stakeholders—through their interactions at multiple levels of an organization—contribute to the creation of either a risk-aware or risk-vulnerable culture. Each individual responsible for risk management activities forms a *mental model*[4] of various risk situations. So how does understanding people's mental models, and the collective mindset of groups, influence risk decisions and outcomes?

In general, research in social psychology suggests that people's *subjective beliefs* are derived from how they judge the likelihood of events, and that people judge event likelihood chiefly through emotions. For example, a risk manager of third party vendors may strongly believe that a majority of vendors' security levels are not optimized and are putting the organization at risk. Such beliefs help to form this risk analyst's mental model, which is established during his/her tenure as a security analyst at a vendor. *Value systems*, in turn, are derived from beliefs. This risk manager's beliefs can be classified as a part of a particular value system or principle-based policy (i.e., *verify, then trust*). Value systems structure and unify groups and, as a result, shape *group norms and behaviors*. Thus, a network operations team, which strongly values network system performance, may value system access standards to a lesser degree than an IT risk compliance team. Negotiating acceptable risk decision options involves the sharing of power and building of trust among groups, because decision problems are perceived differently within and between groups. Ultimately, most *decisions* are the product of the groups that produce them (see Figure 9.2).

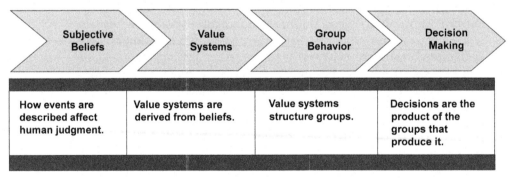

Subjective Beliefs	Value Systems	Group Behavior	Decision Making
How events are described affect human judgment.	Value systems are derived from beliefs.	Value systems structure groups.	Decisions are the product of the groups that produce it.

FIGURE 9.2

From Individual Beliefs to Collective Decision Making.

---

[4]When thinking about risk management, mental model representations can help summarize and compare disparate views of risk management and stakeholder groups. Simply defined, a mental model is a person's internal, cognitive representation of how things appear in the world, either historically, currently, or projected into the future.

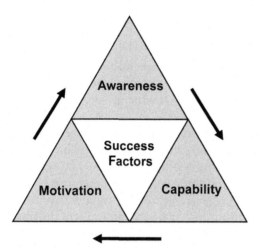

FIGURE 9.3
Program Success Factors: Awareness, Capability, and Motivation.

As individuals and groups work to acknowledge a foundational mindset such as secure, vigilant, resilient, a shared cognitive framework from which to start allows risk management negotiations to occur. As a final note, however: more often than not, those most well positioned to manage risk do not have the awareness, capability, or motivation to do so. Each of these capabilities (see Figure 9.3) is necessary at the individual and group level for successful program implementation.

Actively promoting an secure, vigilant, resilient mindset throughout an organization is the first step toward the first key success factor, *awareness*. The remaining two success factors, *capability* and *motivation*, can be engineered into organizational units through well thought out job descriptions and incentive structures or programs that tie risk management actions to individual performance management.

COMMON CHARACTERISTICS: SECURE, VIGILANT, RESILIENT PROGRAMS

Transforming from a traditional, standards-driven IT security program to a robust, cyber risk secure, vigilant, resilient mindset and program is not just about spending money differently. Instead, it is a fundamentally different approach, and programs will vary according to organizational maturity, needs, and business drivers. The balance, therefore, of investment in secure, vigilant, and resilient capabilities will vary between organizations and will even be applied differently to various areas within organizations.

Nevertheless, secure, vigilant, resilient mindsets and programs do share some common characteristics:

1. **Executive-led**. Executive leaders must set the stage by defining cyber risk management priorities, risk appetite, and mechanisms of accountability. Sponsorship at the top is essential in rallying diverse groups and departments to collaborate in new ways.
2. **Involve everyone**. Although specific roles need to be well defined, the program is not the sole responsibility of a single part of the organization; it requires broad horizontal and vertical participation, and behavioral change throughout the enterprise.
3. **Programs, not projects**. Although it usually requires a series of projects to get off the ground, secure, vigilant, resilient programs are agile and adaptive programs requiring continuous review and improvement cycles to adapt to changes in the business risk and threat landscapes.
4. **Comprehensive and integrated**. The individual secure, vigilant, resilient components are not distinct silos of activity—they are a set of lenses through which every essential business process and growth initiative should be evaluated or planned. Each involves people, process, and technology components. Done well, each will improve the others.
5. **Extend to broader ecosystem**. An organization's ecosystem includes various partners, suppliers, and vendors. Significant cyber incidents that directly impact them may also substantially affect the home organization.
6. **Governance for transformation**. Programmatic transformations cannot take place without strong governance. Instituting an secure, vigilant, resilient program requires a carefully guided evolution: changes in roles, processes, accountability measures, well-articulated performance metrics, and, most of all, an organization-wide shift in mindset.

KEY TAKEAWAYS

Robust cyber risk assessment and management comes from an effort to understand what is happening internally and externally to an organization, the perceptions and beliefs of stakeholders, and how these beliefs drive actions that influence risk management decisions. One way to ground such decisions is to adopt and maintain a robust cyber risk management mindset organized around secure, vigilant, resilient capabilities. How to begin forming such a mindset depends on where an organization is today. If an organization is at the beginning of a transformation process, the following steps can help an organization move in the targeted direction:

Assign a senior executive as program manager. A cyber crisis situation requires a strong leader to drive cohesive, decisive action. But establishing the foundation requires someone with broad influence who can generate collaborative engagement among the diverse players that are essential to the success of the program, most of whom may be unaccustomed to thinking holistically and systemically about cyber risk. The person in charge of an secure, vigilant, resilient program must be able to lead in both capacities, and be respected among a wide range of leaders, including at the board level.

Map threats to critical business assets. Create a high-level cyber risk guidance matrix by gathering top business leaders and threat intelligence specialists to preemptively discuss the potential threat actors and trusted insiders who could cause harm, the damage they could impose, and how they might do it. Through this threat-centric lens, identify significant areas of unaddressed cyber risks. Set stakeholders' risk appetites and prioritize program areas that embody the organization's strategy for becoming secure, vigilant, and resilient.

Launch priority projects for early "wins." Establish momentum by focusing on several areas or pilot initiatives that directly impact business success or mission achievement and have objectives that can be measured and built-in continuous improvement processes. By maintaining focus and demonstrating results, risk managers and executives can begin to plant the seeds of an secure, vigilant, resilient culture that has a long-term, sustainable impact.

Accelerate behavioral change through incentives and experience-based awareness. Traditional security training is an important program component, but on its own it is not enough, as evidenced by the number of breaches that can be traced back to stolen laptops, weak passwords, or failure to follow secure application development protocols. In a typically busy and stressful work environment, a policy manual alone will not prepare people to take the right action. Instead, organizations can work to create active learning scenarios that deepen understanding of the impact of day-to-day activity on the organization's cyber risk posture, and identify visible opportunities to reinforce the right behavior through programs that reward speaking up, raising questions, and achieving core secure, vigilant, resilient program objectives.

In summary, becoming secure, vigilant, and resilient requires that organizations embrace a fundamentally different view of what we've previously called "security." Yesterday's security program was often perceived as a burden, an externally imposed set of restrictions, rules, and procedural hurdles that impeded business initiatives. Security rigor has been pitted against progress, striking up battles over the budgets and timelines of strategic initiatives. Depending on which prevailed at any given point, the net result has too often been either recklessly risky innovation or a degree of caution that leads to lost opportunities.

Such limited mindsets do not have a place in management cognition today. Given the pace of today's global business climate, organizations cannot afford to slow innovation simply because it cannot be perfectly secured. But neither can they innovate without appropriate regard for the inherent risks being generated. Cyber risk and innovation are inextricably linked: rather than subordinating one to the other, senior executives must harmonize these important elements of business performance through a bold change in mindset and a robust cyber risk management program and operations.

CHAPTER 10

Threats Posed by Third-Party Insiders: Considerations for a Vendor Vetting Program

INTRODUCTION

Organizations are now more susceptible to risks posed by their vendors than ever before because today's globalized economies rely increasingly on multitiered supply chains. A heightened reliance on contractors, subcontractors, suppliers, business partners, and third parties is an integral element of doing business in the 21st century (this chapter collectively refers to these terms as "vendors"). Partnering with vendors can substantially lower operational costs and allow organizations to focus on their core business. However, engaging with vendors introduces potential new risks to the parent organization. This can range from sabotage, workplace violence, theft, and data breaches, to less commonly considered risks, such as commercial cover for mal-intent and infiltration of critical infrastructure. Given the multitude of risks that vendors can present, it is imperative that organizations expand their concept of "insider" to include all members of their supply chain. Nearly any member of a vendor organization could perpetrate threats as an insider, from the cleaning crew who enters the building every night, to the truck driver who takes possession of goods for delivery, to the accountant who accesses internal computer files, to the contracted company that conducts background investigation on new employees.

Addressing risks posed by vendors requires a thorough understanding of the vulnerabilities associated with a supply chain and a robust capability to identify and mitigate any potential issues. The first step in this process— vendor vetting—is an essential element to any comprehensive insider threat program. This chapter explores trends driving the growth of vendor support to commercial and public organizations, reviews real-world examples of vendor threats, discusses the importance of vetting vendors, and proposes a robust vendor vetting model that will contribute to mitigating the insider threat.

Insider Threat. DOI: http://dx.doi.org/10.1016/B978-0-12-802410-2.00010-1

TRENDS DRIVING PREVALENCE OF VENDORS IN THE U.S. MARKET

In particular, two trends have driven both commercial and public sector organizations to look externally, as opposed to internally, for sourcing goods and services in their supply chains. An advantage of a globally-networked economy is that companies can expand their supply chains to virtually every corner of the world. Companies increasingly outsource business functions and source goods from external providers, both domestically and abroad, to take advantage of inexpensive labor and materials, less stringent regulatory environments, or to seize on other competitive advantages. Second, in the U.S. public sector, budget caps and a desire for fiscal restraint have driven federal, state, and local agencies to rely on vendors to assist them in executing their missions while reducing their number of full-time employees. Governments of other countries are similarly resource constrained, and seek cost and process efficiencies through external vendors. The result of these two trends is that organizations now often have a significantly larger "insider" population of vendors to contend with than ever before.

In the private sector, companies are outsourcing non-core business services at an unprecedented level. In 2014, outsourcing was estimated to be a $507 billion global industry, generally focusing on information technology (IT) services, financial and human resources services, and logistics and distribution (business functions that are particularly vulnerable to the malicious acts of insiders).[1] In addition to looking for less expensive labor, companies "think globally" when sourcing goods, and as a result, supply chains have grown complex, multitiered, and international. For example, the supply chain for Lockheed Martin's F-35 Joint Strike Fighter includes nine countries, several thousand suppliers, and more than 40,000 parts.[2] Given the imperative for managing labor costs coupled with rapid advances in technology, it is certain this trend of sourcing globally will continue.

Like the private sector, public sector use of contractors has grown substantially in recent years. In some cases, to rein in government spending, lawmakers have capped federal employee headcount, causing agencies to contract for needed support. Responding to an inquiry from the House Budget

---

[1] "Introduction to the Outsourcing & Offshoring Industry," Plunkett Research, September 2014, <http://www.plunkettresearchonline.com/ResearchCenter/Trends/display.aspx?Industry=29>.
[2] Global Logistics & Supply Strategies, "In an Outsourced Supply Chain, Lockheed Keeps the Raw Materials Flowing," SupplyChainBrain, n.d., <http://www.supplychainbrain.com/content/research-analysis/supply-chain-innovation-awards/single-article-page/article/in-an-outsourced-supply-chain-lockheed-keeps-the-raw-materials-flowing-1/>.

Committee about the size and cost of the federal government's contracted workforce, in March 2015 the Congressional Budget Office explained that it was unable to accurately derive the number of full-time contractor employees but notes, "federal agencies spent over $500 billion on contracted products and services in 2012."[3] New York University Policy Professor Paul Light estimates that in 2013, there were approximately 7.5 million contract jobs, compared with 2 million federal civil servants.[4] These massive shifts in staffing and employment in the government have serious implications for maintaining security. Overall, while outsourcing has become a desirable solution for both commercial and public sector organizations, the attendant number of insiders affiliated with many businesses or government agencies now introduces far greater risk to organizations.

EXAMPLES OF THREATS POSED BY VENDORS

The following section discusses a number of examples where the employees of a vendor caused considerable harm to the organization contracting goods or services. In many cases, red flags existed that, if they had been appropriately recognized, may have prevented damage from occurring altogether.

Information Breach

Perhaps the most recent and well-publicized example of an insider threat committed by a vendor is that of Edward Snowden. Working as a defense contractor at the National Security Agency, Snowden leaked massive amounts of classified information in 2013. Media reports suggest that the hiring screeners at Booz Allen Hamilton, the company for which Snowden worked, noted anomalies in his resume such as claims about his educational achievements, but ultimately Snowden "convinced screeners that his description of his education was truthful."[5] Snowden's disclosures resulted in one of the most damaging information breaches in history. As a vendor, Snowden caused as much harm, or more, than many actual NSA employees could have.

---

[3] Douglas Elmendorf, "Re: Federal Contracts and the Contracted Workforce," Congressional Budget Office, March 11, 2015, <https://www.cbo.gov/sites/default/files/cbofiles/attachments/49931-FederalContracts.pdf>.

[4] Nick Schwellenbach, "Is the Federal Civilian Workforce Really Growing? Some Important Context," Center for Effective Government, February 11, 2014, <http://www.foreffectivegov.org/is-federal-civilian-workforce-really-growing-some-important-context>.

[5] Mark Hosenball, "Exclusive: NSA Contractor Hired Snowden Despite Concerns about Resume Discrepancies," Reuters, June 20, 2013, <http://www.reuters.com/article/2013/06/21/us-usa-security-snowden-idUSBRE95K01J20130621>.

Workplace Violence

Aaron Alexis was a vendor who committed a horrific act of workplace violence in 2013. Using a Department of Defense Common Access Card to enter the Washington Navy Yard, Alexis shot and killed 12 U.S. Navy civilian employees and contractors.[6] Alexis was a subcontractor with a company providing IT services to the Navy through a prime contractor. This additional layer of separation from the parent organization makes it difficult to know what hiring standards were applied by Alexis's employer and whether the employer adequately screened for red flags that could have indicated issues in his past, including past arrests and mental health issues. Of note, the prime contractor has severed all contracts with Alexis's employer since the Navy Yard Shooting. In a statement after the shooting, the prime contractor commented, "Based on what we now know about subcontractors conduct, including its failure to respond appropriately to Aaron Alexis's mental health issues and certain incidents recently reported in the press, the prime contractor has terminated its relationship with the subcontractor."

Commercial Cover

Another example demonstrates how an adversarial nation likely used commercial cover to gain insider access to spy on government officials. In August 1999, an eavesdropping device was discovered in the chair rail molding of a seventh floor conference room of the main U.S. Department of State building in Washington, DC. The device was planted in a piece of material that was fabricated to blend precisely into the molding of a conference room down the hall from Secretary of State Madeline Albright's office. Investigators were "concerned the job may have been done by a workman hired by the Russians and posing as a contractor,"[7] because it would likely require recurring access to photograph, measure, match, and install the piece of wood and eavesdropping device. In a Senate Foreign Relations Committee hearing following the incident, the issue of unfettered vendor access to the building was discussed at length.[8] In fact, CNN reported that during the time in question, at least "350 nongovernment employees, including maintenance and custodial workers,

---

[6] Department of Defense, "Internal Review of the Washington Navy Yard Shooting, A Report to the Secretary of Defense," November 20, 2013, <http://www.defense.gov/pubs/DoD-Internal-Review-of-the-WNY-Shooting-20-Nov-2013.pdf>.

[7] John Diamond, "To Catch a Spy," *Chicago Tribune*, December 10, 1999, <http://articles.chicagotribune.com/1999-12-10/news/9912100269_1_aggressive-russian-intelligence-presence-chechnya-bugging>.

[8] Senate Hearing 106-565, "Russian Intelligence Activities Directed at the Department of State," February 10, 2000, <http://www.gpo.gov/fdsys/pkg/CHRG-106shrg64654/html/CHRG-106shrg64654.htm>.

were often allowed to move about the building without escort."[9] The failure of the Department of State to properly vet vendors at that time created a vulnerability that was exploited by the Russian service. Theft of trade secrets is a comparable threat to private sector companies, where vendors may be used by competitors to penetrate the organization.

Supply Chain Infiltration

In May, 2012, the Senate Armed Services Committee released a bipartisan report on a year long investigation into more than 1,800 cases of counterfeit parts in the Department of Defense's supply chains. Programs as diverse as Special Operations helicopters to the Navy's newest surveillance aircraft were compromised.

The private sector is no less vulnerable to exploitation of complex chains. A good example are commercial airlines, who rely on thousands of domestic and overseas vendors—from caterers to travel agents to ticketing and gate agents—in various worldwide locations. In 2014, a major commercial airline employee and a former employee were arrested for gun smuggling at Hartsfield-Jackson Atlanta International Airport. Officials reported that the "two men worked together to smuggle guns and ammunition on at least 20 flights from Atlanta to New York from May to December"[10] using ramp agent Eugene Harvey's credentials to orchestrate the smuggling ring. In 2013, another major commercial airline identified a plan that ultimately resulted in five unknown individuals (an Afghan and four Iranians) boarding a plane in Caracas, Venezuela, destined for North America. A vigilant flight attendant, who counted the passengers onboard, noticed the discrepancy between the head count and flight manifest, ordered the plane to return to the terminal, and had the individuals removed from the plane. When the plot was deconstructed, it was revealed that an immigration official, several airport employees, and a travel agent used their insider access to falsify boarding pass documentation and bribe individuals at various points in the check-in and boarding process.[11] In this instance, the travel agent and vendors working at the airport should have been vetted thoroughly to ensure that any risks to air safety were identified and properly mitigated.

---

[9] "Espionage Probe Regarding Russian Listening Bug Planted in State Department Reveals Troubling Security Scenarios," CNN.com *Transcripts*, February 3, 2000, <http://www.cnn.com/TRANSCRIPTS/0002/03/wt.04.html>.

[10] Ashley Fantz, "DA: Guns Smuggled on Planes in Atlanta an 'Egregious' Security Breach," *CNN*, December30, 2014, < http://www.cnn.com/2014/12/23/us/delta-employee-gun-smuggling/>.

[11] "Afghan, Iranians Found on Canada Flight with Fake Tickets," *Agence France Presse*, *The Daily Star*, November 3, 2013, <http://www.dailystar.com.lb/News/Middle-East/2013/Nov-03/236679-afghan-iranians-found-on-canada-flight-with-fake-tickets.ashx>.

Unethical Sourcing

Unethical sourcing is another type of insider threat that organizations face from vendors in their supply chain. This can occur when a supplier of goods or services does not meet standards set by the parent organization, such as prohibitions around the use of child labor or inhumane treatment of animals or safety standards (like fire and building codes) that if disregarded could cause serious harm to all associated entities. In 2013, a garment factory in Bangladesh collapsed, killing more than 1,100 workers, despite the fact that alarming cracks were observed in the building the previous day and employees were ordered to return to work. Shortly after the disaster, it was discovered that the factory had at one time provided clothing to a major U.S. retailer, against an existing company policy that prohibited subcontracting to factories with substandard working conditions. Media outlets reported that a "rogue employee" of the intermediary vendor placed the order with the Bangladeshi factory without the knowledge or consent of senior company managers.[12] The retailer faced considerable reputational damage, as well as a class action lawsuit alleging that with "the exercise of reasonable diligence" the retailer should have known that the facility was not safe.[13]

In Summary

These are just a few examples demonstrating the wide range of threats posed by vendors. In each of these cases, screening the vendors (and importantly, subcontractors at lower levels of the supply chain) may have raised red flags that could have alerted the parent organization to a potential threat. As the previous example illustrates, claiming ignorance around the activities of a vendor at any tier of a supply chain no longer satisfies "reasonable" expectations of due diligence. Consequently, in today's world, it is imperative for all organizations, public and private, to sufficiently monitor, assess, and mitigate risks posed by members of their supply chain.

VENDOR VETTING DEFINED

The good news is that many companies and public sector entities are already vetting their vendors in some fashion, even if not for insider threat purposes. Within most successful businesses, the General Counsel's Office, the procurement or supply chain office, and internal audit all conduct various types of third party due diligence. Therefore, adoption of vendor vetting techniques to address

---

[12] Matthew Mosk, "Wal-Mart Fires Supplier after Bangladesh Revelation," *ABC News*, May 15, 2013, <http://abcnews.go.com/Blotter/wal-mart-fires-supplier-bangladesh-revelation/story?id=19188673>.
[13] Abdur Rahaman as Personal Representative of Sharifa Belgum and Mahamudul Hasan Hridoy v. JCPenney Corporation, Inc., The Children's Place, Wal-Mart Stores, Inc., and the People's Republic of Bangladesh, United States District Court for the District of Columbia, April 4, 2015, <http://pdfserver.amlaw.com/nlj/Rahaman%20Rana%20Plaza%20complaint.pdf>.

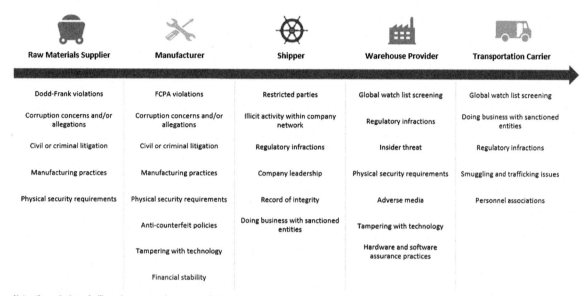

Raw Materials Supplier	Manufacturer	Shipper	Warehouse Provider	Transportation Carrier
Dodd-Frank violations	FCPA violations	Restricted parties	Global watch list screening	Global watch list screening
Corruption concerns and/or allegations	Corruption concerns and/or allegations	Illicit activity within company network	Regulatory infractions	Doing business with sanctioned entities
Civil or criminal litigation	Civil or criminal litigation	Regulatory infractions	Insider threat	Regulatory infractions
Manufacturing practices	Manufacturing practices	Company leadership	Physical security requirements	Smuggling and trafficking issues
Physical security requirements	Physical security requirements	Record of integrity	Adverse media	Personnel associations
	Anti-counterfeit policies	Doing business with sanctioned entities	Tampering with technology	
	Tampering with technology		Hardware and software assurance practices	
	Financial stability			

Note: These criteria are for illustrative purposes. They represent the baseline criteria for a due diligence investigation and not intended to be comprehensive.

FIGURE 10.1
The Above Illustrative Supply Chain Outlines Baseline Criteria for Performing Vendor Vetting.

potential insider threats should not—in most cases—be a "Herculean lift." Vendor analysis, or vendor vetting, is defined in Black's Law Dictionary as the "assessment of strengths and weaknesses of current and prospective suppliers in terms of their capacity, sales revenue, reputation, stocks, markdowns, markups, gross margins, quality, reliability, service, pricing policies, payment terms, etc."[14] Although this definition offers a useful business-centric view, it overlooks a key component by failing to include employees as an element of analysis—after all, it is people, rather than companies, who constitute insider threats by exhibiting harmful behaviors. Therefore, an effective vendor vetting program should also include some method for investigating the employees of associated vendors, or for determining the sufficiency of existing processes. Figure 10.1 is illustrative of a multifaceted vendor vetting program and the criteria that can assist in the identification and mitigation of potential risks and red flags.

APPROACH TO VENDOR VETTING

Vendor vetting is underpinned by the due diligence approach used to assess parties for commercial Mergers and Acquisitions (M&A) transactions. This standard approach seeks to uncover all aspects of a company that may pose risks to a potential acquirer. To ease the burden of thoroughly investigating

---

[14] Bryan A. Garner, Black's Law Dictionary (St. Paul, MN: Thomson West, 2009).

Industry Standard Approach to Due Diligence

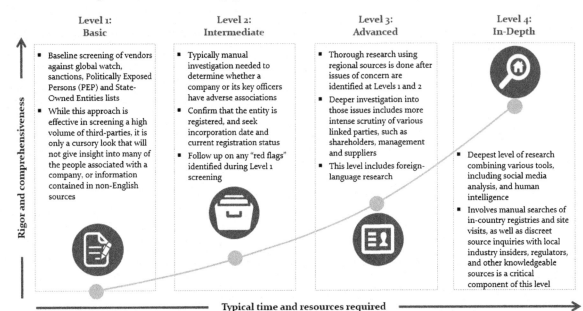

FIGURE 10.2

Professional Providers of Third-Party Due Diligence Structure Typically Structure Their Investigative Approach as Captured in the Tiered Diagram Above.

a company, organizations can employ a tiered due diligence approach to identify commercial risk indicators with increasing levels of scrutiny. The approach begins with basic screening and culminates in a robust investigation of the vendors posing the most risk (see Figure 10.2).

Basic: Level 1

At the most basic level, organizations should conduct an initial screen to determine whether a vendor is a bona fide operating entity, identify any overt red flags, and uncover potential links between the vendor and any government and/or political entities. This involves checking vendors against global watch, terror, sanctions, politically exposed persons (PEPs), and state-owned entities lists to determine whether the vendor has been designated by such oversight bodies as potentially concerning. Many commercial data providers offer this preliminary screen, though it can also be achieved internally with the appropriate data subscriptions. The intention of a Level 1 assessment is to ensure compliance with U.S. regulations rather than offer insight into the people associated with a company. As a result, this level of due diligence is generally insufficient for identifying risks posed by insiders.

Intermediate: Level 2

For greater insight into a vendor and its employees, and for the purposes of identifying potential insider threat issues, an intermediate screening should be conducted. Level 2 supplements a Level 1 review with online public record searches in English and in the native language of the vendor and key officers and employees in question. Topics of investigation cover registration information, business activities, corporate affiliations, and business partners; civil litigation and/or criminal records; financial history, tax liabilities, and revenue reporting; and any regulatory violations. Media searches, both traditional and social, are conducted at this level to uncover any reputational concerns. Additional social media analysis can be undertaken on individuals at this level to identify potential links to bad actors or questionable organizations. This is the standard level of investigation necessary to determine whether a vendor or its employees have significant red flag issues that could pose significant risk.

Advanced: Level 3

An advanced investigation is usually initiated after issues of concern are identified in the Level 1 or Level 2 assessments, or when there is a requirement for a more intense scrutiny of individuals associated with the vendor. This would include manual searches in public records filed at national, local, and municipal agencies into the relevant country, and further research into the vendors and employees to develop a more comprehensive background on all. In addition, this level would review the principals' curriculum vitae and attempt to corroborate the information with that reported in media, executive biographies, and other online public records. Company literature or other similar information would be used to assess business and technical qualifications. This type of investigation is typically used as part of an insider threat mitigation program when it is deemed important to "put eyes on" the vendor and directly engage with them at their facilities.

In-Depth: Level 4

A Level 4 assessment focuses on information-gathering beyond the public record. It involves conducting discreet, confidential interviews with industry experts and members of law enforcement, as well as business references provided by the vendor. Level 4 research is the deepest level of research, usually conducted in cases where the risk to the parent organization could be significant, or when an absence of information is noted regarding a vendor or individual. This level of investigation employs a site visit by functional subject matter experts or individuals with deep knowledge of the parent organization. These types of investigations also are conducted "ex post facts" as part of a damage assessment or damage limitation effect.

Automated Vendor Vetting Solutions

A combination of increased "big data" availability on companies and their employees, together with new analytic techniques is revolutionizing the third party due dilligence market. A number of automated solutions are under development or are already in use. For instance, the Department of Defense and Deloitte have pioneered the *Marigold* Software, which allows for automated bulk screening of vendors at a Level One degree of security. The F-35 Joint Strike Fighter program (discussed at the beginning of this chapter) includes thousands of vendors in its supply chain. It would seem implausible to thoroughly vet each one. To ease the burden, automated solutions like Marigold are emerging that assist in a baseline vendor assessment so that limited resources can be directed toward vendors with the highest risk profile.

MARIG LD

Due Diligence. Simplified.

Substantially more entities can now be investigated in a shorter amount of time than previously. Another key attribute of systems such as Marigold are that they are capable of continuously monitoring a company and its executives for risk, a feature highly valuable to Insider Threat mitigation programs once the initial investigation has been completed.

KEY TAKEAWAYS

- Two trends are driving both commercial and public sector organizations to engage vendors at unprecedented levels. First, companies are diversifying and expanding their supply chains globally. Second, a desire for fiscal restraint has driven some agencies to cap their number of government employees, thereby increasing reliance on vendors to help execute their missions.
- Risks associated with vendors range from workplace violence, theft, and data breaches, to commercial cover for mal-intent and infiltration of critical infrastructure.

- An effective vendor vetting program must assess business attributes but also include an investigation of the employees of associated vendors, and must include all levels of a supply chain. This type of program is essential for protecting an organization from potentially catastrophic financial, legal, reputational damage.
- Most organizations already engage in some form of third party due diligence, but usually not for insider threat detection. By capitalizing upon existing efforts, an organization can mitigate insider threats posed by vendors using a tiered due diligence approach with increasing levels of scrutiny.
- To ease the resource burden of investigating every vendor thoroughly, automated solutions are emerging, such as Deloitte's *Marigold* application, to assist with the baseline assessment of vendor risk. Moreover, high risk vendors can now be persistently monitored for a wide range of red flags and warning indicators.

CHAPTER 11

Employee Engagement: Critical to Mitigating the Risk of Insider Threat

INTRODUCTION

For centuries, defining and measuring loyalty to a person, place, or organization has been a struggle. Loyalty is defined as the state or quality of being *loyal*, faithfulness to commitments or obligations, and faithful adherence to a sovereign, government, leader, cause, etc.[1] Following World War II, President Truman instituted a loyalty program. In the more recent past, loyalty in a government context has been a construct directly tied to eligibility for security clearances. The question of loyalty is a routine, key question in background investigations, used to determine if a person is eligible to have access to classified information that impacts national security. Loyalty is an important construct in the prevention, detection, and mitigation of an insider threat. A background investigation holds similar weight in the private sector, where the vetting of potential new hires is a common practice.

Many leaders of companies and corporations generally assume that the workforce is loyal and committed to the goals of the organization. However, the workforce demographic is changing—in the younger generations, loyalty to careers often trumps loyalty to current employers. Cathy Benko of Deloitte makes an interesting distinction between loyalty and trust in the workforce. She views loyalty through an employee engagement lens—specifically, the meaningfulness of the work and how the work fits with an employee's lifestyle. If deemed not fit, younger employees leave and take the experience with them.[2] In some instances we are learning from our work that they take the IP they created with them as well.

In looking more closely at this phenomenon as it relates to insider threat, it makes sense to think about the dimension of employees' loyalty to an organization through the degree to which they are engaged with the organization and with their work. Specifically, this can be defined as the degree to which

---

[1] "Loyalty." Def. 2. *Merriam-Webster Online*, Merriam Webster, n.d. Web. 31 Jan. 2016.
[2] Korkki, Phyllis. "The Shifting Definition of Worker Loyalty." *The New York Times*, 23 Apr. 2011. Web.

149

Insider Threat. DOI: http://dx.doi.org/10.1016/B978-0-12-802410-2.00011-3

employees feel satisfied, productive, and innovative with their work and the organization that provides it. The level of engagement of a workforce (or worker) has clear ramifications when looking at approaches to prevent and mitigate the risk of an employee exploiting an organization's critical assets or stealing proprietary information to further their own careers. Many employers assume that a rigorous hiring and verting process means an employee can be trusted, and will not exploit, steal, or damage the organization's critical assets. This may be a false sense of confidence if just completed at initial hiring with no periodic updates or attention to the level of engagement an employee experiences.

From the perspective of detecting the insider threat, the default would be to a focus on the disengaged employee, whose low level of engagement fosters dissatisfaction and eventually disgruntlement, which inhibits loyalty. Employees who display potential risk indicators could be detected and investigated, as discussed in previous chapters. However, it is equally important to explore what it takes to create a workforce that is highly engaged. The extent to which an organization can focus on how to improve overall engagement and lower the risk of dissatisfied and disgruntled employees is a preventive strategy in and of itself. Specifically, the at-risk employees are those who are disengaged, who could imperil an organization, either through malicious acts or carelessness. A highly engaged employee is far less likely to exploit assets than an employee who is disengaged and, potentially, disgruntled. Ensuring employees are engaged also enhances a workforce's productivity, efficiency, and innovation.

UNDERSTANDING WHY EMPLOYEE ENGAGEMENT IS A CRITICAL ISSUE

Today's workplace is rapidly shifting—technology enables new ways to work, a new generation of employees bring an increased entrepreneurial spirit, and economic realities add ongoing budget constraints and pressure to improve the bottom line. Plus, increased transparency at work, the rise of contingent and freelance work models, and the provision of health care separate from work (i.e., the Affordable Care Act), make it easier than ever for employees to move or change jobs. Combined, these pressures intensify the focus on the employer's value proposition, including providing employees with new experiences, opportunities for advancement, and continuous feedback. Organizations must reconsider how to engage talent in this new reality.

Employee engagement has become a central focus for organizations, as the newest generation enters the workplace with thirst for information and a propensity to seek out challenging endeavors. Employee engagement has become a cornerstone to retaining talent and building a high-performing workforce. From the perspective of a secure workforce and the mitigation of the insider threat, employee engagement is a critical factor for organizations to protect their people and information. As the concept of employee loyalty evolves, it may be that the level of employee engagement provides a new security metric. If employees are highly engaged and feel their environment allows for innovation, creativity, and growth, they are less likely to become disgruntled, seek new opportunities elsewhere, or steal critical assets. Understanding the role of employee engagement can be a key preventive pillar and a catalyst to securing a workforce, and thus mitigating insider threat.

ENGAGEMENT IS A CRITICAL WORKFORCE CHALLENGE TODAY

Employee engagement and culture are currently the top human capital challenges for business leaders, according to Deloitte's 2015 Human Capital Trends report. The report found that 78 percent of executives around the world, and in every industry, rate these human capital challenges as urgent or important, demonstrating a cross-sector need for prioritizing employee engagement as a business imperative.[3] Both the public and private sectors face this challenge. With employee engagement at 27 percent in the public sector and 31 percent in the private sector, this translates to approximately $18 billion annually in lost productivity.[4] This does not account for costs associated with asset loss. Both federal and commercial organizations alike are investing time and resources into improving employee engagement through formalized programs, but many are not seeing substantial improvement. When the Engagement Institute™ surveyed its members in 2014, it found that only 41 percent of participants believed that their organization's engagement program was meeting its intended outcomes.[5] Further, only 50 percent of those surveyed felt that their leaders know how to build a culture of engagement.

Given that employee engagement is a critical attribute of top-performing public and private sector organizations, leaders should be encouraged to determine ways they can enhance their workforce, especially for those organizations with less engaged workforces. Leaders must recognize that employee engagement is not just a "nice to have" but a necessary component to retain top talent, improve customer service, drive business results, and protect critical assets. By understanding the critical workplace drivers of engagement (e.g., meaningful work, trust in leadership, growth opportunities) and regularly collecting

---

[3] Bersin, Josh, Dimple Agarwal, Bill Pelster, and Jeff Schwartz. *Global Human Capital Trends 2015: Leading in the New World of Work*. Rep. Westlake: Deloitte UP, 2015. Print.

[4] Ander, Steve, and Art Swift. "U.S. Federal Employees Less Engaged Than the Rest." *Gallup*, 16 Dec. 2014. Web.

[5] Ray, Rebecca L., Patrick Hyland, David A. Dye, Joe Kaplan, and Adam Pressman. *DNA of Engagement: How Organizations Create and Sustain Highly Engaging Cultures*. Rep. no. TCB_R-1564-14-R. N.p.: Conference Board, Oct. 2014. Web.

feedback on employees' work experiences, leaders are better equipped to "pull the right levers" to increase and sustain employee engagement.

Organizations are increasingly intensifying their focus on employee engagement, which is not surprising given its impact on mission achievement and business results. A significant number of global workforce studies have demonstrated a positive relationship between employee engagement and performance. Research by Gallup found that there were large differences between organizational units in the top quartile and bottom quartile on engagement on key performance outcomes, including retention, customer satisfaction, productivity, profitability, and safety.[6]

WORKPLACE DRIVERS OF ENGAGEMENT

Today's literature offers many definitions of employee engagement. Typically, employee engagement includes two key components. The first component is commitment to the organization: engaged employees are proud to work for the organization, would recommend it to family or friends as a great place to work, and want to remain at the organization for the long term. The second component is discretionary effort: engaged employees are willing to go above and beyond to help the organization achieve its mission. On the other hand, disengaged employees lack commitment, are dissatisfied and checked out, exhibit negative behaviors in the workplace, and plan to leave the organization in the near term. The disengaged employee is the employee of greatest concern as it relates to protecting assets and people. Simply, the disengaged employee can readily become a complacent insider, who is inattentive or careless in the way he or she manages security responsibilities. This disposition can result in a potential external attack on the organization's IT systems or facilitate unwarranted access to a facility by a malicious outsider. Additionally, those who are dissatisfied and disengaged may begin to ponder intentional ways to compromise an organization's critical assets. The need to secure a new job to find greater satisfaction may goad malicious action. Before departing, an employee leverages critical assets to include IP, R&D, or other proprietary and business critical information to use in their next job, and material that they may have had a hand in developing but is now the company's. Although these are all fictitious examples, it is easy to see that many insiders who separate from organizations as a result of a lack of engagement *willingly* take critical assets with them.

It is critical for leadership to understand the workplace drivers of engagement in order to improve talent retention strategies and develop corresponding

---

[6] Gallup. *State of the American Workplace: Employee Engagement Insights for U.S. Business Leaders*. Rep. Gallup, 2013. Web.

mitigation. Employee engagement strategies are important insider threat mitigators as important as policy, training, communication, and vetting. Bersin by Deloitte recently published a refreshed, research-based model of employee engagement that identifies five major elements that make an organization highly engaging—or *"irresistible."*[7] The *Simply Irresistible Organization®* model draws on years of research and discussions with hundreds of organizations to identify the leading drivers of engagement and outlines distinct, actionable strategies for achieving a highly engaged culture at any organization. The model provides leaders at all levels with specific practices to create an engaging and high-performing workplace environment for their teams. Providing employees with the authority and tools to do their jobs well, coaching and developing employees, setting clear goals, recognizing contributions, appreciating diverse viewpoints, and creating a compelling mission and direction translates into a secure workforce culture. Employees in this culture are more likely to feel that protecting what they develop and contribute is more important and fulfilling than exploiting or stealing what they develop because they are unhappy and disengaged.

Over the past few years, the employee-work contract has changed. The balance of power has shifted from the employer to the employee. This model represents a shift from simply improving engagement to a focus on *building an irresistible organization* where employees are energized, passionate, creative contributors, who are able to do their best work every day. The *Simply Irresistible Framework®* (shown in Figure 11.1) synthesizes 20 distinct levers into 5 employee-focused elements that help organizations attract, engage, and retain talent.

Meaningful Work	Hands-On Management	Positive Work Environment	Growth Opportunity	Trust in Leadership
Autonomy	Clear and Transparent Goals	Flexible Work Environment	Training and Support on the Job	Mission and Purpose
Select to Fit	Coaching	Humanistic Workplace	Facilitated Talent Mobility	Continuous Investment in People
Small, Empowered Teams	Investment in Development of Managers	Culture of Recognition	Self-Directed, Dynamic Learning	Transparency and Honesty
Time for Slack	Agile Performance Management	Inclusive, Diverse Work Environment	High Impact Learning Culture	Inspiration

FIGURE 11.1

Simply Irresistible Organization ® Framework.[7]

---

[7] Bersin, Josh. "Becoming Irresistible: A New Model for Employee Engagement." *Deloitte Review* 16 (2015): 146–63. Deloitte University Press, 26 Jan. 2015. Web.

Meaningful Work: Enriching, meaningful jobs that offer autonomy, decision-making authority, and ample time to reflect, relax, and improve the work lead to higher levels of employee engagement. Individuals tend to desire work that fully utilizes their unique skills and talents. They treasure positions that allow them to create a finished product or contribute to mission success in a personalized and meaningful way. Leaders can increase employee engagement by putting employees in roles that leverage their strengths and designing jobs that encourage talent mobility and diversification of skills. Additionally, employees are more engaged when they work in cohesive teams and have strong relationships with colleagues. Organizations that select employees based on "fit" with the culture, values, and mission (versus solely on technical skills and professional experience) are more likely to build a highly engaged workforce. That is, employees are more likely to be engaged if their values and passions are consistent with the organization's culture and mission. Additionally, candidates should have the opportunity to evaluate the organization and its culture through a realistic job preview. Few employees start a job disengaged. However, early misconceptions about the reality of the work or a poorly defined workplace culture can soon dampen a new hire's excitement. A strong and accurate cultural brand helps potential employees self-select during the application process. This results in higher engagement for those who elect to join the organization.

Hands-on Management: Managers have a more significant impact on the engagement of their teams than organizational programs and processes. The job of managers is to guide, support, and develop their people. Employees are more engaged when their managers set clear goals, support them in their work, provide regular feedback, coach them for high performance, and take a vested interest in developing their careers. Not surprisingly, organizations with highly engaged workforces invest in developing their leaders and managers through formal training and development programs, mentoring, coaching, immersive learning, job shadowing, details, stretch assignments, and informal training (e.g., brown bags), and provide them with the support they need to build highly engaging teams. Additionally, organizations that create more agile performance management programs that focus less on the ratings and more on supporting employees' career desires see significant gains in employee engagement and performance. As highlighted in the April 2015 issue of the *Harvard Business Review* in an article titled "Reinventing Performance Management," Deloitte is reinventing its performance management program to better see, recognize, and fuel performance.[8] Deloitte's

---

[8] Buckingham, Marcus, and Ashley Goodall. "Reinventing Performance Management." *Harvard Business Review* Apr. 2015: 40–50. Web.

research demonstrates that leaders of highly engaged teams check in with their employees on a regular basis to set expectations for the upcoming week, review priorities, determine how they can leverage their strengths, provide feedback, and discuss how employees can do their best work moving forward. Hands-on management is also a critical aspect of mitigating the insider threat. There is a need for organizations to better train managers to connect with their employees to recognize not just when they are high performers but when they need support or may be going through a crisis. For organizations to better utilize resources to get the less engaged employees the support that they need, there needs to be a greater effort on the part of the organization to project to the workforce that management cares, and is here to provide support for employee development and well-being. There are numerous organizations that continue to struggle with gaining an increased sensitivity toward employees by management. Through the implementation of a more focused employee engagement program, managers are engaged with the workforce and able to be attentive to pockets of disengagement that need support. Through this level of hands-on engagement, they are able to promote a secure workforce culture.

Positive Work Environment: Organizations with highly engaged employees provide flexible and supportive work environments, offer health and wellness programs, provide ongoing recognition to employees, and create diverse and inclusive environments where employees are comfortable bringing their true selves to work every day. These organizations create a culture of recognition by regularly appreciating employee contributions through simple thank-you's, praise, and other informal types of recognition, and encouraging peer-to-peer recognition.

Cultivating a diverse and inclusive climate brings about new perspectives needed to promote innovation, create new discoveries, and solve complex problems that lead to the successful accomplishment of the mission. The benefits of diverse employees and an inclusive workplace are well documented and include higher employee engagement, stronger team performance, and more innovative ideas and solutions.

Growth Opportunity: Research consistently shows that learning opportunities, professional development, and career progression are among the biggest drivers of employee engagement and retention. This is particularly true for younger employees. Organizations can engage and keep their talent by providing employees with opportunities to take on new roles and assignments, which is particularly important where advancement opportunities are limited. Furthermore, employee engagement is higher when employees see clear career paths, understand what they have to do to advance in the organization, and are provided the training, support, and coaching to achieve their career goals.

Trust in Leadership: Effective leadership is one of the biggest drivers of employee engagement, but represents a challenge for many organizations in both the private and public sectors. Highly engaging leaders develop a compelling vision for employees and tie employees' work to the mission, set clear direction, build trust, communicate openly and honestly with employees, invest in their people, and inspire employees through their words and actions. Developing engaging leaders requires a focus on the critical behaviors that are required to motivate and inspire teams. Through a sound leadership strategy that is connected to the mission, organizations must identify these critical engagement behaviors, assess their leaders' capabilities, and help current and emerging leaders develop these behaviors through leadership assessment, development, and coaching.

MEASURING EMPLOYEE ENGAGEMENT

In order to create and sustain an engaged workforce, it is necessary to capture feedback from employees regarding their work experiences and engagement levels. Many organizations today conduct annual employee engagement surveys to identify key organizational strengths and opportunities for improvement, identify the workplace drivers of engagement, and develop and implement action plans for increasing engagement. Survey data are often provided down to the unit or team level so managers can understand the unique drivers of engagement for their teams, current levels of engagement of team members, and the levers they need to pull to increase team engagement. This provides an invaluable program measure around potential risk for an insider threat program.

More and more organizations today are recognizing that annual surveys and action planning processes are not sufficient to build and sustain a highly engaged workforce. Instead, they are using pulse surveys to regularly measure progress in creating an engaging workplace environment and the impact of actions taken in response to annual employee surveys. Today's organizations need to capture employee feedback in near real time and locally so that course correction can be made effectively. If used effectively, short employee surveys can provide a quick and cost-effective means to gauge real-time levels of engagement and the impact of leadership actions. This allows corrective action to be taken quickly. Pulse surveys may serve as an additional potential risk indicator (PRI) to be correlated with other indicators. They will track trending in performance in a more frequent time frame than annual or semi-annual assessments.

IMPROVING AND SUSTAINING ENGAGEMENT

Organizations can make lasting improvements in employee engagement when they stop focusing solely on distinct programs or initiatives and begin to build a comprehensive culture of engagement. Effectively building a culture of engagement involves both organizational and team-level activities. Organizationally, building a culture of engagement requires clear mission alignment, effective and consistent communication about engagement, a workplace and organization structure that enables collaboration, the incorporation of engagement measures into leader performance goals, and selection of leaders based on both technical skills and their ability to create engaging workplace environments. Other organizational programs and policies that can foster engagement are formal recognition programs, work-life fit programs and policies, diversity and inclusion programs, health and wellness programs, and employee development programs and career paths, among others. All of these programs contribute to helping employees avert potential crises that could lead to insider threat actions and is key to building a secure workforce culture.

Senior leaders have an important role to play in creating an engaging culture. Highly engaging senior leaders communicate openly and honestly with employees about key changes and decisions made, provide clarity around the vision and strategic direction, connect the work employees do to achieving the organization's mission, coach and mentor high potential talent, and invest in their people. These leaders are visible, approachable, and regularly visit employees at their work locations to build relationships and trust; see firsthand the work employees do on a daily basis; and discuss employee issues and concerns (e.g., "management by walking around").

However, organizations have the best opportunity to increase engagement by focusing on the team level and the behaviors of managers and team members, all of which help mitigate risk on recognizing potential at-risk employees. For example, managers can increase engagement by

- having regular check ins with employees about work priorities, how to leverage their strengths at work, how they can do their best work in the near-term, and how to remove barriers that get in the way;
- providing praise and appreciation (simple thank-you's) and using innovative ways to recognize individuals and teams for their contributions;
- empowering teams and providing them with time to think and create;
- soliciting and listening to employee ideas and suggestions;
- respecting diverse viewpoints and allowing employees to bring their true selves to work every day;
- providing clear direction, goals, and regular feedback;
- coaching employees and providing them with learning opportunities (e.g., stretch assignments, cross-training);
- creating a collaborative environment for employees; and
- sharing information and communicating openly and honestly with employees.

Employee behaviors also have an impact on team engagement. Employees can have a positive impact on the workplace environment by providing constructive feedback and recognizing their colleagues, sharing information and insights, respecting diverse perspectives and thoughts, respecting others, collaborating and supporting colleagues, and taking responsibility for their own career development.

The critical role employee engagement plays in creating a secure workforce cannot be emphasized enough, when trying to prevent the loss of critical assets. Organizations should focus on measuring and improving the engagement of their workforce as a preventive step, equal to other preventive measures to include revising policies, creating targeted training, and enhancing communications.

KEY TAKEAWAYS

- Employee engagement is not just a "nice to have" component but is linked to key organizational performance outcomes, such as retention of talent, customer satisfaction, and business results.
- Employee engagement is also a critical factor in developing a secure workforce and mitigating insider risk.
- Many organizations today have a portion of their workforce that is disengaged.
- Employees are more engaged when they have meaningful work, managers that provide regular feedback and coaching, a positive work environment, development and growth opportunities, believe in the organization's mission, and trust leadership.
- Leaders and managers have a critical role to play in creating an engaging workplace environment.
- Understanding the critical workplace drivers of engagement and regularly collecting employee feedback on their work experiences will better equip leaders to "pull the right levers" to increase and sustain engagement.
- Employee engagement practices provide ample resources and attention to employees to prevent potential crises and disengagement, thus mitigating insider risk.

CHAPTER 12

Workplace Violence and Insider Threat

INTRODUCTION

This chapter will examine how work done to mitigate workplace violence in the past has influenced insider threat programs today. Historically, workplace violence and insider threat have been viewed as separate issues, partially because they lead to different types of investigations, and also because the insider threat has, in the past, had a focus on counterintelligence and counterespionage. Both risks, however, have a similar etiology when an individual begins to move along a continuum of idea to action. Through the use of technology and analytics today, we have the ability to capture and identify behavioral anomalies much earlier. The process of detecting these behavioral anomalies—whether they indicate a traditional insider threat or workplace violence—is the same. The mitigation of these two risks, therefore, can be brought together under one program initiative.

Workplace violence continues to be a priority issue for organizations around the world who have put an enormous focus on mitigating this dangerous threat. Workplace violence statistics from the past years reveal sobering realities about our society, the human condition, and the danger that exists in the workplace. These statistics, which have remained constant in recent years, show that nationwide, workplace violence remains the number one cause of death in the workplace for women, and number two for men. Men are three times more at risk for workplace homicide than women. Workplace violence is the number one cause of death for African American, Asian/Pacific Islander, and Latino employees in the workplace. It is estimated that nationwide, 900 to 1,000 deaths per year are caused by workplace homicide and that 20 workers are murdered each week. Overall, it is believed that these statistics are considered to be underreported by 25% to 50%.[1]

Looking at workplace violence through a historical lens, many positive strides that have been made to mitigate workplace threats have probably saved many

---

[1] Bureau of Labor Statistics, "Injuries, Illness, and Fatalities (IIF)," www.bls.gov/iif/.

Insider Threat. DOI: http://dx.doi.org/10.1016/B978-0-12-802410-2.00012-5

lives. In fact, programs to prevent, detect, and respond to workplace violence have functioned as the foundation for the development of insider threat programs in both the government and the private sector today. The basic components of these programs, which will be described further below, include an emphasis on policy and training, background investigations, termination procedures, and attention to the employee life cycle. Additionally, the initiatives to conduct workplace violence threat assessment led to the development of working teams composed of diverse resources from within an organization. These threat assessment teams can be viewed in a similar light to today's insider threat working groups which govern holistic and proactive anomaly detection programs to identify insider threats such as workplace violence or the loss of proprietary or protected information.

A HISTORICAL BUT CUMULATIVE VIEW OF WORKPLACE VIOLENCE AND INSIDER THREAT

On July 9, 1995, in the City of Industry, a suburb of Los Angeles, a postal worker pulled a gun from a paper bag and shot his supervisor dead.[2] Following this and several other incidents of workplace violence in the 1990s, workplace violence became an area of considerable focus for both the government and the private sector. In 1998, the Office of Personnel Management published a manual entitled *Workplace Violence for the Agency Planner*[3]. This publication was followed by a significant change in corporate America, where many companies and corporations were developing policies regarding workplace safety in response to the government. Many of these policies addressed and defined acceptable behavior in the workplace. Some of this effort was coming on the heels of a frontal assault on harassment in the workplace and the development of policy and response guidance. In many cases, violations of workplace violence policies result in the termination of an employee or, at minimum, a referral for counseling through the company's employee assistance program. Violations might also lead to appropriate law enforcement involvement.

As a result of an increasing number of incidents and a greater awareness of the prevalence of harassment, stalking, and violence in the workplace, a demand for a more focused approach to threat assessment through prevention and mitigation surfaced. In the early 1990s, the Los Angeles Police

---

[2] Stephanie Simon and Edward J. Boyer, "Postal Worker Held in Slaying of Supervisor," LA Times, July 1995. http://articles.latimes.com/1995-07-10/news/mn-22409_1_postal-worker.

[3] United States Office of Personnel Management, "Dealing with Workplace Violence: A Guide for Agency Planners," February 1998. https://www.opm.gov/policy-data-oversight/worklife/reference-materials/workplaceviolence.pdf.

Department, under the supervision of Lieutenant John Lane, initiated the first threat assessment unit in a police agency. In response to the increase in stalking cases among Hollywood stars, as well as several significant workplace violence incidents in Los Angeles, the need for a threat assessment unit was recognized. During this same time, the United States Marshals Service and the FBI were developing a threat assessment methodology, and the Naval Criminal Investigative Service, led by myself and Special Agent Kim Sasaki,[4] stood up the first threat assessment unit within the Department of Defense. At the same time, the independent threat assessment organization, the Association of Threat Assessment Professionals, also under Lane's leadership, was organized to advance the study of violence, including workplace violence and stalking. It was the first association to bring together human resource professionals, psychologists, attorneys, corporate security, and law enforcement to collectively collaborate around mitigating workplace violence and other targeted violence threats. Psychologists Chris Hatcher, Jim Turner, Reid Meloy, and Kris Mohandie were key contributors toward understanding the behavior and the management strategy for these perpetrators. Mohandie was a psychologist at this time with the LAPD.

Also in the 1990s, the United States Secret Service (USSS) initiated the National Threat Assessment Center (NTAC). The USSS, recognized as the premier threat assessment agency based on its mission to protect the President, began to expand its expertise from the threat of assassination to more broadly targeted violence. The NTAC began a number of studies led by Dr. Robert Fein and supported by Dr. Randy Borum and U.S. Secret Service Special Agents Bryan Vossekuil, John Berglund, and Matthew Doherty (who all led NTAC at different times from the 1990s to the mid-2000s). The NTAC focused on the study of targeted violence, including assassination, workplace violence, and school violence.[5-7] These individual case studies of assassins and school

---

[4] Association of Threat Assessment Professionals, "ATAP News," Volume 1, Issue 1, August, 2009. http://c.ymcdn.com/sites/www.atapworldwide.org/resource/resmgr/imported/documents/ATAPNewsletterAugust_JSC.pdf.

[5] Fein, Robert, Vossekuil, Bryan, January 2000. Protective Intelligence and Threat Assessment Investigations: A Guide for State and Local Enforcement Officials. National Criminal Justice Reference Service. https://www.ncjrs.gov/pdffiles1/nij/179981.pdf.

[6] Robert Fein, Bryan Vossekuil, William S. Pollack, Randy Borum, William Modzeleski, Marisa Reddy, "Threat Assessment in Schools: A Guide to Managing Threatening Situations and to Creating Safe School Climates," United States Secret Service and United States Department of Education, May 2002. https://books.google.com/books?id=wHDt1OMyzUYC&dq=robert+fein+publications&source=gbs_navlinks_s.

[7] Randy Borum, Robert Fein, Bryan Vossekuil, John Berlund, "Threat Assessment: Defining an Approach to Assessing Risk for Targeted Violence," University of Southern Florida Scholar Commons, Mental Health Law and Policy Publications, July 1999. http://scholarcommons.usf.edu/cgi/viewcontent.cgi?article=1145&context=mhlp_facpub.

shooters examine the behaviors, activities, and signals that perpetrators exhibited before engaging in violent events. They are the first empirical validation of risk indicators that brought visibility to the continuum of idea to action for targeted violence. These findings became critical for training law enforcement, security personnel, and the community to begin proactively identifying early signals of potential violence. Further, these indicators or sequence of behaviors contributed to our understanding of how an individual moves along a path toward violence. They support the belief that workplace violence is not an impulsive act, but rather, that perpetrators demonstrate a discernible pattern of behavior, and that by recognizing this pattern, it is possible to lead an intervention and interrupt the forward motion toward violence and save lives. Later, in the mid-2000s, the NTAC sponsored a study in collaboration with CERT to look at the insider threat and information technology sabotage.[8]

Although a different focus, these findings were very similar to the findings of Project Slammer, led by Drs. Neil Hibler and Richard Ault, conducted in the late 1980s and throughout the 1990s by the intelligence community, FBI, and Department of Defense. Project Slammer studied convicted spies to better understand their motivation, behavior, and activities.[9] Again, although insider threats and workplace violence were viewed as separate categories and perpetrated by different groups of professionals, their themes were identical, specifically the concept that these actions were not impulsive and followed a continuum from idea to action. These and other similarities with the advent of behavioral analytics and early detection of risk indicators have contributed to a convergence of these two threats today under the insider threat. In retrospect, we can now see that beyond alignment of the continuum of idea to action, they both also result from some form of a real or perceived crisis and having access to information or people as part of being an employee, contractor, or vendor. While the choice of action is different from exfiltration and theft to targeted violence, the ability today to detect movement early makes sense to incorporate both under an insider threat program for an organization. The sooner a crisis can be detected and an adaptive solution implemented the less risk of the organizations data or personnel being exploited and assets of all kind are protected.

All of these studies were critical to better understanding targeted violence and espionage as actions that unfold across a continuum of idea to action. It is important to note that although there are statistics around workplace violence perpetrated by customers or other outsiders, for the purpose of this

---

[8] Band, Stephen R., Cappalli, Dawn, Fischer, Lynn, Moore, Andrew, Shaw, Eric, Trzeciak, Randall, December 2006. Comparing Insider IT Sabotage and Espionage. Software Engineering Institute. http://resources.sei.cmu.edu/asset_files/technicalreport/2006_005_001_14798.pdf.

[9] Central Intelligence Agency, "Project Slammer Interim Report (U) – CIA FOIA," accessed online, April 1990. http://www.foia.cia.gov/sites/default/files/document_conversions/89801/DOC_0000218679.pdf.

discussion we are referring to an insider who has access to an organization's information, people, facilities, or material.

An insider does not impulsively engage in either espionage or workplace violence. All have access to information, facilities, material, or people. All display a pattern of behavior that, if detected early, can be interrupted. Although difficult to empirically validate, the review of anecdotal cases and investigations has provided great insight into how a person moves along the continuum. This movement often starts with a shift in attitude toward an organization or individual. The findings from these studies conducted over the past 20 years continue to be reflected in more recent incidents and have informed what risk indicators need to be monitored today to detect the anomalies that warn of potential insider activity.

In 2004, Dr. James Turner and I devoted an entire book, *Threat Assessment: A Risk Managed Approach*,[10] to understanding workplace violence. The book's popularity endures because it provides a comprehensive understanding of workplace violence and a methodology for developing a mitigation program to manage targeted violence.

Most recently, in 2014, with a continued focus on workplace violence, OSHA amended its federal data regulations to require all agencies to annually report their collected data to the Bureau of Labor Statistics.[11] This regulation was intended to allow the agencies and the public to compare workplace safety information across the government, and will also be used by OSHA to target its inspections on Federal entities with high incidence rates within the agencies. Today, policies and metrics are becoming key components of insider threat programs. Policies must define the behavioral expectations of employees as they directly relate to protecting people, information, material, and facilities. To manage a secure workforce, policies become actionable when those designed to protect the organization are violated or ignored.

KEY CONCEPTS

The 2004 book presents a set of key concepts to further advance an understanding and a mitigation strategy for the detection of a potential workplace violence perpetrator. We developed categories that align with different behavioral sets, motivations, and intentions that illustrated how a workplace violence perpetrator could move back and forth along the continuum of idea

---

[10] Turner, James, Gelles, Michael, 2004. Threat Assessment: A Risk Management Approach. Routledge, New York.

[11] 29 C.F.R. § 1960.55, OSHA Docket # 2013-0018, Fed. Reg. 2013-18457.

to action. Furthermore, we proposed specific mitigation steps to manage the escalation for the potential for violence and inform steps to mitigate the threat. We postulated five different categories, an individual who had engaged in an act of violence (Category 1); a conditional threat (Category 2); the individual who engaged in a series of acts or communications that intended to create emotional distress (Category 3); an individual who engaged in a single act and who expressed remorse (Category 4); and finally, an individual who was identified as a false positive (Category 5). The purpose of this taxonomy was to not only begin to define the different stages at the individual level but how that person could move back and across categories in both a trend of escalation as well as deescalation. For example, although a Category 4 may have been a single event, if it reoccured then the individual would be moved to a Category 3.

Additionally, we defined some key triage factors for workplace violence that could be applied to an individual's behavior or communication (written or voiced). The triage process was developed across five key concepts or criteria: Organization, Fixation, Focus, Action imperative, and Time imperative. The potential for violence could be assessed by evaluating the degree to which an individual's behavior was organized versus disorganized. The underlying premise was that the more disorganized a person, the less likely that he or she could develop and execute an effective attack. *Fixation* refers to the degree to which the individual is preoccupied with a specific theme or aspect of the organization. For example, an individual becomes preoccupied with how an organization may be changing the day-to-day operations and the way business is conducted. This may include changes in business processes that impact workflow, implementation of a new technology that requires employees to learn something new, or a change in organizational structure impacting who a person reports to. As a result, the individual perceives what the company is doing as wrong and having a direct negative impact on his or her job status or life situation. Often, those who become fixated blame an organization for changes that they feel directly impact them and, thus, have caused them a degree of distress or crisis. Individuals who exhibited characteristics of fixation have articulated—in either communication or behavior—a sense of being persecuted or targeted by specific individuals. The individuals who become targeted by a potential perpetrator are often viewed as potential targets for targeted violence. *Action imperative*, when articulated by the perpetrator, generates greater concern. If an individual articulates a specific plan that he or she intends to carry out against a specific person or organization, it is assessed as behavior that is further along the continuum, moved beyond ideation, and the potential for violence is assessed as escalating. Lastly, if the individual articulates a specific time frame or *time imperative* in which the plan will be carried out, it is further assessed as another step along the idea to action continuum and with increased potential for violence and the need for immediate action. These concepts have been used to help assess communication and behavior to identify escalation toward a potential action directed against a person or organization.

What is important to point out for the purpose of this book is that in 2004 we were able to begin to articulate the movement of a potential insider through recognizing and observing behaviors in the world of bricks and mortar that helped to "proactively" identify and categorize specific actions with the goal of interrupting forward motion and aligning specific mitigation strategies. In addition, the 2004 book focused on the importance of policy and activities associated with workplace violence to include the development of an integrated workplace violence management team composed of stakeholders from HR, legal, and security with advice from a behavioral science expert.

Today, there are still many organizations in both the public and private sector that view insider threat and workplace violence as separate and distinct programs. But, the trend is moving toward grouping them together given that there are significant conceptual similarities, and behavioral analytics has facilitated the ability to detect anomalous behavior that could be an early indicator of either violence or the exfiltration of proprietary information. For example, an employee contractor or vendor who would either exfiltrate considerable intellectual property or research and development from an organization follows a similar path in the early stages as a person who would choose to commit violence. Although both acts are separate and distinct, malicious insiders appear to demonstrate behavior consistent with being disgruntled, dissatisfied, or feeling undervalued. Therefore, if those behaviors can be identified earlier through the collection of potential risk indicators or behaviors that suggest someone is moving down a path toward a negative action such as workplace violence, the behavior can be detected much earlier when viewed holistically and with the use of behavioral analytics. Furthermore, although I think it is fair to say that complacent and ignorant insiders do not commit violent acts, their actions or lack of actions may in fact lead to others exploiting their lax attitude to policy and procedure, which would be advantageous to others who may have other intentions.

An example of a malicious insider would be an individual who begins to feel disgruntled and dissatisfied, and who then may begin to fixate on the organization. Such an individual may feel that he or she has been treated unfairly or is undervalued and begins to blame the organization for having a direct impact on his or her well-being. Such individuals experience a crisis. The insider then focuses on specific information, material, or people that could provide a solution for the perceived crisis at work. The solutions an insider chooses at this point differentiates what an insider will do, either exploiting assets or committing a violent act.

As has been discussed in previous chapters, by taking a holistic view of an employee and proactively monitoring behaviors in both the virtual and non-virtual space, we are able to proactively detect the movement of a potential workplace violence threat. Whether the individual is moving toward violence or exploitation of company assets, the early-stage behavior will be similar. The developmentally appropriate escalation and triage processes, in order to detect anomalies in mere detail, will inform effective interventions that interrupt forward motion of a potential violent perpetrator in the workplace.

Over the past couple of decades, we have made significant strides in preventing, detecting, and responding to incidents of workplace violence within organizations. The early seeds of management teams, behavioral indicators, and the continued validation that targeted violence is not an impulsive act has contributed to the evolution of insider threat programs today where behavior can be captured in data, from declining performance to disgruntled and threatening emails through keyword searches to sites visited on a Web site that may be early warning signs of a perpetrator preparing for some action. Today, we are able to use analytics to correlate multiple indicators simultaneously and track changes in a person's baseline behavior and discrepancies in his or her actions from peer groups. The future should continue to brighten, and our ability to continue to evolve and detect the potential for violence by an insider only get better. As we look at additional resources on behavioral indications, what is monitored in the workplace will better enable protection of an organizing personnel and assets in far more diligent ways.

There remain a number of myths around workplace violence that still exist today as they have for several decades. Although the concerns don't change, the realities have evolved. The chart below seeks to dispel some of those myths with the realities of what we are capable of doing today in 2016.

MYTHS REGARDING WORKPLACE VIOLENCE

There are a number of myths regarding workplace violence that reveal some of the misconceptions held about this phenomenon.[12] We have updated the following table to clarify the myths surrounding insiders who can be both violent and nonviolent actors.

---

[12] Turner, James, Gelles, Michael, 2004 . Threat Assessment: A Risk Management Approach. Routledge, New York.

Myth	Reality
A profile of an insider exists	**Reality:** Perpetrators of workplace violence or asset exploitation do not fit any profile.
	Reality: Focus upon demographic profiles may cause us to ignore potential threats.
	Reality: Paying attention to behavioral cues/risk indicators is important to illuminating anomalous behavior.
The workplace violence problem is all about homicide	**Reality:** The workplace violence problem is less about homicide and more about assaults, intimidation, and fear in the workplace, all of which occur far more frequently.
Insider threats are most typically disgruntled employees	**Reality:** There are three types of insider threats: those who are malicious with intent to do harm (i.e., commit workplace violence). These individuals may be disgruntled. Violence can also be perpetrated by a person who has no relationship with the company, for example, by a customer or service recipient, or by someone with a non–employment-related relationship with the company.
	Reality: A disgruntled employee is one of several types of perpetrators. An insider incident, however, is the most publicized and most preventable. A disgruntled employee can be identified through monitoring and the use of behavioral analytics and the right set of correlated potential risk indicators/behaviors.
Individuals who pose an insider threat possess malicious intent	**Reality:** Individuals who are potential insiders may be unwilling actors. Some employees may view policies, procedures, and controls to protect an organization's assets as less applicable to their work because of an overvalued sense of importance or entitlement. These employees may subsequently enable external actors who wish to harm the organization to exploit the organization's people, information, materials, and facilities.
Violent employees just snap; they strike without waning or clues	**Reality:** Violent employees provide clues—often multiple clues—to coworkers and others prior to engaging in violent behavior. These clues can be captured in data when using a holistic approach to monitoring a person's behavior, i.e., when a person begins to deviate from his established, behavioral baseline, or the baseline of his peer groups. Although there is no way to predict employee violence, there are now ways to identify anomalous activity that can trigger a mitigating action before an act of violence is undertaken.
There is no way to predict employee violence	**Reality:** Potentially dangerous individuals present multiple clues to multiple people prior to an incident. Capturing and observing these clues with reporting mechanisms adds to the value of monitoring potential indicators of individuals.
	Reality: Clues are not reported to appropriate individuals or entities, which can contribute to losing observable behavior by coworkers and managers.
	Reality: Clues can be verbal or physical, and may include obsessions, bizarre statements, and unusual behaviors that suggest interest in an organization's business that extends beyond an employee's job.
Violent and threatening employees are chronic losers	**Reality:** Violent employees have major job and personal losses and are experiencing a perceived sense of crisis.
	Reality: Violent employees have a degree of success.
	Reality: Violent employees feel entitled and undervalued.
Even if you can identify violent employees, you can't do anything about them	**Reality:** Effective interventions are possible by developing appropriate escalation and triage processes to inquire, interview, or investigate anomalous behavior detected through employee monitoring.
	Team management works, and has worked for many years, managing incidents and validating a policy for communicating and training the workforce.
	Define the appropriate potential risk indicators and ensure that those indicators reflect a holistic approach; then monitor for anomalies in a person's actions in virtual and nonvirtual spaces.

WARNING SIGNS

There are many lists of warning signs for workplace violence published by a variety of sources. We have organized significant indicators into specific areas to assist with evaluating behavior and communications from a holistic perspective. Many of the behaviors that are warning signs of potential workplace violence can be captured today in potential risk indicators and data that can be correlated to detect anomalous behavior (Chapter 5). Linking these indicators to potential risk indicators that can be monitored as a potential insider threat moves along a path to action.

KEY TAKEAWAYS

- Workplace violence has been a key focus since the early 1990s and has laid the foundation for today's insider threat program structure to include the concept of a working group and focus on behavioral indicators.
- Mapping idea to action for an individual who has an intent to commit workplace violence has been postulated by Turner and Gelles through a system of Categories.
- Potential risk indicators today capture the behavior that has been a longtime focus and enables a more proactive approach to pinpoint movement, thus allowing interruption of forward motion of a potential perpetrator.
- As a result of technology today, and specifically behavior analytics, the identification of anomalous behavior enables the detection and merger-of workplace violence and the traditional insider threat.

CHAPTER 13

Monitoring and Investigating

A holistic and mature insider threat program should have a monitoring and response mechanism to detect and investigate anomalous behavior to interrupt forward motion. A robust monitoring capability allows an organization to prioritize the use of limited resources to analyze virtual, nonvirtual, and contextual indicators to detect anomalies. Monitoring informs the inputs of a set of identified potential risk indicators aligned to an organization's prioritized threats that they seek to identify, in which a team responds to correlated data to make a determination as to the nature of an event. The determination of the inquiry should feed into the response allowing an organization to interrupt an insider's forward motion or correct nonmalicious but complacent or ignorant behavior. Figure 13.1 illustrates the monitoring and investigating life cycle. The escalation and triage process should be continually evaluated, modified, and tested to adapt to the changing

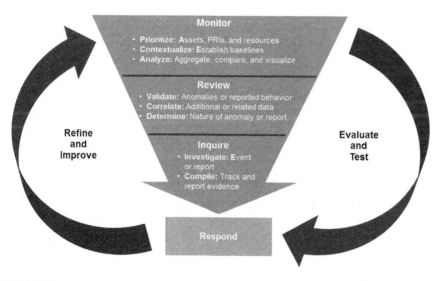

FIGURE 13.1

Monitor and Investigate Life Cycle.

169

Insider Threat. DOI: http://dx.doi.org/10.1016/B978-0-12-802410-2.00013-7

threat environment. Developing these capabilities involves decisions for the organization, with regards to privacy, ethics, and legal concerns. Navigating this process requires predetermined agreements by key organizational stakeholders, an understanding of what must be protected and the associated policies and communications to accomplish it.

MONITORING

The monitoring function of an insider threat program should review alerts resulting from the correlation of virtual, nonvirtual, and contextual indicators. There is no one-size-fits-all solution to insider threat monitoring. An organization's risk appetite (or what they want to protect) dictates the content that is monitored and the depth and breadth of the monitoring program.

Establishing a monitoring program requires participation from multiple stakeholders in an organization. As outlined previously, an insider threat program is a shared responsibility that requires collaboration and ongoing coordination across functional areas (for example, human resources, information technology, and compliance). This group is responsible for defining risk tolerance, critical assets, and the path forward for developing and implementing a comprehensive program. What is especially important today is for an organization to understand the privacy and employment law that varies by state, including the limitations and conditions associated with monitoring employees that require organizations to inform the individuals.

Organizations will face a variety of challenges when structuring a monitoring program. One persistent challenge is linking information from sources that traditionally exist in silos, such as IT data and HR records. An effective program integrates nonvirtual potential risk indicators (PRIs grounded in psychological and social expressions) with more traditional PRIs that exist in virtual form to raise red flags early enough for further analysis and mitigation.[1] Therefore, when designing a program, organizations need to develop processes that connect these sources of information. It is important, however, to acknowledge the limits of connecting data. Some information, like HR complaints, is not accessible in real time.

Another challenge is scoping a monitoring function. An organization must consider what data will be collected, how it will be aggregated and analyzed, and how meaningful outputs will be derived. When standing up a

---

[1] Securities Industry and Financial Markets Association (SIFMA). *Insider Threat Best Practices Guide*. 2014. Web.

monitoring function an organization should begin by identifying key behaviors that are captured in data and identified as potential risk indicators, and then develop the capabilities to monitor for those key indicators (e.g., identify data sources that reflect the PRIs that can't be correlated using an analytical tool, based on new threats and newly identified gaps in business process that could expose the organization to vulnerabilities). By collecting and analyzing key PRIs over time, an organization can begin to identify gaps in its monitoring function and identify new PRIs. It is important to note that when scaling a monitoring function it can be effective to develop the program in stages, improving monitoring processes as the organization's capabilities mature.

Prioritizing a Monitoring Capability

A monitoring function is intended to protect critical assets, information, and people while being time- and cost-efficient. The inclination that more monitoring is always better is not necessary if what is monitored is well thought out. Too many indicators can generate too much data to process and evaluate in a timely manner. Under these constraints, a monitoring capability can fail to identify red flags of an imminent insider incident or generate too many false positives. Organizations should make strategic decisions about how to invest resources when it comes to its internal monitoring capability. Prioritizing monitoring efforts can make the insider threat program more efficient. It can also help the organization separate the signal from the noise by selecting the right indicators.

Organizations should first conduct a risk assessment to prioritize critical assets and tailor PRIs to align to their critical assets. In other words, rather than collecting all data all the time, organizations should focus their attention in areas with the highest risk. This targeted approach allows organizations to overcome barriers to effective monitoring such as volume and complexity. Simplifying and focusing monitoring efforts reduces the amount of data to aggregate and analyze. Focusing on essential assets can potentially reduce the systems used in monitoring, and reduce the burden of linking disparate data sources. Best practices suggest that, at a minimum, organizations should monitor HR data (declining performance), undue access, policy violations, and common exfiltration means (e-mail, removable media) as foundational indicators to identify anomalous behavior.[2]

---

[2] Cappelli, Dawn M., Andrew P. Moore, and Randall F. Trzeciak, *The CERT Guide to Insider Threats: How to Prevent, Detect, and Respond to Information Technology Crimes* (Upper Saddle River, NJ: Addison-Wesley Professional, 2012).

Monitoring functions should also tailor PRIs according to specific employee characteristics and behavior. Rather than uniform monitoring of all PRIs, it should depend on an employee's access to critical databases, systems, or information. Organizations can prioritize data collection based on what accessible data sources align to what they want to protect.[3] Certain employee groups are higher risk due to what they have access to, an example would be privileged users system administrators.[4]

Monitoring should also be attached to certain organizational and individual triggers. A focus on specific areas of monitoring should increase when significant organizational changes, such as layoffs, adjustment in compensation, or the performance management cycle, occur.

Baseline Behavior

Establishing a baseline for behavior is a key component of a monitoring program: in other words, routine behavior for an employee in a particular position should be defined to then identify anomalies.

Baselines should be developed at individual and peer levels. An individual baseline is a baseline for routine activity on the organization's network and systems. To establish this baseline, select the PRIs to be monitored, and collect the related data points over a determined period of time.

Peer baselines establish routine activity for individuals who are doing the same job in subunits of an organization or classes of employees. Classifications of peer type will vary based on organizational structure, but at a minimum, a monitoring program should define behaviors for levels of employees and different functional areas.

Although it can be difficult, defining individual and peer baselines up front can help to quickly flag when an employee deviates from routine behavior on networks and in non-virtual areas (e.g., badging, time entry, and attendance).

Communication

Effective communication is a crucial part of a successful monitoring function. Legal counsel can help ensure that all legal and privacy requirements are met when communicating monitoring activities to employees. In addition to the

---

[3] Securities Industry and Financial Markets Association (SIFMA). *Insider Threat Best Practices Guide*. 2014. Web.

[4] Cappelli, Dawn M., Andrew P. Moore, and Randall F. Trzeciak, *The CERT Guide to Insider Threats: How to Prevent, Detect, and Respond to Information Technology Crimes* (Upper Saddle River, NJ: Addison-Wesley Professional, 2012).

legal imperative, appropriate program communication can mitigate workforce fears and objections to monitoring. In some cases, communication of monitoring and investigation procedures can serve as an additional deterrent to malfeasance and assure employees that the organization is working to protect assets and the workforce.

Proper communication requires senior management buy-in. Leaders in the organization must convey the importance of the program, and set an example of compliance from the top down. The importance of leadership buy-in reinforces the importance of involving the right stakeholders in developing an insider threat program, and monitoring and analyzing anomalous behaviors that could suggest potential risk to the organization.

All policy communication and controls should be documented in a concise and coherent way, and documentation should be accessible to all employees. Additionally, policies and communications should be aligned to training. Communication policy and training should be updated in a timely manner in response to changes to the program. CERT recommends communication should emphasize[5]:

- acceptable use of the organization's systems, information, and resources
- use of privileged or administrator accounts
- ownership of information created as a work product
- processes and procedures for addressing employee grievances

Further, communication should be refined based on how policies affect specific employees.

Training is also beneficial for communicating with employees about monitoring policies and acceptable behavior. Training provides an opportunity for organizations to inform employees about the proper channels to report suspicious behavior or suspected wrong-doing, which also complicates the capture of nonvirtual PRIs. Properly training employees can help reduce violations that occur from complacency or ignorance.

The Intelligence and National Security Alliance (INSA) recommends holding annual formal training programs on topics such as IP, ethics, and standards of conduct. All training should be monitored and documented with IP agreements, NDAs, and other documentation as appropriate.[6]

---

[5] Cappelli, Dawn M., Andrew P. Moore, and Randall F. Trzeciak, *The CERT Guide to Insider Threats: How to Prevent, Detect, and Respond to Information Technology Crimes* (Upper Saddle River, NJ: Addison-Wesley Professional, 2012).

[6] Intelligence and National Security Alliance (INSA), Cyber Council: Insider Threat Task Force. *A Preliminary Examination of Insider Threat Programs in the U.S. Private Sector* (Arlington, VA: INSA, 2013). Web. 3 Mar. 2015.

D'Arcy, Hovav, and Galletta found that three practices deter system misuse: user awareness of security policies; security, education, training, and awareness programs; and computer monitoring.[7] When users are aware of the resources and policies devoted to monitoring, it deters infractions by creating a perception (hopefully one that reflects reality) that security is taken seriously and infractions will result in certain punishment.

Escalation and Triage Process

An Escalation and Triage (E&T) Process is a vital component to establishing an insider threat program. It enables organizations to methodically assess, prioritize, and act on risk behaviors via a coherent and structured strategy. This is important from a legal perspective as well as establishing a repeatable process that consistently and logically analyzes employee behavior. The components of an E&T Process can be broken down into four phases:

1. Lead Generation
2. Review and Validate
3. Due Diligence
4. Course of Action

1. **Lead Generation:** Leads will be generated when anomalies are detected based on a set of PRIs correlated through the use of a advanced analytics tool. Working with various stakeholders in the organization, data will be collected and scored, or weighed, for risk. The tool will, in turn, generate the correlated data, shaped in a manner that displays a "dashboard" of users. This constitutes potential leads for analysts to review. If an organization does not use a behavioral analytical tool, the insider threat program analyst will accumulate the data and follow the same process, but the system will be more rudimentary.

2. **Review and Validate:** The analyst will conduct a review of the users and their associated risk scores shown as alerts on the dashboard. An analytical tool and its associated algorithms are critical for reviewing large amounts of data and winnowing down the data to a digestible and prioritized amount. At this juncture, the analyst initiates a subjective but informed analysis of the data points, behaviors, and associated risk scores. The analyst initially looks at the anomalous alerts to identify the following: Is the analytical tool aggregating and correlating data

---

[7] D'Arcy, John, Anat Hovav, and Dennis Galletta. "User Awareness of Security Countermeasures and Its Impact on Information Systems Misuse: A Deterrence Approach". *Information Systems Research* 20.1 (2009): 79–98. Web.

properly? Does any specific behavior jump out as an immediate risk to the organization (e.g., a workplace violence issue or an employee downloading a large amount of highly sensitive data)? Are there certain users that warrant more scrutiny than others?

3. **Due Diligence:** Due Diligence is the investigative phase of the Escalation and Triage process in which the analyst examines behaviors to ascertain the origin of an anomaly and to determine risk to the organization. This is driven by understanding the context of the behavior and applying investigative and analytical principals to the data being reviewed. The analyst evaluates the individual behaviors in both a singular and aggregate fashion to determine the nature of the activity (e.g., benign, legitimate, malicious, or complacent). The analyst also attempts to ascertain the possible intent of the individual and the potential risk to the organization to based on the behavior being exhibited. Generally, it is unusual to have a complete picture of the why, what, and how of the individual's behavior at this stage. The analyst will prioritize the alerts requiring follow-up action depending on the severity of the incident, seriousness of the behaviors, and the time sensitivity of the alert. Frequently, there is incomplete or unexplainable behavior at this step that will drive the process to the next decision point.

4. **Course of Action:** At this point, data has been collected and analyzed, but to be of true value, it must be acted upon. The next step is for the analyst to follow a "decision process" to act on Due Diligence results. There should be a course of action for each of the results in the Due Diligence phase. These results can often be broken down into the following:

   ▪ legitimate work
   ▪ benign behavior (not work related but not overtly harmful or against policy)
   ▪ confirmed violations of organizational policy/regulations
   ▪ behavior requiring additional investigative work by the ITP or a stakeholder within the organization

The last option is often the most frequent result. Organizations can leverage existing processes to address findings. To reach a conclusion, this may require additional efforts by the Security Department, Human Resources, Information Technology or other components to fill in the gaps of information uncovered by the Insider Threat Program. If the assessment concludes that the behavior is tied to legitimate work, then no further action is needed other an evaluating the original behaviors and risk scoring to see if there should be an adjustment to eliminate "false positives." If the result is complacent behavior, one outcome may be to recommend additional training, education, or a policy adjustment that highlights the uncovered behavior that, although benign, may cause the organization to be vulnerable. An example could be someone downloading internet-based programs for personal use to their work computer.

As an organization builds out its E&T Process, it is important that each of the phase are completed in substantive consultation with legal counsel and stakeholders that are part of the governance process.

Continuous Improvement

A monitoring function should not be static. There should be a plan for continuous evaluations of efficacy that are flexible enough to adapt to changing threat environments. Organizations should develop formal processes and schedules for evaluating and testing monitoring systems, and the overall program, for example, by using red teams and audits.

An organization should be able to quickly change what data is being monitored if the data is not successfully detecting at-risk behavior. Risk indicators that are monitored should be renewed or modified in response to current events, changes in the organization's threat environment, and any major business changes (e.g., acquisitions, changes in strategy, or market expansion).

An organization should determine if trainings are held on time, if processes are updated in a timely manner, how often the program is reviewed, and other key measures. While this will not necessarily provide insight into how well the program is performing (i.e., if it is successful in identifying anomalies), it can provide insight into the culture around the monitoring function.

A formal review process—one that involves the stakeholders from the program's design and implementation—should be developed to review the monitoring function, review PRIs and identify any that are inefficient, superfluous, or misleading. It should also identify gaps in PRIs, and supplement the program with new PRIs as appropriate. The evaluation should include a review of the tools used to monitor, and ensure that they still meet program needs. The review should also evaluate current policies and monitoring practices for potential gaps or updates.

Lastly, a monitoring function should be tested. Regular war gaming or red teaming should be a part of the monitoring function evaluation process. Organizations should design tests specific to their environment and the risks they have prioritized. Although organizations should plan testing frequency, routine audits should be conducted on a semi-annual basis.

RESPONDING TO AN INSIDER THREAT

Once monitoring allows organizations to identify anomalies, an effective response capability is critical to appropriately dealing with potential insider threats before the individuals engage in damaging behavior. An important consideration of a response process is its focus on the individual. Responding to an incident involves more than detecting and disrupting a threat. A properly constructed response process brings the focus back to the individual by directly addressing the person. A response process involves conducting an inquiry or investigation, and in some cases taking legal action. The primary goal is to identify individuals moving along the idea-to-action continuum, and to bring them back into the fold, before an incident occurs. Not all insider threats are operating in a malicious manner. A response capability must proactively respond to malicious threats, but also recognize and appropriately deal with individuals who are complacent or ignorant. A response process must also recognize that counseling or training needs to take place to remediate an individual's actions. In addition, the organization must take responsibility for evaluating its policies, the frequency and quality of training, and its communication with the workforce.

Another important consideration when responding to an insider threat is confidentiality. Not all anomalies constitute malicious, complacent, or ignorant insider threat behavior. Some anomalies are false positives. It is therefore imperative that at the beginning of the response process, the information triggering the response is thoroughly reviewed. It is important that the information is shared only with those parties who may participate in the review process, for example, HR, a supervisor or manager, and a systems administrator. Insider threat investigation records cannot be fully retracted once initiated, regardless if a person is wrongly accused. An organization must balance discretion and privacy while proactively monitoring and searching for insider threats. Defining the process by which information is shared prior to an investigation can assist information flow and help prevent possible data leaks that could compromise an investigation or damage a person's career. The program, therefore, needs to be located in a part of the organization that is firewalled from other functions, for example, an operations center.

Response Team and Process

Organizations should structure their response capabilities to be proactive, with processes designed to interrupt forward motion and address the root cause of issues. Responding to an insider threat requires the same holistic approach as the insider threat program itself. The response team should establish response processes that engage all parts of the organization, including: physical security, IT, privacy, policy, human resources, legal, business units, information assurance, compliance, and executive management. Lastly, the response team should have a trained interview team that will engage the identified employee and have a prepared conversation to clarify the anomalous activity that has been detected.

The response team should be ready to address anomalies and other indicators that a high-risk individual might display to include verbal statements and nonverbal behaviors, with consistent and predictable response processes outlined in an insider threat playbook. The response team can be triggered in two ways: either by an anomaly, or by an incident. In both instances, the response team should follow the processes outlined in its insider threat playbook that addresses how an organization conducts a review of an anomaly, how and when legal approval is obtained for an inquiry, how inquiries are conducted and who is involved, and how inquiries are turned over to law enforcement authorities or legal entities for investigations or legal proceedings.

When a threat occurs, an executive-level leader should be briefed on the "cause, all actions taken by the company, and the end result".[8] A best practice, outlined by SIFMA, is to develop a "decision tree" that includes guidance for leaders to make decisions on the following:[9]

- When to intervene versus continue to monitor concerning behavior
- When to involve noninsider threat team personnel in an inquiry or investigation
- When to escalate incidents up the management chain within the organization
- When a circumstance warrants consultation of third-party experts and/or legal counsel
- When to include security personnel, an employee assistance program, or other employee support entity
- When a situation warrants notification of law enforcement

Conducting a Review: Escalation and Triage

The first step after identifying an anomaly or receiving a report of a possible insider threat is to validate the information. For the purposes of this book, a review is defined as an Escalation and Triage Process. Inputs to the review process are the identified anomalies or reported behaviors and other associated behaviors that may be peripheral but still related. For example, if an anomaly is being driven by virtual behavior, the review should include a review of all the other PRIs that may provide insight into the activity that has caused an alert. The goal of the review process should be to validate the anomaly to determine if further inquiry is needed. The review process should help identify when additional information is needed and if an individual poses a likely insider threat.

---

[8] Intelligence and National Security Alliance (INSA), Cyber Council: Insider Threat Task Force. *A Preliminary Examination of Insider Threat Programs in the U.S. Private Sector* (Arlington, VA: INSA, 2013). Web. 3 Mar. 2015.

[9] Securities Industry and Financial Markets Association (SIFMA). *Insider Threat Best Practices Guide*. 2014. Web.

The Escalation and Triage Process should start with a review of the data on PRIs that an organization has at its disposal. For instance, a report may come in of an individual who has inquired about entering a facility that he or she does not need to access to fulfill his or her daily duties. The initial review should check the individual's performance, online behavior, and other virtual and nonvirtual PRIs to determine the validity and urgency of the report. Anomalous behavior should be reviewed in a similar manner. For instance, the event that someone is resigning or planning to resign may trigger an immediate alert to the insider threat program. Reviews of the individual's virtual, nonvirtual, and contextual PRIs will help determine if further inquiry into the resignation is needed.

The output of a review is a determination of the nature of the incident or anomaly. The determination helps an organization decide how to respond. Table 13.1 outlines individual and organizational outputs based on the review determination.

Insider threat programs have analysts specifically trained to assess anomalies. The organization determine whether or not inquiries are conducted. The insider threat program should develop an analyst playbook that defines actions that should be taken that align to prioritized risks and the investigative process. The playbook helps to develop a consistent model of conducting an inquiry, interview, or investigation for alerts and anomalies that are identified.

Table 13.1 Responses to Monitor Output in an Escalation and Triage Process

Output	Possible Responses
False positive	No action, continue monitoring, potentially evaluate monitoring system.
Ignorance likely (e.g., phishing, or other negligent or ignorant actions that allowed access or compromised information)	Individual: Counseling on policies and retraining. Organization: Depending on the number of ignorant actors, could indicate an area of weakness in insider threat training program.
Complacency likely (e.g., using Gmail as a means to accomplish tasks, but good overall performance)	Individual: Counseling on policies, retraining, reprimand, or termination. Organization: Depending on the number of incidents, could indicate inefficient software or system design.
Malevolence likely (e.g., undue downloads in topics not relevant to an individual's job)	Individual: Depending on the circumstance, increase monitoring, consider cutting accesses, conduct formal inquiry. Organization: Identify weak or compromised areas, make necessary adjustments, and support formal inquiry or law enforcement referral.

What Escalation and Triage Looks Like

Legal counsel's involvement in the Escalation and Triage response process should be documented and validated by the organization's key stakeholders and an insider threat working group that includes legal counsel. Legal counsel should help validate the process and ensure that the reviews are in accordance with the labor law of the particular state and aligned with privacy considerations. Some organizations may want legal counsel to be involved in reviews of all anomalies and reports, while other organizations may want legal counsel involved only before conducting an inquiry or at some predetermined threshold of review. Privacy laws and considerations for insider threat programs are covered in depth in Chapter 14.

Commercial e-forensic tools enable a team to "acquire employee's hard disks in a forensically sound manner for analysis and use in criminal prosecution."[10] The ability of the inquiry team to legally and accurately acquire digital or physical evidence is indispensable in the event that the inquiry is turned over to law enforcement.

Results of an Inquiry

> Whether it is gathering data for law enforcement or legal action, the response activities must be thorough, but conducted expeditiously and judiciously.
>
> **—Insider Threat Task Force Whitepaper**[11]

The results of an inquiry depend on the findings of the response team. If the response team finds that there are possible criminal or foreign intelligence activities, then the results of the inquiry must be brought to the proper authorities to conduct a formal investigation. Organizations should establish triage criteria based on law enforcement and federal government guidance to determine when to contact the proper authorities for investigations. If an investigation is not warranted based on the outcome of the inquiry, then there are several steps an organization can take with an employee, including counseling, remediation (e.g., reduced access, action plan by organization), and termination.

Organizations should also consider what steps, if any, must be taken from an insider threat program perspective based on the outcome of the inquiry. For

---

[10] Intelligence and National Security Alliance (INSA), Cyber Council: Insider Threat Task Force. *A Preliminary Examination of Insider Threat Programs in the U.S. Private Sector* (Arlington, VA: INSA, 2013). Web. 3 Mar. 2015.

[11] ibid.

instance, an inquiry may have uncovered a part of the organization that is not currently monitored or that requires more training to address deficiencies. In either case, organizations should evaluate their programs after each investigation to ensure that the program is adapting and changing to the most current threats.

KEY TAKEAWAYS

- All data collected as part of a monitoring program must be contextualized. Establishing a baseline for behavior is a key component of a monitoring program.
- A monitoring program must adequately protect critical assets while being time and cost-efficient. Prioritizing monitoring efforts can make a program more efficient and easier to navigate.
- Monitoring in different states is subject to different legal limitations and conditions.
- Establishing a baseline for behavior is a key component of a monitoring function.
- Baselines should be developed at organizational and peer levels. An organizational baseline looks at normal activity on the organization's network and systems. Peer baselines establish normal activity for subunits of an organization or classes of employees.
- Monitoring systems should not be static. They must be constantly evaluated for efficacy, and adapted in response to changing threat environments.
- Monitoring systems need to be adaptable. An organization should be able to quickly change what data is being monitored and the level to which data is reviewed.

CHAPTER 14

Privacy Considerations for Insider Threat Mitigation Programs

At no point in history have employers had more access to information about job applicants and employees than they do now. Some of this is benign, such as discovering a potential hire's favorite musician through Spotify. Other information can be useful, such as evaluating someone's experience as stated on their LinkedIn profile. But inherent in our hyper-public, transparent world is the risk for abuse and discrimination, raising legitimate questions about whether employer investigation and surveillance comply with the existing law or if those laws simply do not go far enough.[1]

—*New York Law Journal*

INTRODUCTION

Technology has changed the context of behavior in business. In the past, we were only able to observe behavior in the physical setting. Today, as business is conducted in the virtual space and work is digital, there are a variety of mechanisms to capture behavior. Organizations can now observe behavior by monitoring a variety of different indicators that reflect what a person does in both the virtual and nonvirtual space. As a result, the trend toward monitoring the workforce to protect people, information, material assets, and facilities has become the risk mitigation strategy of choice for many organizations. Organizational leadership should acknowledge that effective insider threat mitigation must be part of a broader enterprise-wide risk mitigation strategy. Despite an evolution in how organizations account for insider threat, the fact remains that insider threat mitigation opens many questions about data privacy and the legal precedent associated with monitoring employee behavior. The fact remains that the collection of information on employees, contractors, and vendors is foundational to

---

[1] Lazar, Wendi S., "1984" in 2015: Protecting Employees' Social Media From Misuse; Employees in the Workplace, *New York Law Journal* (Online), July 7, 2015.

Insider Threat. DOI: http://dx.doi.org/10.1016/B978-0-12-802410-2.00014-9

an insider threat mitigation capability. However, this activity raises legal and privacy risks for both the workforce and the organization regarding the potential for improper collection, use, or disclosure of information. Among these risks is the perceived concern that employee information, gathered through an insider threat program, could be used in a manner for which it was not intended, such as informing staffing or employment decisions.

This chapter outlines how to balance employee privacy protection with the implementation of effective and appropriate insider threat mitigation strategies. We will introduce a series of cases that established a legal precedent outlining how courts have historically ruled on employee privacy matters, and discuss the necessary steps organizations should take to comply with data privacy and legal requirements.

DATA PRIVACY AND THE COLLECTION OF POTENTIAL RISK INDICATORS (PRIs)

An organization's ability to detect insider threats depends on how it collects information on actions, conditions, or events that serve as precursors to harmful insider activity. These PRIs can include personal, organizational, or behavioral data with varying requirements, regulations, and expectations around data privacy. In addition to the varying privacy concerns associated with different PRIs, organizations themselves fall along a spectrum of data privacy and regulatory compliance considerations based on their industry, customers, and organizational history.

To visualize this spectrum, we have identified common PRIs organizations may incorporate in an insider threat program based on their organizational objectives, critical assets, and overall risk tolerances. Those organizations that fall within Tier 1 (Low Risk) in Figure 14.1 are generally smaller organizations that have limited means to collect a broad spectrum of PRIs. At the other end of the maturity spectrum, Tier 5 (High Risk) organizations are typically larger and cast a wider net in terms of the breadth of PRIs collected and correlated. These PRIs come from a variety of sources, including recurring background investigations (externally available data, such as financial, criminal civil), use of internal organizational data, and external data such as social media postings, forums, and Internet blogs and chat rooms. As organizations mature in their capabilities and ingest a more holistic set of PRIs, the data privacy requirements and regular engagement with the organization's legal council should increase.

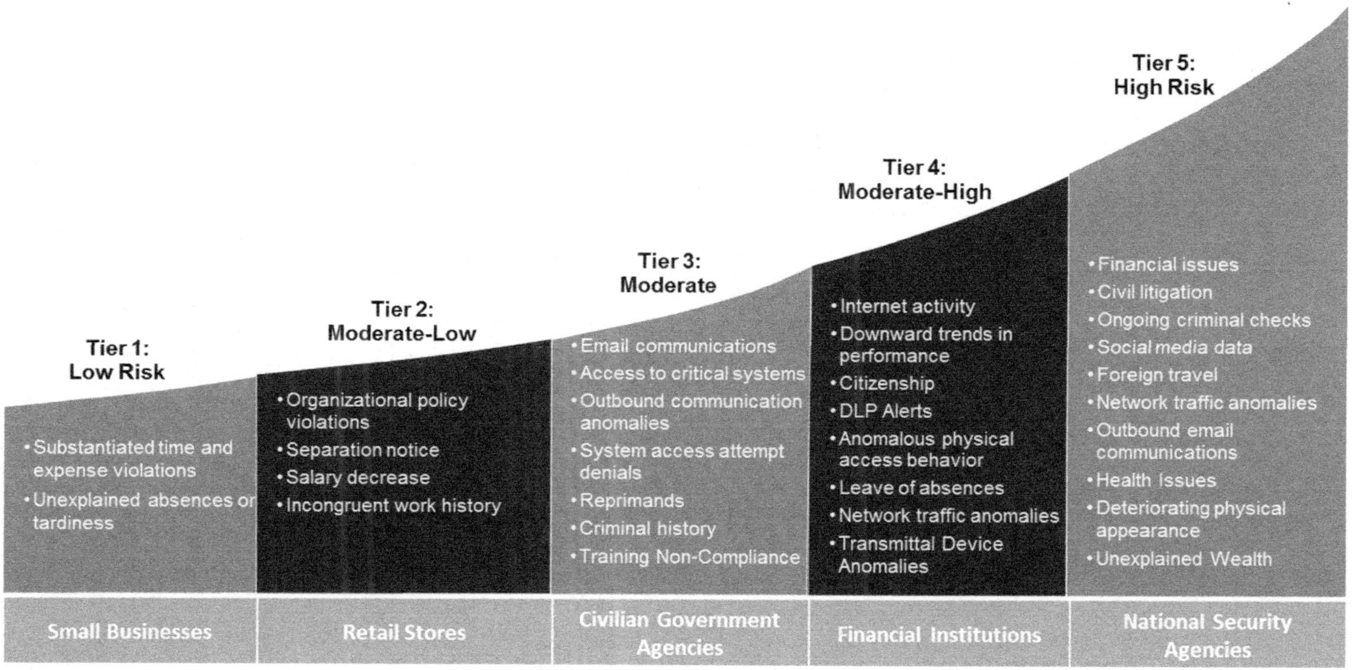

**Tier 1:
Low Risk**

- Substantiated time and expense violations
- Unexplained absences or tardiness

**Tier 2:
Moderate-Low**

- Organizational policy violations
- Separation notice
- Salary decrease
- Incongruent work history

**Tier 3:
Moderate**

- Email communications
- Access to critical systems
- Outbound communication anomalies
- System access attempt denials
- Reprimands
- Criminal history
- Training Non-Compliance

**Tier 4:
Moderate-High**

- Internet activity
- Downward trends in performance
- Citizenship
- DLP Alerts
- Anomalous physical access behavior
- Leave of absences
- Network traffic anomalies
- Transmittal Device Anomalies

**Tier 5:
High Risk**

- Financial issues
- Civil litigation
- Ongoing criminal checks
- Social media data
- Foreign travel
- Network traffic anomalies
- Outbound email communications
- Health Issues
- Deteriorating physical appearance
- Unexplained Wealth

| Small Businesses | Retail Stores | Civilian Government Agencies | Financial Institutions | National Security Agencies |

FIGURE 14.1

Privacy risk tiers for employee data collection.

BALANCING DATA PRIVACY WITH EFFECTIVE INSIDER THREAT MITIGATION

It is critical that organizations take steps to protect the employee data collected in the analysis of PRIs to maintain the insider threat program's support and participation from the workforce, as well as compliance with Federal, state, and organizational regulations and legal requirements. Through the course of developing insider threat assessments, we have documented some foundational principles associated with the protection of employee data when establishing an insider threat program.

Foundational Data Privacy Principles*	
Principle 1 Protection	Appropriate technical and organizational measures shall be taken against unauthorized or unlawful processing of personal data and against accidental loss or destruction of, or damage to, personal data.
Principle 2 Legality	Personal data shall be processed fairly and lawfully.
Principle 3 Intended Use	Personal data shall be obtained only for one or more specified and lawful purposes, and shall not be further processed in any manner incompatible with that purpose or those purposes.
Principle 4 Substantiation	Personal data shall be adequate, relevant, and not excessive in relation to the purpose or purposes for which they are processed.
Principle 5 Accurate	Personal data shall be accurate and, where necessary, kept up-to-date.
Principle 6 Aging	Personal data processed for any purpose or purposes shall not be kept for longer than necessary for that purpose or those purposes.
Principle 7 Organizational Doctrine	Personal data shall be processed in accordance with the program concept of operations and in compliance with the organization's policies and edicts.

The Foundational Data Privacy Principles are primarily sourced from the UK Data Protection Act of 1998 and adapted as applicable.

THE PRIVACY IMPACT ASSESSMENT (PIA)

When implementing an insider threat program, organizations should consider conducting a Privacy Impact Assessment (PIA) to serve as a critical step in determining the level of effort required to protect the privacy of the data collected to inform PRIs. A PIA is an analysis of how personally identifiable information is collected, used, shared, and maintained. These assessments are currently used by public and private sector organizations when deploying new programs or projects (such as an insider threat program). The PIA will identify the need/justification for the collection of new data; define information flows to identify what systems and people will be exposed to the personnel data; and document potential privacy risks and mitigation strategies associated with the data collection. The information documented in the PIA will inform the level and type of legal and privacy coordination needed to protect the organization from potential legal action and ensure that the insider threat program comports with the necessary legal requirements in the state or jurisdiction the organization operates.

It is important to note that different US states may have additional legal requirements associated with the collection and analysis of personnel data. For example, California's Online Privacy Protection Act[2] requires that a notice be distributed to employees when personal information is collected in the online and mobile contexts. Although the considerations noted in this chapter come from our experience with US clients, the data privacy requirements and legal considerations when dealing with organizations operating in other countries vary greatly. As a result, a PIA is useful here in determining the data privacy risks and mitigation strategies with respect to the legal or regulatory environment in which an organization operates.

Determining the Need for a PIA

To determine whether or not a PIA is required, there is a series of questions that organizations should consider when implementing a project that involves the collection or analysis of organizational data. If the organization answers "yes" to any of the below questions,[3] it is recommended that a PIA be conducted:

- Will the project involve the collection of new information about individuals?
- Will the project compel individuals to provide information about themselves?
- Will information about individuals be disclosed to organizations or people who have not previously had routine access to the information?
- Are you using information about individuals for a purpose it is not currently used for, or in a way it is not currently used?
- Does the project involve you using new technology that might be perceived as being privacy intrusive, for example, the use of biometrics or facial recognition?

---

[2] "California Online Privacy Protection Act (CalOPPA)" Education foundation. Consumer Federation of California, 29 July 2015. web, <https://consumercal.org/aboutcfc/cfc-education-foundation>.
[3] "Conducting Privacy Impact Assessments Code of Practice." Data Privacy Act. Information Commissioner's Office, Feb. 2014. Web. <https://ico.org.uk/media/for-organisations/documents/1595/pia-code-of-practice.pdf>.

- Will the project result in you making decisions or taking action against individuals in ways that can have a significant impact on them?
- Is the information about individuals of a kind particularly likely to raise privacy concerns or expectations, For example, health records, criminal records, or other information that people would consider to be private?
- Will the project require you to contact individuals in ways that they may find intrusive?

Conducting the PIA

The way in which an organization conducts the PIA can be tailored to the organization's structure and project management processes. The below steps for conducting a PIA can be considered a baseline framework for an assessment encompassing the core elements for a PIA[4]:

- **Identify the need for a PIA** – Explain the intention of the project and the impact it will have upon the organization. To address this element, organizations can use the previously mentioned questions and any project documentation (e.g., Project Management Plans) to provide the objectives and justification for the project.
- **Describe the information flows** – Describe the collection, use, and retention/deletion processes associated with personnel data that will be included in the program or project. It is recommended that the organization illustrate all systems and individuals will have access to the personnel data, potentially using process flow diagrams.
- **Outline consultation measures** – Explain what practical steps will be taken to communicate and review the identified privacy risks that emerge over the course of the project. These consultation measures can and should occur throughout the project, involve internal stakeholders (e.g., HR, Legal), and potentially involve external stakeholders (e.g., consultants).
- **Identify the privacy and other related risks** – Identify the risks to individuals and the downstream impacts to the organization (e.g., regulatory noncompliance, additional or costly business processes) associated with the collection of personnel data for the project.
- **Define risk mitigation actions** – Describe the actions that the organization can take to address the identified risks and the anticipated result of the mitigating action (e.g., risk eliminated, risk reduced).

---

[4] "Conducting Privacy Impact Assessments Code of Practice." Data Privacy Act. Information Commissioner's Office, Feb. 2014. Web. <https://ico.org.uk/media/for-organisations/documents/1595/pia-code-of-practice.pdf>.

- **Approval and recording of PIA actions** – Document the risks, approved actions, and approving party for the sake of record keeping and potential compliance adherence.
- **Integrate PIA actions with project** plan – Define the owners and timelines associated with the actions defined by the PIA. This information would ideally be captured in the existing project plan as additional actions.

Throughout the execution of the PIA, a policy review should be conducted to guide the identification of privacy issues and ensure adherence to regulations that impact the organization. Following the PIA, as part of the consultations with internal and external stakeholders, any new regulations should be reviewed to assess how the current PIA actions and overall project may need to be altered for compliance.

ADDITIONAL PRIVACY CONSIDERATIONS

Through assisting a number of organizations establish insider threat programs and conducting a series of PIAs, we have defined a number of additional considerations related to data privacy and protection that organizations should note when implementing an insider threat program.

- **Notification Procedures:** When considering what PRI information to collect, an organization should abide by the principles of transparency and proportionality. The Electronic Communications Privacy Act of 1986 (ECPA) (18 U.S.C. § 2510-22) allows employers to monitor activities on their own networks and equipment, where monitoring serves a legitimate business purpose and is conducted with employees' express or implied consent. Clearly articulating when and where an employee has an expectation of privacy is critical to protecting the organization from legal ramifications, especially in regards to monitoring electronic communications and physical movement. This can take the form of a Mandatory Acceptable Use Policy and/or Mandatory Employee Notices.

  Case Study[5]: Although several courts have upheld monitoring with no notification of a monitoring policy, lack of a monitoring policy may present difficulties later on, as courts often look to announced policies as one factor when determining privacy protections. Notification and consent fall under one of the overarching principles discussed in this

---

[5] Huth, Carly L., The insider threat and employee privacy: An overview of recent case law, *Computer Law & Security Review* 29 (2013), May 18, 2013, 368–81. (Case Study citations in text refer to original citations in article.)

article: transparency by informing employees of policies. Privacy guidelines such as the US Fair Information Principles and the APEC Framework also incorporate notice and consent into their frameworks. For example, in *Curto v. Medical World Communications*, the court held that attorney-client privilege applied to several emails retrieved from an employer-owned laptop. Whether or not the employer consistently enforced their computer usage policy was deemed a relevant consideration.

- **Required Filings with Protection Authorities:** In many countries, entities that are collecting data on individuals must comply with certain standards and data privacy frameworks at the national and international level. The EU is a particularly advanced example of this type of system with EU-level data protection bodies such as the European Data Protection Supervisor (EDPS), an independent EU body responsible for monitoring the application of data protection rules by EU institutions, and a Data Protection Officer (DPO) in every EU institution.[6] Additionally, each EU country has an identified national data protection authority. Data controllers, or those who collect and process personal data, are subject to a number of obligations as per the EU's Data Protection Directive.[7] Notably, one requirement states, "all data controllers must notify their supervisory authorities when they process personal data."[8] Although some consider the United States less protective of personal data, pieces of legislation such as the Fair Credit Reporting Act (FCRA) of 2003, Health Insurance Portability and Accountability Act (HIPAA) of 1996, Electronic Communications Privacy Act of 1986 (ECPA), and Stored Communications Act are used to both justify collection of data and defend privacy, depending on the specific context and case. Regardless, organizations must be aware of any required filing obligations and cooperate with data protection authorities as required by relevant laws.

- **Data Collection and Storage:** Understanding what information can be collected and aggregated, as well as the rules governing appropriate collection methods, access, storage requirements, and any restrictions on the duration that data can be held is an important aspect of an insider threat program and should be established in conjunction with an organization's legal counsel. For example, the Stored Communications Act (ECPA 18 U.S.C. § 2701) exempts employers

---

[6] "Data Protection Bodies." Directorate General for Justice and Consumers. European Commission, 26 Mar. 2016. Web. <http://ec.europa.eu/justice/data-protection/bodies/index_en.htm>.
[7] ibid.
[8] ibid.

from liability for accessing employee email messages stored on their computer systems.[9]

- **Investigations:** Determining how data can and should be used from an investigative perspective from a legal perspective is an important protective measure. Some data elements are more heavily protected under anti-discrimination policies whereas others may relate to articles of free speech. This is especially relevant for PRIs from social media or "dirty word" searches of employee email or messaging systems. An organization should work with in-house counsel to ensure the program comports with the organization's policies and legal requirements. The case study of *The City of Ontario v. Quon* highlights an example of collected data being used as part of an investigation.[10]

  Case Study: In *The City of Ontario v. Quon*, several SWAT team members were issued pagers that received texts. When a team member went over his prescribed limit of texts, the police department scrutinized his texts and discovered sexually explicit messages. The Court found that even if Quon had a reasonable expectation of privacy, the government employer fell within the work-related exception to the Fourth Amendment prohibition to a warrantless search. Several factors played into this decision: the employer's clear policy of auditing (which was updated to include the pagers), the employer's consideration of messages sent only during work hours, the employer searching only two months out of all the months that the pager had been used, and the fact that the employer had given the pager.

- **Program Scaling:** Restrictions on data collection and use vary by country, which can complicate scalability for multinational organizations. Such an organization may have to tailor the collection, correlation, and visualization of PRIs to the privacy restrictions and legal environment of the country the employee operates out of. Similarly, the ability for the organization to exchange data that is internal to the organization may be limited if this transaction is transnational in nature. Lastly, local counsel should be engaged in all decisions to expand insider threat programs across borders to ensure that efforts are informed by applicable data privacy laws.

- **External Data:** Currently, there are no legal restrictions on gathering publicly available information, such as that collected through social networking sites, blogs, consumer feedback, etc. Additionally, no

---

[9] Determann, Lothar, and Robert Sprague, Intrusive monitoring: employee privacy expectations are reasonable in Europe, destroyed in the United States, *Berkeley Technology Law Journal Volume* 26, Issue 2, Article 3 (March 2011), 1001.

[10] Huth, Carly L., The insider threat and employee privacy: An overview of recent case law, *Computer Law & Security Review* 29 (2013), 18 May 2013, p368–381. (Case Study citations refer to original citations in article from The City of Ontario v. Quon 130 S. Ct. 2619 [2010].)

overarching federal privacy law governs the collection and sale of personal information among private sector companies, including information resellers.[11] However, the Fair Credit Reporting Act FCRA limits resellers' use and distribution of personal data—for example, by allowing consumers to opt out of allowing consumer reporting agencies to share their personal information with third parties for prescreened marketing offers.[12] Organizations should consider establishing a "trigger" where external data are only pursued once an individual's risk reaches a certain point to mitigate the risk associated with continuous collection.

- **Social Media:** Among the various external data types, social media data can be considered especially sensitive. It represents one of the largest sources of external data about an individual and due to its relative nascence, employers, legislators, and employees are still working to understand the implications, uses, and misuses of these data. The *New York Law Journal* notes that "while some state and federal laws prohibit using certain types of information as noted above, there are no federal laws that protect an employee from an employer's use and abuse of information that is not related to employment and was intended as a recreational activity, such as social media communications. Some states, including Maryland and California, have prohibited employers from requiring or requesting their employees or job applicants to provide social media or password-protected websites."[13] The issue of social media can be further complicated as employees frequently use employer-provided hardware and networks to access, post, and download information from social media sites.

CONCLUSION

Collecting data on employee's actions is the bedrock of an insider threat program. As a result, data privacy safeguards are "must-haves" for successful insider threat mitigation programs. An organization must be informed on the relationship between information collection and legal and privacy issues to determine where issues fall on the data privacy continuum. Identifying potential insiders is important, but equally important is ensuring that the manner in which the insider was identified is appropriate and reasonable within the regulatory environment. The complex legal and organizational

---

[11] Government Accountability Office, Information Resellers: Consumer Privacy Framework Needs to Reflect Changes in Technology and the Marketplace (September 2013).
[12] GAO, ibid.
[13] Lazar, Wendi S., "1984" in 2015: Protecting Employees' Social Media From Misuse; Employees in the Workplace, *New York Law Journal* (Online), July 7, 2015.

impacts of data collection beget the need for consultation with legal counsel and insider threat experts.

KEY TAKEAWAYS

- An organization should understand the relationship between information collection and legal and privacy issues.
- As organizations mature in their capabilities and ingest a more holistic set of PRIs, the data privacy requirements and regular engagement with the organization's legal council should increase.
- It is critical that organizations take steps to protect the employee data collected in the analysis of PRIs to maintain the insider threat program's support and participation from the workforce, as well as compliance with federal, state, and organizational regulations and legal requirements.
- The information documented in a Privacy Impact Assessment informs the level and type of legal and privacy coordination needed to protect the organization from potential legal action. The PIA will help ensure that the insider threat program comports with the necessary legal requirements in the State or jurisdiction the organization operates in.

CHAPTER 15

What the Future Holds

INSIDER THREAT: A LOOK FORWARD

In the past few decades, insider tactics have evolved from "dead dropping" small packages of classified information to the use of removable media and other computer technology to extract terabytes of data. As technological change continues to facilitate workforce mobility and productivity, it also exposes organizations to emerging risks. This chapter highlights risks from insider threats that are likely to emerge in the next five years, and the technological, socio-economic, and political context that is likely to enable them.

The previous chapters provide an actionable roadmap for developing a program to effectively manage insider threats. But what does the future of the insider threat look like? How does an organization effectively prepare to manage the new threats posed by a rapidly evolving world? What additional information from public source data will become common place in an insider threat program in the future? Looking ahead, what scenarios should cause the most concern for organizations?

This chapter explores the future of the insider threat and discusses the trends, changes, and potential scenarios for which organizations must prepare to prevent insider-based attacks. While it is impossible to predict what the future holds, these scenarios reveal emerging trends to help organizations stay ahead of evolving threats. Organizations must adapt their insider threat management practices to manage risk effectively.

THE CHANGING DEFINITION OF INSIDER

> The disproportionate attention and resources given to outsiders understates the current response to the insider threat, even though the financial implications may be considerable.
>
> **David Wall, Symantec**

Insider Threat. DOI: http://dx.doi.org/10.1016/B978-0-12-802410-2.00015-0

The insider threat from careless or complacent employees and contractors exceeds the threat from malicious insiders (though the latter is not negligible). . . . This is partially, though not totally, due to the fact that careless or complacent insiders often unintentionally help nefarious outsiders.

U.S. Security Expert Johnston[1]

Previous chapters have defined an insider as an employee of an organization who has the potential—out of greed, malice, ignorance, or complacency—to wittingly or unwittingly exploit his access to proprietary information. As the economy becomes increasingly interdependent, however, the definition of an insider should expand beyond those employed directly by an organization. The increasing prevalence of outsourcing and subcontracting, and even the modest and predicable growth of business-to-business enterprises, open the door to a secondary layer of insiders. These insiders have access to a company's information and networks, but can lack loyalty to organizational values and norms. Furthermore, in some instances, their online actions may be unmonitorable. The definition of insider must expand beyond the traditional employee to include any individual who has access to a company's proprietary information networks or facilities.

For example, the rise of the shared economy poses an emerging threat to organizations and the individuals who have access to the organizations' information and networks. If an individual has access to an employee's belongings—his car (GetAround), apartment (AirBnB), or lifestyle (TaskRabbit)—it becomes easier to access that employee's information through online means or social engineering. Moreover, the insider of the future is anyone who services a company and has access to the knowledge and technology of an employee.

UNDERSTANDING THE MACRO ENVIRONMENT

It is important to recognize that both future insider activity and an organization's mitigation strategies will be increasingly driven by factors largely outside of organizational control. To plan for future insider activities, organizations should work to expand their enterprise risk profile and continually reevaluate associated contextual factors.

Impact of Economic Downturns

An economic downturn, though largely unpredictable, significantly increases an employee's likelihood to engage in behavior that can harm an

---

[1] Bunn, Matthew, and Scott D. Sagan. *A Worst Practices Guide to Insider Threats: Lessons from Past Mistakes* (Cambridge: American Academy of Arts & Sciences, 2014). Print.

organization. The recent Great Recession highlights how economic down-turns can significantly increase the risk of insider activity. Job uncertainty, layoffs, and other financial strains can create the motivations to engage in harmful insider behavior. Similarly, shrinking margins and budgets caused by economic turmoil can lead managers to reduce investment in security measures that are critical to insider threat mitigation.

Privacy Expectations

Unlike preceding generations, individuals today are more willing to share personal information on the Internet. Understanding the current workforce and how it reacts to technology enables organizations to anticipate the future threat environment. Many joining the workforce today were born into the digital age and understand technology as if it were their native language. The prevalence of social networking and online information sharing, however, may expose organizations to increased risk of ignorant or complacent insider activity.

Many Millennials are comfortable sharing information online and have less concern over privacy and the boundaries of what should and should not be shared than their parents' or grandparents' generations. They are typically comfortable and trusting with technology, and often opt out of the controls that are popular among earlier generations (i.e., passcodes, locks, and innate restraints against sharing too much). As more Millennials enter the work-force, changing privacy expectations may inadvertently expose organizations to additional risk of insider events.

Policy Implications

As instances of government spying or companies use of individuals' personal information for financial gain come to light, how will this affect laws and public opinion regarding privacy? Where will opinion and legislation fall on a spectrum with monitoring at one end, and privacy rights at the other? Unless a massive societal event alters the spectrum, it is plausible to assume that there will be an increase in public support for legal protection against monitoring by private and public entities. Technology that allows users to search and conduct online activities without being traced are already in use and will continue to be incorporated into mainstream devices. A number of major telecommunications and electronics conglomerates have already begun encrypting communications on their devices and channels to limit government snooping (Figure 15.1).

These technologies, coupled with new laws, could make data collection and monitoring more difficult, and limit progress on the development of cutting-edge insider threat mitigation strategies, such as insider threat analytics.

FIGURE 15.1
Locked Out.

EMERGING TRENDS

As organizations enhance security spending budgets and implement more advanced systems, attacker threat vectors will continue to evolve. Organizations lacking an adequate level of preparedness will be targeted by hostile actors and easily victimized. As recent cyber-attacks in the entertainment industry illustrate, internal networks and data are even more vulnerable to external attacks if an attacker has inside knowledge of the processes, codes, people, or procedures protecting it.

Targeting Employees

Moving forward, employees who do not see themselves as targets, appreciate the importance of security measures, or lack training in the value of the information to which they have access, may pose a more significant threat to organizations than ever before. According to Joel Brenner, former NSA Inspector General and author of *America the Vulnerable*, "technical capabilities that a decade or two ago could be found only in advanced military aircraft-GPS, for example, now come standard in your rental car and can be bought at RadioShack for a few bucks. Computing capacity greater than governments could muster during the Cold War now resides in mobile devices that fit in a pocket."[2] These innovations help to make workers more productive, but also increase the potential risk to organizations from a data leak.

Global competitors, foreign governments, and external attackers will also continue to manipulate unwitting employees to access information or infiltrate a system. This trend is illustrated by the increase in the overall number of insider breaches. Interestingly, the percentage of nonmalicious, insider–driven breaches is increasing whereas the number of malicious driven acts is decreasing (Organizational Security and the Insider Threat: Malicious, Negligent and Well-Meaning Insiders). A study by Carnegie Mellon University CERT revealed that about a quarter of insiders in one particular study were recruited by an outsider who had targeted the data, and around 20% of data thefts involved the collaboration of another insider. This trend reinforces the importance of behavioral monitoring and a holistic insider threat program, because it forces companies to identify employees who demonstrate traits that would increase susceptibility to targeting.

Protecting the Entire Value-Chain

Globalization has led to the increased integration of economic activities across space, time, and political boundaries.[3] This phenomenon has generated remarkable economic growth across the globe and enhanced the power of nonstate actors, including corporations. Although most corporations value globalization for the profits and market growth it has provided, it has also made them more vulnerable to attack. Jesse Goldhammer, Associate Dean at U.C. Berkeley's School of Information and coauthor of *Deviant Globalization*, believes this phenomena is in "the process of changing the landscape and distribution of power in the world economy." Gaps in security widen as corporations expand operations globally; the workforce becomes more mobile, and supply chains become more integrated with multiple users. One example of this shift is the recent Target Corporation retail data breach, in which attackers leveraged a small HVAC contractor to ultimately breach all of Target's systems. The fallout of this breach cost the company billions in fees, claims, upgrades, depressed earnings, and leadership turnover.

---

[2] Brenner, Joel. *America the Vulnerable: Inside the New Threat Matrix of Digital Espionage, Crime, and Warfare* (New York: Penguin, 2011). Print.

[3] Gilman, Nils, Jesse Goldhammer, and Steve Weber. *Deviant Globalization: Black Market Economy in the 21st Century* (New York: Continuum, 2011). Print.

In spite of these risks, commercial and government enterprises will undoubtedly continue to expand into developing markets, acquire smaller firms, and encourage global cooperation. Although these are laudable business objectives, they require proper security controls to mitigate risk and protect the organization's most critical assets. Organizations that neglect their entire value-chain and only work to protect themselves will still be vulnerable to insider attacks.

Another obstacle organizations will face as a result of globalization is trying to maintain security and protect assets while navigating different privacy laws across borders. From an insider threat program perspective, this is a significant challenge and requires deft operational control to maintain access to the most critical indicators that detect risky behavior. In the future, mature insider threat programs will devise methods and leverage expertise to efficiently manage this growing challenging.

The Virtual Environment

In the future organizations will continue to unveil new corporate offices with "open-space" plans, "bring your own device" (BYOD) policies, virtual working arrangements, and file-sharing and cloud service operations. All of these efforts are designed to increase integration across offices and entities as well as enhance business processes and productivity. Organizations that facilitate convenience and work–life balance for their employees will permit the use of personal tablets for business purposes and a variety of virtual work arrangements. Although these changes have the potential to increase job satisfaction and worker productivity, they provide new challenges for security managers. Personal devices that are not secured using organizational IT protocols will leave proprietary data susceptible to attack. When an employee leaves an organization, it will be difficult to ensure his personal device is properly cleared of all sensitive information. Personal devices also make monitoring virtual activity very difficult, as they are not part of an organization's network. Despite the convenience and low cost of BYOD, organizations must make a detailed risk assessment to ensure that its "crown jewels" are not needlessly accessible.

Other security protocols can also help organizations balance between security and mobility. Studies from CERT demonstrate that insiders typically act when they believe they will not be caught because an organization lacks controls.[4]

---

[4] Cappelli, Dawn M., Andrew P. Moore, and Randall F. Trzeciak, *The CERT Guide to Insider Threats: How to Prevent, Detect, and Respond to Information Technology Crimes* (Upper Saddle River, NJ: Addison-Wesley Professional, 2012).

Personal devices that are not monitored by the organization or subject to security audits undermine this deterrent. Organizations that employ and promote the use of a virtual private network (VPN) can mitigate some of these risks of mobile technology. Monitoring is the mechanism that enables an organization to observe behavior and thus let employees know that behavior is observable in virtual spaces.

BIG DATA AND RISK ANALYTICS

Although technology is enabling insiders to more easily extract data and inflict significant harm on critical assets (e.g., sabotage), it also provides more advanced solutions to counter threats. Security technology (e.g., DLP, SIEM, IDS, and IAM) helps organizations to better understand the risks they face in real time. In addition to these capabilities, the rise of user-based analytics tools have also provided a new opportunity for prevention and detection. Advanced analytics systems built for the sole purpose of insider threat monitoring are coming into the marketplace and appealing to C-suite executives. These tools will need to become smarter and scalable for the largest multinational organizations. Increased focus on behavioral studies and updates to risk scoring algorithms will only enhance the accuracy and scope of these tools.

SCENARIO PLANNING

In the future, the scalability and accuracy of insider threat detection tools will improve as technical sophistication grows. The critical question, however, is how will organizations use these tools and will they be able to legally monitor all of the key risk indicators. To explore this question, we have plotted each of the following four scenarios in Figure 15.2.

> Changes in technology and privacy protections could alter the insider dynamic.

Scenario 1.0: Nearsighted/Farsighted

In this scenario, there are lots of data solutions available, all of which are imperfect because of privacy protections and other regulations. As public opinion clamors for greater protection and large-scale breaches continue to happen there is potential for governments to aggressively fight data aggregation and monitoring, thereby limiting the use of analytic tools to detect

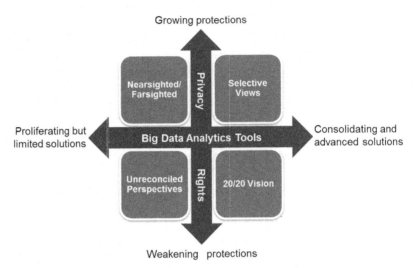

FIGURE 15.2
Scenario 1.

risky behaviors. In this scenario, malicious insiders become more common and destructive, while external actors actively recruit complacent insiders to exploit vulnerabilities. To effectively counter this scenario, organizations must find new ways to baseline risky behaviors and define new processes to carefully adhere to compliance guidelines.

Scenario 2.0: Selective Views

In this scenario, technology becomes much more powerful and has expansive capabilities to detect behavior (Figure 15.3). Yet, despite this increased capability, the use of analytics is limited by stringent privacy protections. As a result, data collection is limited and opportunities abound for complacent and malicious insiders. There is little fear of detection because it is well understood that monitoring is limited to a very small set of indicators. As a result, organizations leverage enhanced technical controls, invest in training, and utilize advanced technical tools to collect what data is permitted.

Scenario 3.0: Unreconciled Perspectives

In this scenario, privacy protections are limited and data solutions remain highly imperfect and scattered. Malicious insiders become a more significant threat than complacent insiders, because the latter can be monitored, if ineffectually. Organizations increase manpower and training investments to monitor disparate tools and curb complacent insiders.

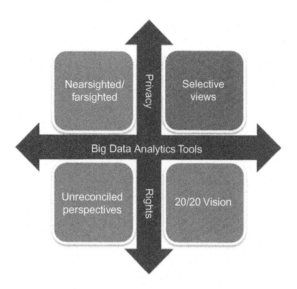

FIGURE 15.3
Scenario 2.

Scenario 4.0: 20/20 Vision

In this scenario, real-time insider threat mitigation capabilities become available and operate at scale. As a result of the ability to quickly identify malicious insiders, the focus shifts to external actors who recruit complacent insiders. To effectively manage this type of insider threat, organizations make significant insider technology investments accompanied by process changes to improve their return on investment and enhance safeguards.

WHAT'S NEXT?

The future is fundamentally forecasting advances in technology, or the regulatory burdens that may impact them, is a difficult task. By using scenario planning exercises, organization can begin thinking beyond the conventional wisdom to imagine new and more effective ways to mitigate insider threats. In the future, the use of insiders to access information will grow, exposing organizations to additional risks. Those enterprises that are most prepared will utilize the best strategies and technologies available to leverage the power of big data analytics. Because an organization's risk will never be zero, the key is to find the most efficient and effective way to manage residual risk.

Appendices

An insider threat program's ability to detect threats is based on the collection of potential risk indicators (PRIs). The table below includes 25 PRIs, including attributes and behaviors across three key categories: virtual, nonvirtual, and contextual.

Appendix A: What data is needed to proactively identify potential insiders?

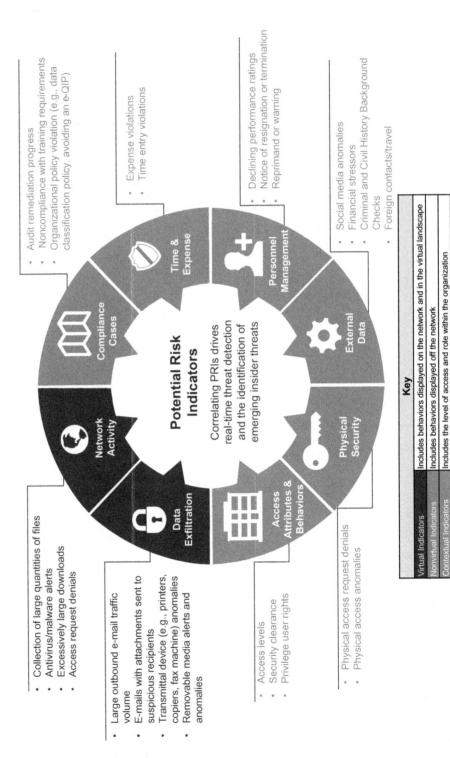

- Collection of large quantities of files
- Antivirus/malware alerts
- Excessively large downloads
- Access request denials

- Large outbound e-mail traffic volume
- E-mails with attachments sent to suspicious recipients
- Transmittal device (e.g., printers, copiers, fax machine) anomalies
- Removable media alerts and anomalies

- Access levels
- Security clearance
- Privilege user rights

- Physical access request denials
- Physical access anomalies

- Audit remediation progress
- Noncompliance with training requirements
- Organizational policy violation (e.g., data classification policy, avoiding an e-QIP)

- Expense violations
- Time entry violations

- Declining performance ratings
- Notice of resignation or termination
- Reprimand or warning

- Social media anomalies
- Financial stressors
- Criminal and Civil History Background Checks
- Foreign contacts/travel

Potential Risk Indicators

Correlating PRIs drives real-time threat detection and the identification of emerging insider threats

Compliance Cases
Time & Expense
Personnel Management
External Data
Physical Security
Access Attributes & Behaviors
Data Exfiltration
Network Activity

Key	
Virtual Indicators	Includes behaviors displayed on the network and in the virtual landscape
Nonvirtual Indicators	Includes behaviors displayed off the network
Contextual Indicators	Includes the level of access and role within the organization

The following tables represent a sample set of potential risk indicators. The indicators were down-selected from an initial set of more than 100 PRIs through analysis of relevant insider threat cases.*

Appendix B: Potential risk indicators

Access
Multiple failed log-in attempts
Deviations from clearance/access level; undue access requests on the network
Failed physical access attempt
Request for lost uniform
Request for lost (SIDA) badge
Security clearance Level
Position sensitivity level
Administrative rights or privilege user level
Physical security access level (e.g., SCIF)

Communication
Keyword alerts (e.g., e-mail, instant message, etc.)
Outgoing e-mail to suspicious sources (e.g., foreign government)
Unauthorized/excessive overseas calls

Network Activity
Plugging in unapproved devices
Deviations from baseline activity
Unusual VPN log activity
Data loss prevention (DLP) alert
Excessive downloads
Malware alerts
Printing log alerts
Attempts to access restricted sites

Conduct (Outside of Work)
Unreported criminal event
Previous misconduct
Arrests
Reported DUIs
Foreign travel
Foreign contacts

Internal Conduct
Suspicious incident report
Adverse action (e.g., suspension)
Destruction of property
Falsifying data
Sexual harassment incident
Theft (property or public property) incident
Workplace violence incident
Associating with suspicious parties

Employee Work Schedule
Excessive/unexplained absenteeism
Frequent sick leave
Late work arrivals
Unusual work patterns (e.g., comes into work during off shift)

Finance
Unexplained wealth
Excessive debt

Performance
Negative response to review
Historical poor performance ratings
Promotion passed over/demotion
Staffed during failure of performance management field test
Frequent position/airport transfers
Noncompliance (e.g., training)
Notice of termination

Employee Status
Employee unique ID
Employment status
Geographic location
Airport code
Position level
Tenure

Citizenship
Country of citizenship
Dual status

*The PRIs listed are only a sample representative and do not represent the full scope of those available.

The following core principles can help leadership proactively address common concerns and effectively communicate insider program benefits to the workforce.

Appendix C: How do i position an insider threat program to my workforce?

Core Principles

Employee Well-being

Insider threat program will align to the organization's culture and seek to ensure that employees and contractors can trust one another. Program has built in mechanisms for employee support, where needed (e.g., Employee Assistance Program)

Balanced Approach

Too many security restrictions can impede an organization's mission and agile workforce, while having too few increases vulnerabilities. Program will strike a balance between countering the threat and conducting business

Brand Protection

To protect the business and maintain organization's reputation, implement technologies, policies, and procedures that go beyond satisfying baseline requirements. Employees will benefit from a strong brand in the marketplace

Privacy Protection

Leadership is committed to protecting employee privacy and will continuously strive to improve privacy controls. Routine, semiannual evaluations of the insider threat program will address evolving threats and reinforce program compliance with legal policy

Risk-based Monitoring

As the perceived risk of an insider threat incident increases as a result of the detection of contextual, virtual, and nonvirtual precursors, the amount of monitoring should also increase

Critical Assets

Insider program is designed to protect critical assets: people, data, etc.; without these protections, the business could be at risk if there is an incident

An effective insider threat program employs staff with a well-rounded set of skills across a variety of organizational functions (Human Resources, Security, Law Enforcement, Information Technology, Counterintelligence, etc.). The organization should have these skill sets — some will reside within the program and some will be in separate functions that will interact with the program.

Appendix D: What are the skill sets that a leading program needs to have?

National Insider Threat Policy (NITP)*
Staffing Recommendations

The NITP outlines five key areas that insider threat personnel should be trained in:

1. Counterintelligence and security fundamentals to include applicable legal issues.

2. Agency procedures for conducting insider threat response action(s).

3. Applicable laws and regulations regarding the gathering, integration, retention, safeguarding, and use of records and data, including the consequences of misuse of such information.

4. Applicable civil liberties and privacy laws, regulations, and policies.

5. Investigative referral requirements of Section 811 of the Intelligence Authorization Act for FY 1995, as well as other policy or statutory requirements that require referrals to an internal entity, such as a security office or Office of Inspector General, or external investigative entities such as the Federal Bureau of Investigation, the Department of Justice, or military investigative services.

In order to enhance an insider threat program, the following skill sets are recommended:

 Privacy Specialist: Provide subject matter expertise for legal issues that organizations need to consider when standing up and maintaining the program.

 Data Scientist: Conduct correlation and analysis of risk indicators to detect anomalous behavior on the network, as well as visualize employee risk trends over time using analytics dashboards.

Psychologist: Provide input on employee attitudes or behaviors and provide analysis on behavioral indicators.

Social Media Expert: Gather relevant data from a variety of social media outlets to use for insider threat detection.

Policy Specialist: Provide subject matter expertise on relevant insider threat policies and provide guidance on how to educate executives, managers, and employees on policy adherence.

*National Insider Threat Policy, Office of the National Counterintelligence Executive, http://fas.org/sgp/obama/insider.pdf

The core components associated with foundational and advanced insider threat programs vary. Organizations seeking to mature their program will establish foundational components first and progress toward advancement over time.

Appendix E: What capabilities differentiate an industry-leading program?

Foundational Program Attributes

Coordinated

The program should have one owner but a broad set of invested stakeholders* that can serve as change agents and ensure organizational buy-in across departments. Response procedures are well defined and codified.

Holistic

Includes the development of business processes, policies, technology, controls, training, and organizational change components. Program components include prevention, detection, and response capabilities.

Risk-Based

Employee risk levels are based on the collection, correlation, and visualization of PRIs which allows the organization to take a proactive and risk-based approach to mitigating emerging insider threats.

Proactive

Risk-mitigation strategies are developed to allow for proactive threat detection that can stop or disrupt an emerging insider threat. The program's emphasis is on prevention but includes robust detection and response capabilities.

Advanced Program Attributes

Continuous Improvement is incorporated throughout the program's operations. Randomized testing of new PRIs, simulated tests (red teaming) to evaluate detection capabilities, and development of feedback loops to manage program effectiveness.

Behavior Change is a programmatic goal and includes approaches to improve compliance with business processes and policies through targeted outreach.

Return on Investment is captured through the quantification of metrics including number of business processes improvements, policy enhancements, technical control updates, cases initiated, documents retrieved, and law enforcement referrals.

Proactive Outreach includes proactive initiatives such as Employee Assistance Programs (EAPs) designed to provide counseling and outreach to individuals that may be at increased risk for committing an insider threat act.

There are different organizational components that are essential for the governance structure of insider threat programs.

Appendix F: Insider threat program governance structure

Governance Structure

Consistent coordination with key Organization X stakeholders is critical to the success of the insider threat program and the ability to identify potential insider threats in a proactive manner. The following governance components have been established to guide and inform the project:

Global Risk Compliance Council
Provides strategic oversight and ultimate authority

Executive Steering Committee
Ensures program alignment and provides oversight

Insider Threat Working Group
Provides routine engagement and oversight

Global Security
Coordinates across the key stakeholders and operates the program

Organization X Investigative Resources
Responds to leads and provides mitigating actions

Algorithm Working Group
Manage updates to the risk algorithm based on historical and ongoing cases

Vendor
Provides system support for the analytics capability

CHAPTER 5

The following charter is a sample document for use in standing up an Insider Threat Working Group (ITWG).

APPENDIX G: BUSINESS ASSURANCE/ INSIDER THREAT WORKING GROUP CHARTER

Introduction

The Organization X Business Assurance/Insider Threat[1] Working Group (ITWG) brings together multidisciplinary stakeholders from across key components of Organization X to assist Office X and the Office Y to develop a robust insider threat program capable of mitigating insider threats. The ITWG will assist in defining Organization X's critical assets, identifying existing and future capabilities to mitigate risk and vulnerabilities, and serve as agents of change for transitioning Organization X to the future state of insider threat mitigation in support of corporate business objectives.

Phase I Project Background

Phase I of the project provided a 12-week assessment of aspects of Organization X, and Office X. The insider threat team worked with Organization X stakeholders to execute an additive, three-tiered project assessment that provided a current state assessment, a future state gap analysis, and the development of an actionable roadmap. The roadmap prioritized recommendations and provided the foundation for transitioning to the envisioned state of insider threat mitigation capable of protecting Organization X's sensitive U.S. government information/programs, intellectual property, and people. Recommended steps included IT solutions, security awareness training, business processes improvement, and policy creation.

Phase II Project Objectives

The objective of Phase II is to move forward with the assessment recommendations and roadmap developed in Phase I. Specifically, the team will develop a Concept of Operations (CONOPs) document outlining how the Insider Threat program will operate, the governance structures, and their roles and responsibilities and outline the use of an advanced analytics tool within

---

[1] Insider threat is a specific, intentional violation associated with an employee or contractor who has a trusted and verified position and access within the company and not solely the result of actions conducted by external agents or threat actors. Insider threat refers to acts by insiders to commit information technology sabotage, data or information theft, fraud, or espionage that could potentially jeopardize the company's competitive advantage, business continuity, financial standing, brand reputation, and employee or customer safety.

Organization X. The team will conduct a review of commercial analytics tools capable of scaling across Organization X's workforce and able to satisfy ITWG requirements. Additionally, in coordination with the ITWG, key systems and data elements will be identified for use within the advanced analytics prototype that will be developed in the next phase of the project.

Roles and Responsibilities

The ITWG will represent key stakeholders and Organization X leadership whose involvement and support in the development of an insider threat program are critical for project success. The ITWG's primary purpose is to

- validate outputs and ensure key executives are informed and committed to the development of an insider threat program
- ensure roadblocks are addressed and risks properly mitigated
- attend meetings and come prepared to provide input, address issues, and share knowledge
- serve as advisors and agents of change for transitioning to the validated, future state of insider threat mitigation

Membership

Member	Position	Office

Authority

The ITWG shall have authority over the project and key decisions. To promote consensus, the ITWG process requires members to consider legitimate views, proposals, objections, and endeavors to reconcile them. When unanimity is not possible, the ITWG will agree on final decisions supported by the available evidence.

Communication

The ITWG will meet at least three times during the 8-week project, or as needed to discuss progress, address issues and risks, and agree on next steps. Meeting coordination will be administered by an insider threat team representative and held at a convenient location for ITWG members. If Working Group members are unable to attend, they may elect to send delegates to meetings in their stead.

The model below displays different levels of program maturity across organizational components that are essential for insider threat programs. The criteria included in the model is meant to be thematic in nature, rather than comprehensive, and each stage of the maturity model builds on the previous stage's criteria.

Appendix H: How do i assess the maturity of my insider threat program?

Many organizations are in Stages 1 and 2 of the maturity model.

Stage 1:
Initial / Ad Hoc

- **ITWG:** Purely reactive posture with limited to no coordination
- **Program Foundation:** No standardized threat mitigation processes, training or policy
- **Advanced Analytics:** PRIs are not collected or standardized

Stage 2:
Repeatable but Intuitive

- **ITWG:** Coordination across key functions exists but not formal or routine
- **Program Foundation:** Limited business processes, policies, formal training, and communication of procedures
- **Advanced Analytics:** Early stages of developing a collection, correlation, and visualization capability

Stage 3:
Defined Process

- **ITWG:** Established and meets periodically with the core group of stakeholders
- **Program Foundation:** Baseline business processes, training and standardized policies in place; limited communication and enforcement on insider threat mitigation
- **Advanced Analytics:** Initial capability including a limited subset of data and workforce population

Stage 4:
Managed and Measurable

- **ITWG:** Meet routinely, have executive buy-in and deliver recommendations
- **Program Foundation:** Majority of business processes including segregation of duties, least privilege, training and awareness, and physical and logical programs in place
- **Advanced Analytics:** Virtual, nonvirtual, and contextual risk indicators are collected and analyzed generating leads
- **Escalation and Triage:** Clear and defined

Stage 5:
Optimized

- **ITWG:** Coordinate changes across key functions and serve as agents for change
- **Program Foundation:** Satisfy all leading practices for segregation of duties, least privilege, access control, network controls, physical controls, training, hiring, vetting. Built in continuous improvement mechanisms
- **Advanced Analytics:** Provide the full scope of peer-based and individual baselines, network controls, and alerts; routine monitoring
- **Escalation and Triage:** Robust processes that are routinely evaluated and tested

APPENDIX I: BUSINESS RULE DEVELOPMENT

The methodology for managing rules is designed to obtain the proper validation from personnel within the Insider Threat Working Group (ITWG) before implementing business rules. The methodology spans from discovery to ongoing rule analysis by using an agile and iterative approach. Activities fall into the four steps outlined below:

1. **Business Rule Discovery & Refinement** – Includes designated ITWG members working with system developers to evaluate existing rules and capture suggestions on new rules for consideration. The cross-functional and multidisciplinary ITWG members meet on a reoccurring basis to examine the business rule engine and modify and adjust the scoring methodology according to Organization X's risk threshold, priorities, and the need to manage false positives.
2. **Business Rule Validation** – Involves designated personnel on the ITWG across legal, ethics, and privacy sign-off on new business rules and potential risk indicators (PRIs). Business rule validation is a reoccurring agenda item for ITWG discussions and a means to improve the scoring methodology and recalibrate false positives.
3. **Business Rule Design, Authoring and Deployment** – Includes the programing and development of new rules as well as the modification and existing rules based on direction from the ITWG.
4. **Business Rule Analysis** – Includes reports on false positives and the recalibration of rules to provide manageable and timely outputs of risk levels associated with internal threats. Rule analysis factors in business process changes and operational shifts that may impact the utility of business rules.

The tables below list sample policies requisite for an insider threat program and the imperatives for evaluating current or drafting new policies, respectively.

Appendix J: How do i address insider threat from a policy and training perspective?

	Policy / Agreement	Description
1.	Acceptable Use Agreement Policy	Provides guidelines on the acceptable use (e.g., describes the employee's roles and responsibilities when using the organization's information systems).
2.	Account Management Policies	Provides policies that identify how accounts are created, reviewed, and terminated and should address who authorizes the account and what data they can access.
3.	Cloud Computing Policy	Provides guidelines on cloud computing services and safeguards that will prevent employees from data exfiltration and provides guidance on how to restrict and/or monitor what employees put into the cloud.
4.	Employee Assistance Program (EAP) Policy	Provides Company X employees with counseling and other options for coping with issues from external factors, including financial and personal stressors.
5.	Data Transfer Policy	Provides guidelines on appropriate data transfer procedures that will allow sensitive Company X information to be removed from organizational systems only in a controlled way.
6.	Information Classification Policy	Provides guidelines on what constitutes different types of Company X information, how they can and cannot be shared, handled, and stored.
7.	Intellectual Property Agreements (i.e., Employer Agreements)	Outlines what constitutes IP and the consequences for taking it. The use of such clauses is premised on the possibility that upon termination or resignation, an employee might begin working for a competitor or starting a business, and gain competitive advantage by exploiting confidential information about Company X's operations, trade secrets, sensitive information.
8.	Least Privilege Policy	Provides guidelines that require individuals to only have access to the data and systems needed to perform their duties. Ensures that access is evaluated when employees move throughout the organization (i.e., promotions, transfers, relocations, and demotions).
9.	Log Management Policy	Provides guidelines for addressing log retention (i.e., consult legal counsel for specific requirements), what event logs to collect, which key systems are included, and who manages the logging systems.
10.	Mobile Device Policy	Provides guidelines on how mobile devices can and cannot be used in the workplace. Outlines the necessary protocols to prevent mobile devices from being used as mass storage/removable media and includes protections to mitigate any risks associated with them.
11.	Non-Disclosure Agreements	All employees, contractors, and trusted business partners sign NDAs upon hiring and termination of employment or contracts.
12.	Password Policy	Provides guidelines regarding accounts and passwords. For example, these policies should state that account information should not be shared with anyone outside of the organization, and violations of the policy must be handled accordingly.
13.	Removable Media Policy	Provides guidelines regarding how Company X will track documents copied to removable media (common removable media types were USB devices, CDs, and removable hard drives).
14.	Social Media Policy	Provides guidelines that address what is and is not acceptable employee participation in social media sites. For example, a policy prohibiting the posting of company projects or even company affiliations may be appropriate because social engineers or competitor could use this information to their advantage.
15.	Separation of Duties Policy	Provides guidelines on the separation of duties leading practices for privileged functions (i.e., require at least two people to perform critical actions, administrators should have no control over the auditing function, and disable system access to former privileged users.)

This use case includes a malicious employee who purposely seeks to cause harm to the firm by exfiltrating data for financial gain and new employment.

Appendix K: Use case: e-mail exfiltration

John Doe	Use Case: Exfiltration Through Email
Case Summary	*John Doe is a contractor that works for a large multinational in India. He received declining performance reviews for the past three years and John has become increasingly disgruntled. A supervisor becomes concerned that John is disgruntled to the point that he may want to retaliate against the organization, but the supervisor does not know how to report or log this concern. John begins interviewing with other employers. He takes short trips to nearby foreign countries (e.g., Bangladesh) to interview with competitors. John uses his access to look for information that he can take to give him a competitive advantage. His search through company systems yields no alerts. John submits a request to access a sensitive pricing database that is not required in the performance of his duties. His access request is denied but is not evaluated in a broader context. After his access denial, John puts in his two-week notice. In his final two weeks, John is able to obtain sensitive data interpretations of markets and contract bids. He uses an administrative ID to change the permission levels on restricted folders to access data with his regularly used ID. This data is e-mailed to his personal e-mail address in a series of emails, each below 10 MB. In his exit interview, he expresses that the company will "regret how they treated him," referring to his perceived low pay, performance ratings, and negative interactions with his supervisor. Despite this, no action is taken to assess his network activity after John separates. John is able to covertly exfiltrate approximately 20 MB of highly sensitive business information.*
Exhibited PRIs	<ul><li>Contractor with high level of access and privileged user rights</li><li>Located in a country with a high risk of competitive intelligence due to a high volume of closely located competitors</li><li>Historically declining performance</li><li>Work-related dispute; supervisor notices John is highly disgruntled</li><li>Short trips to foreign countries for unexplained reasons</li><li>Attempts to access data outside of the scope of his duties</li><li>Concerning sentiment expressed in exit interview</li><li>E-mail anomalies with attachments to personal webmail</li></ul>

This use case focuses on a privileged-access employee, working in a competitive market, who commits malicious acts in order to secure new employment. The primary means of exfiltration is an approved removable media device.

Use case: Removable media

John Doe

Use Case: Exfiltration Through Removable Media

Case Summary

John Doe is a domain administrator who works for a large technology company at an office in Brazil. As a domain administrator, he was granted an exception to use an approved removable media device. He received an unexpected poor performance rating and has been placed on a Performance Improvement Plan (PIP). A few weeks later, John begins to research competitor websites from his company laptop. John decides he is going to leave the organization. John accesses the network remotely and late at night through VPN and begins to transfer pricing data, mergers and acquisitions data, and other sensitive documents associated with restricted data to an approved thumb drive inserted into a USB port in his organization's machine. He explores the shared drive and other databases to see if there is information he can take to a competitor in exchange for a higher-paying position. In total, John is able to exfiltrate 50 GB of data through e-mail and removable media without detection.

Exhibited PRIs

- High level of access with privileged user rights, including exceptions for removable media usage
- Located in a country with a high risk of competitive intelligence due to a high volume of closely located competitors
- Poor performance rating and PIP
- Web activity associated with potential competitive preference
- Unusual work hours
- VPN baseline anomalies including time and bandwidth consumed
- Exfiltration through removable media

This use case focuses on a privileged access employee who coordinates with another privileged access employee to exfiltrate data for financial gain and new employment.

Use case: Transmittal device and FTP

John Doe

Use Case: Exfiltration Through Transmittal Device and FTP

Case Summary

John Doe is a Linux Administrator who works for a large energy company in Papua New Guinea. He has access to a variety of upstream data as part of his administrator functions. He is going through a divorce and is dissatisfied with his career and professional achievement. He has recently encountered mounting debt and is in a worsening financial situation. John files for bankruptcy. John is approached by a competitor that knows the type of data he has access to based on his LinkedIn profile. The competitor, a small oil and gas company, offers him significantly more than he makes with his current company if he is able to bring certain information with him. John reaches out to one of his friends, Jane Doe, and recruits her for the opportunity to come with him to the competitor for a similarly higher pay. Jane is part of the tech service and supports the help desk function as a security administrator. Together John and Jane identify seismic, leasing, and drilling data that they plan to exfiltrate. They use corporate communications (i.e., company e-mail) to discuss their plans. John begins to print documents as he suspects nobody is monitoring transmittal devices. He also uses FTP to transfer the documents outside of the company network. Jane grants herself administrator access to a number of systems without a ticket and without going through the approval process because of her role as a security administrator. In doing so, Jane is able to get root access to high-risk applications that house restricted documents. She begins to transfer the documents through an approved cloud sharing portal (e.g., Dropbox) that she has access to for a proof of concept pilot. Together, John and Jane exfiltrate more than 16 MB of sensitive data. John puts in his notice and abruptly leaves.

Exhibited PRIs

- High level of access with privileged user rights including exceptions for FTP and Cloud Pilots
- Located in a country with a high risk of competitive intelligence due to a high volume of closely located competitors
- Overwhelmed by crises and career disappoints
- Mounting debt and worsening financial situation
- LinkedIn profile that makes him a target for social engineering
- Corporate communications highlighting their exfiltration plans
- Printing large quantities of documents
- FTP activity
- Abrupt separation with no context

This use case focuses on a privileged access employee who changes sensitive data and site assessment information in order to compromise a proprietary exploration project. He uses removable media to exfiltrate the correct (unaltered) data for financial gain.

Use case: Data subversion

Use Case: Data Subversion

John Doe

Case Summary

John Doe is IT systems administrator who works for a large energy company in Brazil. As a IT administrator he has high levels of access to company systems; this access includes the ability to grant permissions and create new user IDs. He received an unexpected poor performance rating and expresses his frustration to his supervisor during a performance review. A few weeks later, John begins to research competitor websites from his company laptop. John decides he is going to leave the organization and does not look back. John accesses the network remotely and late at night through VPN and begins to alter upstream research and site assessment data that will affect the firm's business, drilling, and exploration plans. Prior to changing the data contained within company systems, he moves the correct information about certain site assessments, exploratory R&D, and company regional expansion plans to an approved USB device. He plans to use this data as leverage to obtain a position at a competitor (there are many located closely together in his area of Brazil). As a result of John's subversion of company drilling data, he causes losses as a result of misallocated resources and untapped oil.

Exhibited PRIs

- High level of access with privileged user rights to highly sensitive upstream data
- Located in a country with a high risk of competitive intelligence due to a high volume of closely located competitors
- Poor performance ratings
- Explicit frustration expressed toward the organization
- Web activity associated with potential competitive preference
- VPN baseline anomalies including time and bandwidth consumed
- Changes made to highly sensitive documents and information
- Logs associated with removable media
- Notice of separation

This use case focuses on ignorant/complacent (as opposed to a malicious) employees whose lack of adherence to the organization's policy compromises sensitive client data.

Use case: Ignorant insider

 **John Doe**

Use Case: Download and Deployment of Unapproved Programs

Case Summary

A project team based out of an office in India, but is currently working with a client in the United States on a technology project. As they came close to finishing a key client deliverable, the team decided they needed to test the client's software to ensure it was foolproof against hackers. They agreed the best way to accomplish this was to hack the client to uncover any vulnerabilities, such as revealing passwords. They downloaded a hacking tool to test on the client network and conducted the hack on the client.

The client 's monitoring system discovered the hack attempt. The employees had not notified their client they were hacking against their data.

Following the incident, the organization collected all laptops belonging to the team to conduct an e-forensics analysis. As a result of Team X's actions they put their client's data at risk, as well as the firm's relationship with the client.

Exhibited PRIs

- Employees have a high level of access to client information and data
- Employees download and install unapproved program (hacking tool)
- Employees run an unapproved tool, presumably multiple times during a short period of time
- Large amounts of sensitive data (e.g., passwords) are downloaded as a result of running the test

This use case includes a malicious employee who purposely seeks to cause harm to the organization by exfiltrating data for a foreign intelligence service.

Use case: Espionage

Use Case: Foreign Intelligence Services Environment

John Doe

Case Summary

A foreign government tasked the insider to acquire information on other specific technologies. The insider sent multiple e-mails with extremely large file attachments. The next day, the insider inserted a computer disk into her laptop and exfiltrated a large amount of data. The insider went to agency headquarters late at night every day for two weeks and accessed the network to go through sensitive files.

Exhibited PRIs

- Send large files to foreign-country e-mail address
- Accessed the building during off hours late at night
- Accessed the network during off hours late at night
- Use of computer disks to exfiltrate data

This use case includes a hostile employee who purposely seeks to cause harm to the organization through violence to extract revenge.

Use case: Hostile employee

John Doe

Use Case: Hostile Employee

Case Summary

Insider was a government contractor at an intelligence agency. Insider had performance issues at work. He planned to open gunfire at the office as a form of revenge to those who gave him poor performance reviews. He was overdue for his security clearance reinvestigation. The insider's prior employer did not report in the security system of record multiple incidents of adverse information during the insider's prior employment. The insider expressed visible anger toward his supervisor and is given a formal reprimand and a Corrective Action Plan to deal with the behavior.

Exhibited PRIs

- Performance issue
- Noncompliance with security clearance reinvestigation
- Formal reprimand from supervisor
- Corrective Action Plan

APPENDIX L: FAQs

Q1. What are the objective(s) of the Insider threat program?
- To protect critical assets from unauthorized disclosure as well as mitigate a broad spectrum of insider threats (workplace violence, espionage, fraud) that could impact Organization X's business continuity, financial standing, brand reputation, and employee safety.

Q2. Is there a requirement to have an insider threat program?
- The Defense Security Service (DSS) will provide requirements in 2016 to all cleared Federal contractors to establish a formal insider threat mitigation program. This program will become a requirement to conduct business with the U.S. Federal government within a year.

Q3. How will Organization X ensure the program comports with existing Organization X policies?
- The program will be developed and administered in accordance with Organization X privacy requirements, policies, and standards and will be routinely briefed to members of the ITWG and oversight committee to ensure alignment.

Q4. How will Organization X ensure the program comports with legal requirements?
- Information collected regarding individuals will be done in accordance with Organization X's legal standards, including Organization X's privacy policy, and with the proper approval of Organization X's legal counsel. Weekly meetings are being held with points of contact from legal and privacy teams. The program will be lawful and abide by the rules and regulations that bind the company.

Q5. Are individuals profiled as part of the program?
- The program and the analytical tool do not profile individuals. The program helps correlate data in order to identify potential indicators of risk behavior. The focus is on behavior exhibited by the individual and not on who they are (e.g., gender, age, race).

Pilot Questions

Q6. What is the purpose and scope of the pilot?
- The purpose of the pilot is to demonstrate a proof of concept for evaluating elevated risk behavior and to shift Organization X toward a proactive risk mitigation approach to protect our employees and company. The insider threat program tool will identify high-risk patterns of behavior that can be further reviewed by the necessary stakeholders and triaged into an existing Organization X escalation process. The tool will provide

Organization X with a centralized view of virtual and nonvirtual behavior and of contextual factors (access, clearance, etc.) used to provide a converged view of security. The initial proof of concept will be piloted within Organization X's Y business segment for a subset of personnel (approximately X) that work in the practice.

Q7. Will any insider threat program communications go out to Organization X employees?

- Employees will receive communications to ensure that they understand the basic, high-level concepts associated with the Organization X insider threat program with regards to protecting Organization X's business viability through security education, awareness, and protection of critical assets. Communications will be tailored to three critical audience groups, with each group having "need to know" knowledge of the program: Organization X Executives, Organization X Managers and Supervisors, and Organization X Staff. Messaging for the insider threat program will provide general information to staff and focus on roles and responsibilities associated with mitigating insider threats and existing mechanisms for reporting suspicious behavior.

Q8. What types of data will be collected?

- Data will be classified into three categories including virtual behavior (e.g., antivirus alerts), nonvirtual behavior (e.g., policy violations) and contextual factors (e.g., security clearance and access). All data for the pilot phase will include data that is currently collected by Organization X. The pilot will simply correlate this data and use it to identify areas where there may be elevated risk or an improvement opportunity with regard to an existing business process, technical control, or policy.

Q9. How is the insider threat program analyst selected that will manage the tool on a day-to-day basis?

- The insider threat program manager will select the insider threat program analysts based on experience, performance, and alignment to existing responsibilities.

Q10. How is the insider threat program analyst governed?

- The insider threat program analyst will be required to log in and log out of the system on a daily basis. Activities within the tool will be governed by insider threat leading practices, including segregation of duties and role-based access. Activities will be captured in a log and audited on a routine and random basis.

Q11. What happens after an employee is identified by the tool as engaging in high-risk activity?

- The behavior will be evaluated and identified by the insider threat program tool and then routed to the necessary stakeholders across, human resources, Legal, Privacy, Security, and Ethics point of contact. A determination will be made as to the proper action and the time sensitivity of that action. This determination will utilize the existing triage and escalation processes established at Organization X. The escalation and triage process will ensure false positives are sufficiently managed and the tool is properly calibrated based on Organization X's risk tolerance.

Q12. How will the confidentiality of inquiries and investigations be maintained?

- Inquiries and investigations will be controlled by the existing Organization X Ethics and Security process and systems that ensure privacy and confidentiality and are entrusted to a limited group of individuals for resolution. The information handled throughout various aspects of this program will be sensitive, requiring individuals to handle cases with the utmost discretion, protection, and due diligence.

Developing a holistic insider threat program

Many organizations continue to face a myriad of challenges associated with insider threats. It is critical that organization's take a broad approach to insider threat mitigation, viewing it as a people-centric challenge that should be addressed as part of an enterprise-wide program with broad stakeholder engagement and executive buy-in.

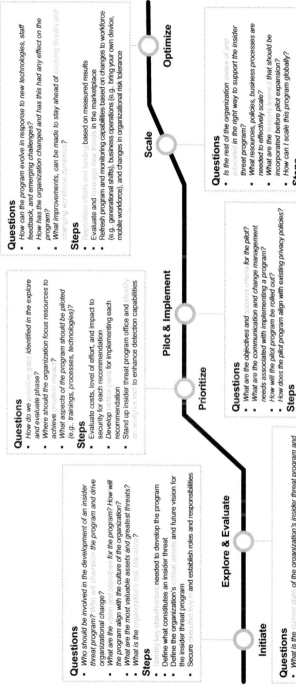

Initiate — **Explore & Evaluate** — **Prioritize** — **Pilot & Implement** — **Scale** — **Optimize**

Initiate

Questions
- Who should be involved in the development of an insider threat program? Who will champion the program and drive organizational change?
- What are the vision and objectives for the program? How will the program align with the culture of the organization?
- What is the organization's risk tolerance?

Steps
- Identify key stakeholders needed to develop the program
- Define what constitutes an insider threat
- Define the organization's critical assets and future vision for the insider threat program
- Secure executive buy-in and establish roles and responsibilities

Explore & Evaluate

Questions
- What is the current state of the organization's insider threat program and how does the organization align to leading public, private, and academic practices**?
- What are the organization's core strengths and vulnerabilities associated with mitigating insider threats?
- How mature are the organization's current capabilities?

Steps
- Benchmark business processes and technical and non-technical controls against leading practices
- Identify evidence-based strengths and vulnerabilities
- Develop actionable recommendations for realizing the future-state vision

Prioritize

Questions
- How do we prioritize gaps identified in the explore and evaluate phase?
- Where should the organization focus resources to achieve greatest impact?
- What aspects of the program should be piloted (e.g. trainings, processes, technologies)?

Steps
- Evaluate costs, level of effort, and impact to security for each recommendation
- Develop tactical plans for implementing each recommendation
- Stand up insider threat program office and identify an analytics tool to enhance detection capabilities

Pilot & Implement

Questions
- What are the objectives and success criteria for the pilot?
- What are the communication and change management needs associated with implementing a program?
- How will the pilot program be rolled out?
- How does the pilot program align with existing privacy policies?

Steps
- Develop a concept of operations for the program
- Collect potential risk indicators to monitor activity critical assets; work with counsel to ensure program alignment with privacy policies
- Conduct a pilot proof of concept to evaluate detection and mitigation capabilities focusing first on areas of the organization with the highest risk
- Utilize pilot program to prioritize and correlate alerts to calibrate analytics tool
- Develop a communications and change management plan

Scale

Questions
- Is the rest of the organization aware of and educated in the right way to support the insider threat program?
- What resources, policies, business processes are needed to effectively scale?
- What are the lessons learned that should be incorporated before pilot expansion?
- How can I scale this program globally?

Steps
- Execute trainings and communications plan
- Evaluate pilot outcomes against success criteria and calibrate the program based on results
- Engage key stakeholders to serve as champions for program roll out
- Develop a roadmap for expansion to include a focus on privacy considerations for different geographies

Optimize

Questions
- How can the program evolve in response to new technologies, staff feedback, and emerging challenges?
- How has the organization changed and has this had any effect on the program?
- What improvements, can be made to stay ahead of evolving threats and changing workforce dynamics?

Steps
- Reprioritize efforts and funding based on measured results
- Evaluate and leverage new trends in the marketplace
- Refresh program and monitoring capabilities based on changes to workforce (e.g. generational shifts), business operations (e.g. bring your own device, mobile workforce), and changes in organizational risk tolerance

* Leading public, private and academic practices include: The National Institute of Standards and Technology (NIST), Federal Bureau Investigation (FBI) guidance for threat mitigation, Carnegie Mellon's Computer Emergency Response Team (CERT), the Intelligence and National Security Alliance (INSA), and the International Organization for Standardization (ISO).

Index

Note: Page numbers followed by "*f*" and "*t*" refer to figures and tables, respectively.